How to be a Real Gay

How to be a Real Gay

Gay Identities in Small-Town South Africa

GRAEME REID

UNIVERSITY OF KwaZulu-Natal Press

Published in 2013 by University of KwaZulu-Natal Press
Private Bag X01
Scottsville, 3209
South Africa
Email: books@ukzn.ac.za
Website: www.ukznpress.co.za

ISBN: 978-1-86914-243-8

Managing editor: Louis Gaigher
Editor: Alison Lockhart
Proofreader: Elana Bregin
Typesetter: Patricia Comrie
Indexer: Ethné Clarke
Cover design: Nicolene van Loggerenberg, IdeaExchange
Cover photograph: 'Bheki and Nhlanhla' by Sabelo Mlangeni, 2008

Typeset in 11pt Garamond

Printed and bound by in South Africa Ultra Litho (Pty) Limited

To Graeme, Kieran and Luke

Contents

Acknowledgements

I am deeply indebted to so many people who have helped me in a multitude of ways – from the mundane to the sublime. I am immensely grateful to you all. In particular, my sincere gratitude goes to Peter Geschiere, Carolyn Hamilton and Gert Hekma. I have benefitted enormously from their generosity, as well as their intellectual rigour and vigilance.

During my fieldwork I was embraced into lively social circles and was inspired and rewarded by the generosity of the many people whose life stories are the substance and texture of this book. In particular, I would like to thank Bafana Mhlanga who continues to be a passionate advocate for gays and lesbians living in the South African countryside.

During the course of researching, writing and editing this manuscript I have been based at three universities: the Wits Institute for Social and Economic Research (WISER) at the University of the Witwatersrand; the Amsterdam School for Social Science Research (ASSR) at the University of Amsterdam; and at Yale University in Lesbian, Gay, Bisexual and Transgender Studies and Anthropology. In each setting I enjoyed extraordinary support and helpful critical engagement from my colleagues.

Anne-Marieke Steeman and Dirk-Jan Veldman hosted me in Amsterdam providing a quiet 'room of my own', which was invaluable to me. During my fieldwork, Phineas Riba did excellent translations, while Sabelo Mlangeni shared his talents as a photographer. Anthony Manion, director of the Gay and Lesbian Memory in Action (originally the Gay and Lesbian

Archives of South Africa, GALA) has been exceptionally helpful. I have also drawn on two interviews conducted by Busi Kheswa, formerly of GALA.

For research funding I thank the Netherlands Foundation for the Advancement of Tropical Research (WOTRO) of the Netherlands Organisation for Scientific Research (NWO) for funding this research. I also gratefully acknowledge the Fund for Lesbian and Gay Studies at Yale.

I have been fortunate to work with Debra Primo and Louis Gaigher of University of KwaZulu-Natal Press. They were most attentive, persistent and patient. I also want to thank Alison Lockhart for her meticulous editing.

Abbreviations

ACDP	African Christian Democratic Party
ANC	African National Congress
BBC	British Broadcasting Corporation
GALA	Gay and Lesbian Archives of South Africa (also Gay and Lesbian Memory in Action)
GGC	gay gossip column
GLOM	Gays and Lesbians of Mpumalanga
GLO-QUE	Gay and Lesbian Organisation of Queenstown
GLOSA	Gays and Lesbians of Sakhile
GLOW	Gay and Lesbian Organisation of the Witwatersrand
HUMCC	Hope and Unity Metropolitan Community Church
IFP	Inkatha Freedom Party
LGBT	lesbian, gay, bisexual and transgender
LGEP	Lesbian and Gay Equality Project
MC	Master of Ceremonies
NGO	non-governmental organisation
NHTL	National House of Traditional Leaders

Local Meets Global

Small-Town Gay Identities

This book was inspired by the unexpected discovery of gay spaces proliferating in the South African countryside in the wake of the transition to democracy. It grew out of a video documentary project that I worked on in 2000, a 52-minute film entitled *Dark and Lovely, Soft and Free*.[1] Research for this documentary, a project of the Gay and Lesbian Archives of South Africa (GALA), which I established in 1997, took me to small towns throughout South Africa.[2] However, in some ways, making the film left me with more questions than answers. For one thing, I had expected to find gay people living in secrecy and fear and dreaming of migrating to the cities. Instead, I found niches where gay identities were being expressed in the most unexpected places. In order to explore processes of gay self-identification and emerging forms of gay self-understanding during South Africa's democratic transition, I focused my research on the creation of gay public spaces in small-town settings and the bricolage of local and global elements in such processes. In queer studies, a rapidly developing field, especially in North American academia, the evolving of one global gay identity may be seen by many as an irreversible trend, but the people I worked with seemed to insist on combining elements of a global identity with local elements that are often in stark contrast (see Chapter 1 for a more detailed exploration of some of the relevant academic theories, as well as a brief history of same-sex relations in South Africa prior to 1994).

Local gays proved to be highly inventive in creating gay spaces that seemed to be new, but were at the same time marked by all sorts of (pseudo-) traditional traits. Chapter 2 focuses on the ways in which dichotomies (among others, sex/gender, urban/rural and traditional/modern) were imagined and invoked in relation to processes of self-identification.

In most of the towns I visited, hair salons (saloons) turned out to be quite visible meeting places for gays.[3] Sanele, a friend and Johannesburg-based hairstylist, who had helped with the documentary, was also instrumental in introducing me to a network of stylists who lived and worked in small towns.[4] Using the few contacts and cell phone numbers that he gave me, I set out to do background research, which took me to diverse places in South Africa, from Heidelberg on the outskirts of the Gauteng province to Ermelo,[5] a regional economic node in the Mpumalanga province,[6] to the gold-mining town of Virginia in the Free State. The hairstylists I met, as well as their friends, associates and families became the main protagonists in the documentary and (at least some of them) also in this book.[7] Through an ethnographic account of hair salons in Chapters 3 and 4, it becomes clear how gays are seen to be particularly skilled at hairstyling (associated with femininity and fashion) and hence have a strategic edge in a highly competitive informal industry.

My intensive fieldwork in Ermelo started towards the end of 2003 and took place mainly during 2004–5. During this period I commuted between Johannesburg and Ermelo spending as much time in the field as work and other commitments would allow. My base was in Wesselton, a historically black township in Ermelo, which is one of the larger towns in the region, surrounded by countryside, agricultural land and mining enterprises. On the way to the Kruger National Park, it is also a popular stop-over place for tourists. The town remains typically divided along the lines of apartheid-era planners: Wesselton is located on the outskirts of the historically white town. At first I stayed in guesthouses or with informants in their homes.[8] In

July 2004 I hired rooms, which I eventually moved out of in October 2005. The rooms were in Wesselton, next door to Bhuti. The rooms became known for a time as the 'gay palace', because a number of gay people stayed there. Given the racially divided nature of residential space, my white presence in a black residential area was exceptional.

Aside from in-depth interviews with individual respondents, my research consisted of paying close attention to informal discussions and interactions and attending innumerable social events (organised parties, ceremonies, church services and pageants). When permitted, I recorded interviews; otherwise I took copious notes. I also recorded, again with permission, small group discussions, such as dinner conversations, which proved to be immensely helpful. An unexpected boon for fieldwork was cell phones. Few of my informants ever had airtime, but almost all of them had cell phones, which proved to be essential in meeting up, making plans or getting directions. Bhuti, who worked as a switchboard operator in Ermelo, kept me informed of developments or alerted me to important functions by calling me when I was in Johannesburg.

My archivist background insists on thorough documenta-tion, so I was pleased to meet a photographer, Sipho, and video-maker, Mrs Mavusa, at an engagement ceremony I attended in 2003 (see Chapter 2). Sipho was from the area and had as a youngster assisted Mrs Mavusa with her photographic and video enterprise in the rural district of Driefontein. Sipho took a lot of photographs for me, while Mrs Mavusa documented some events on video, including Miss Gay Ten Years of Democracy and a workshop on Christianity and homosexuality that was held in Bethal.

Language use was very mixed in Ermelo. Most gays in the region spoke both English and Zulu. I relied on local informants for translations of everyday conversations and exchanges and, very rarely, for interviews. I discussed the pitfalls of translation (as opposed to interpretation) with my informants. Sipho often acted as translator for me. This appeared to work well since he was both a familiar figure within the local gay community, and also at a distance from it, as he lived in Johannesburg.

The documentary and other research projects that I undertook or assisted with while at GALA fed into my research. For example, in October 2000, I attended a workshop run by Bhuti in Standerton (which is about a hundred kilometres from Ermelo), part of a series of workshops billed as 'how to be a real gay' (see Chapter 5). At the time I was working with personal photograph albums, interviewing individuals about their lives, using the albums as a prompt and a framing device. The organisers of the workshops explained to me that other gays in Ermelo did not know how to be 'real gays'; rather, they were accepted as women. These events were a symptom of the political space that has opened up, a space where different ways of conceptualising the self and options for social and intimate engagement were discussed.

Miss Gay Queenstown 2000

The language of gay rights and identity permeated the discussions of gays living in the small towns and rural areas I visited. In some ways it was indistinguishable from the language of activist organisations in South African cities and indeed amongst lesbian, gay, bisexual and transgender (LGBT) organisations across the globe. And yet this global gay identity was combined in ambiguous ways with local ideas about gender and sexuality that appeared to be much more tenacious than I (and many other scholars in LGBT studies) had expected. The following scene (recorded in my field journal) highlights the intriguing mixture that I was to encounter in different settings in my fieldwork.

The Miss Gay Queenstown beauty pageant took place on a Saturday night in April 2000. It was staged in the town hall, which was built in the late nineteenth century. Queenstown was one of the 'frontier towns' established in this turbulent region of the Eastern Cape in the mid-1800s. The town itself radiated out from a hexagonal core, designed to defend settlers from attack during the Cape Frontier Wars, which continued intermittently for a hundred years, ending in 1879. A main road, the N6, which links Bloemfontein to East London, runs through Queenstown. Along this road, at the entrance and exit to Queenstown, were two hand-painted banners fashioned from animal-feed sacks, announcing the event. These were attached to barbed-wire fences, characteristic of this sheep-farming region. One was placed opposite a truck stop on the west side of town, the other outside the entrance to Komani Mental Hospital on the east side of Queenstown.

The Miss Gay Queenstown organisers said that people were waiting for the 'show of the year'. They seemed to be right in their assessment, as Miss Gay Queenstown was very popular. The hall was packed with an enthusiastic audience and a local shebeen owner did a roaring trade selling liquor in the town hall.[9] She was chosen as the supplier because she ran a township shebeen, known as a 'gangster tavern', where 'the girls' (a local term for gays) often went with their boyfriends. She had a poster up in her tavern advertising the event. It consisted of a black and white photocopy with the slogans 'We want "to claim our rights" and to be "Recognised with our relationship" in Queenstown'. The main organiser, Mthetho, explained to me: 'We don't have a problem here in Queenstown, only the uneducated people don't understand.' A lesbian member of the Gay and Lesbian Organisation of Queenstown (GLO-QUE) reported that she had sold 26 tickets for the show from her hawker's stall outside the Ultra Liquor Store. She made her living by selling entrails – offal placed on newspaper on the wooden boards of her makeshift stall. She and her fellow hawkers waved to 'the girls' and remarked on their hairstyles. As 'the girls' did their rounds, straight young men whistled and catcalled, while women laughed and applauded.

I accompanied Mthetho to the home of Luyanda, where he was going to try on his ballgown. I waited with Luyanda's husband and children while measurements were taken, pins adjusted. Luyanda had befriended a number of gays, although it was unusual for her to bring them home when her husband was there. She told me that they were not on good terms with her husband because they made a lot of noise in the house, and also used her make-up. Luyanda worked as a hairstylist and dressmaker and was used to producing outfits for fashion shows in the area. She explained to me that this was the first gay fashion show and she was assisting the competitors. In fact her hair salon was something of a gay meeting place and she was aware that 'people might think that I am promoting this gay and lesbian thing, whereas I have nothing against it'. While she was doing Mthetho's hair, she explained to me that there was a distinction between 'real gays' – in her definition those who were born that way – and those for whom it was just 'a fashion'. She said that Mthetho was a case in point – he was not a real gay – although, with the help of her hairstyling and dressmaking skills he did go on to win Miss Gay Queenstown 2000. Mthetho's mother had a different version. She understood that 'as a mother, I took it that he was created by God and there was nothing I could do'. She first realised that there was something different about her son when 'he started by wearing dresses and stilettos and combing his hair'.

The Miss Gay Queenstown contestants were judged on formal wear, evening wear and traditional wear. They also had to answer questions relating to gay life and the role that they would play in the community, if they became Miss Gay Queenstown. Traditional wear evoked a Xhosa dress style and typically consisted of orange and brown, or white and black dresses, beadwork and headscarves. As the contestants paraded through the hall, the audience clapped, shouted, waved, stamped their feet and danced, at times swarming round and swamping the contestants. The floor of the hall vibrated and the judges' table shook. The Master of Ceremonies (MC) was a well-known presenter from the regional radio station, Radio Ciskei. South African star Brenda Fassie's latest CD blared from the loudspeakers. Formal wear presented a challenge as most of the local contestants had used the same dressmaker and their dresses were quite literally cut from the same gold cloth. Hours later, the show ended in glorious chaos. Shortly after being crowned Miss Gay Queenstown 2000, Mthetho was swamped, kissed and hugged by a swarm of enthusiastic supporters, tears flowing down 'her' cheeks. Interviews with the winners were cancelled though, due to 'very sensitive discussions' backstage. Evidently the MC was not paid her required fee and refused to leave the hall.

Miss Gay Queenstown 2000 was striking in several respects: it was a very public event (the pageant took place in the town hall situated in the centre of Queenstown); most of the audience was not gay and neither was the extensive network of ordinary people who were involved in preparations for the event; there was a clear differentiation along gender lines between gays, or 'girls', and their boyfriends; the language that the organisers and contestants used to speak about the pageant was similar to the rights-based vocabulary used within gay and lesbian organisations in South Africa and transnationally; and there was a close association between gays and fashion. The pageant constituted a public performance of hyper-femininity that appeared to be central both to gays' self-identification and to the level of acceptance they enjoyed within the broader community. I was struck by what appeared to be the flowering of gay spaces in unexpected contexts and, specifically, by the ways in which local and global elements were combined in complex ways. I was aware of three intersecting strands: firstly, the strong echoes of community activism associated with the anti-apartheid struggle; secondly, the rhetoric of what I will refer to as the 'global gay movement', including urban-based South African LGBT organisations; and thirdly, the tentative exploration of the new experiment with a rights-based Constitution.[10]

The widespread and exuberant participation of people who were not gay in an event like Miss Gay Queenstown seemed to contradict widespread assumptions about the supposed intolerance of sexual diversity and the impossibility for gays to make spaces for themselves outside of metropolitan centres. Certainly, it seemed contrary to the popular refrain that homosexuality is not part of 'African culture', although it did little to dispel the equally popular idea that gay lifestyles were 'just a fashion'.

Queenstown had already brought me another surprise. I had worked there previously on the patient files of Doctor Laubscher, a psychiatrist who had worked at the Komani Mental Hospital in the 1930s. I was intrigued by his observation that there was a striking prevalence of homosexuality amongst patients who had been admitted to the mental hospital, but who claimed to have received the calling to become traditional healers. The liminal state associated with the calling, Laubscher suggested, was being inappropriately diagnosed by Western medical practitioners as a form of mental illness.[11] I was intrigued by the use of psychiatric discourse on homosexuality in a cross-cultural context and sought to expand on one of Laubscher's footnotes by going through his patient files, remarkably still housed in a storeroom at the hospital.[12]

While this endeavour did not reveal much more on the topic, a persistent connection between homosexuality and healing was evident in my subsequent fieldwork. In Standerton, for example, Bhuti introduced me to his 'daughter in gay life', Nhlanhla, who worked as a sangoma (traditional healer) on a farm in the rural district of Platrand and in the vicinity of Standerton.[13] Chapter 6 shows how the assertion that homosexuality is un-African has impacted on the lives of gays. Sangomas who are involved in same-sex relationships occupy an important symbolic space as evidence for gays that homosexuality is indeed African. But sangomas needed to show that they are 'genuinely' cultural and traditional in order to establish credibility. In policing this symbolic space, gays distinguished between 'genuine' and 'millennium' sangomas.

Six months after Miss Gay Queenstown, I attended the workshop mentioned earlier, which addressed several issues, including questions such as: 'Is it a fashion thing? How do they show love to each other? Who cooks and cleans the house?' About half the members of the small local gay organisation, Gays and Lesbians of Sakhile (GLOSA), described themselves as gay, the rest were a cohort of women who called themselves 'supporters of gays'.[14] Bhuti explained to me that only one of the gay members was iqenge, while the rest were isikhesana. These Zulu terms refer to a gender-structured arrangement in which there is a masculine (iqenge, alternatively injonga) and a feminine (isikhesana) partner in a male same-sex relationship. The gays who attended the workshop were all isikhesana.

The workshop was attended by about twenty participants, mainly women, as well as colleagues, friends and neighbours. Some belonged to church groups; one woman was from a local school committee and another was from a local branch of the Department of Welfare. The programme also made provision for discussion of topics such as 'homosexuality in the African context' and 'HIV/AIDS and the problems that affect gay and lesbian people in the community'. At Bhuti's invitation, two members of the Johannesburg-based gay advocacy group, the National Coalition for Gay and Lesbian Equality (NCGLE), were there to facilitate the workshop.[15] The gays who attended were either from Sakhile, the township on the outskirts of Standerton, or they had made the one-hour trip by minibus taxi from Balfour. The gays spent most of the day in the kitchen pre-paring the midday meal and the workshop was therefore focused on the men and women who, although not gay themselves, had nevertheless attended to ask questions and to show their support.

The workshop appeared to have two main activist intentions: one was to raise awareness amongst gays themselves and the other was to educate invited members of a sympathetic public about gay and lesbian life. The workshop drew on emerging forms of gay and lesbian activism within South Africa and was also influenced by an understanding of a global gay identity. Yet this activism was coupled, in complex and negotiated ways, with a gendered vision of same-sex relationships, in which there was a clear understanding of locally appropriate gender norms and practices, such as household work being feminine terrain. The gender binary of *iqenge* and *isikhesana* was central to the organisation of gay life in this community.

The workshops confronted me again with this complex mixture of, on the one hand, elements of a budding gay identity that one could term 'global' and that clearly had gained enormously in impact after the collapse of apartheid and, on the other hand, local elements that do not seem to lose their cogency despite all the changes. It is true that same-sex arrangements have a long history in South Africa (see Epprecht 2004 and Chapters 1 and 7). But it is equally clear that the demise of apartheid and the liberalisation of laws pertaining to gender and sexuality coincided with an increased visibility of gays who started to come out in large numbers (Gevisser and Cameron 1995).[16] What surprised me was that this trend was also so apparent in rural areas. Whether in the form of a beauty pageant in the Eastern Cape or a workshop in Mpumalanga, it appeared that gay spaces were visible and public, rather than secretive and private. Andrew Tucker's work on Cape Town (2009), through the rubric of 'queer visibility', provides a compelling account of the ways in which larger social forces, many of which continue to be animated (if not determined) by race, shape divergent experiences of the city for queer men.

Chapter 7 places the rest of the work in historical context. Gays are invested in the idea of history, as the past is seen to legitimate the present. I illustrate this through a discussion on the role of a Zulu gay lexicon in creating a sense of history. Through the experiences of an older informant, which I use as a red thread, I refer to various historical accounts of homosexuality in South Africa and ask the question: can these be seen as antecedent? The gendered ordering of relationships is the most tenacious and consistent thread that links the past to the present. A historical perspective throws light on the question of to what extent the Constitution represents a turning point.

What might be specific to the setting in which I did my research was that the local version of same-sex relations was quite abruptly – due to the sudden liberalisation of the post-apartheid era – confronted with gay activism and the 'global sex' model. In fact, my presence was more or less part of this confrontation.[17] I was certainly attuned to the language of identity politics that had been so much a part of the fabric of South African gay organisations that I had been familiar with since the late 1980s and immersed in since 1990, when the first African gay pride march took place in Johannesburg. Yet it was also clear that what was happening in Ermelo, while often couched in the familiar vocabulary of the gay rights movement, was both similar and profoundly different from my experiences in gay organisations in Johannesburg, for example.

This book thus sheds light on the dynamic interaction between political, social and legal changes on a macro-level and how these are interpreted, translated and incorporated on a micro-level – through individual processes of self-styling and identity-formation, as well as through the creation of gay spaces and nascent social movements. I have tried to capture something of the original and creative combination of local elements and global gay culture by my friends in Ermelo. They (and my informants in other places) show considerable courage in creating their own niche in hostile and quite violent surroundings and also in sticking to their own ideas about what it is to be gay. This book celebrates their courage and their (at times) overwhelming creativity in this process.

Notes

1. Co-directed with Paulo Alberton in 2000. Produced by Franmi (Brazil) and Gay and Lesbian Archives of South Africa. The film can be viewed on http://www.youtube.com/watch?v=Cq4v7Dbu-DA and https://vimeo.com/55796731. If you would like to purchase a copy or host a screening, please contact distribution@frameline.org for more information.

2. The archives were concerned with addressing silences and absences in the historical record and documenting contemporary gay social worlds that existed outside of the metropolitan mainstream. A focus on urban peripheries, small towns and rural areas was part of the acquisition strategy.

3. 'Saloon' was the most common term used to describe hairstyling establishments and it is striking in that it highlights the social nature of the salon space. However, 'salon' was also sometimes used and the owner of a hair salon in Polokwane, the capital city of the Northern Province, was embarrassed when the sign-maker corrected her spelling of 'salon' to read 'saloon'. She felt that 'saloon' was an anachronistic corruption of 'salon' and, as such, showed a lack of sophistication.

4. I have used pseudonyms for all my informants.

5. Ermelo's population in 2001 was 50 000 (according to figures derived from the official census). The town is located 250 kilometres to the east of Johannesburg.

6. Mpumalanga province had a population of about three million, of a total national population of about forty-five million at the time of the 2001 census.

7. While my research base was in Ermelo, several other towns, including Piet Retief, Standerton, Bethal and eMbalenhle and the rural districts of Platrand and Driefontein were also part of it. Although my research findings emerge from this particular region in Mpumalanga, my observations suggest that what is happening in Ermelo and surrounding towns is typical rather than exceptional.

8. Some of the friendships that developed during fieldwork have endured and, in Johannesburg, I have subsequently been able to reciprocate some of the hospitality that I received in Ermelo.

9. A shebeen is an informal drinking establishment.

10. My use of the term 'global gay movement' refers to the hegemonic discourses and practices of rights-based LGBT movements that first emerged in Europe and North America and that have been globally dominant.

11. Based on his work in the mental hospital, Doctor Laubscher published *Sex, Custom and Psychopathology: A Study of South African Pagan Natives* in 1937. Filled with essentialist assumptions, the book is nevertheless interesting, perhaps even ahead of its time, in terms of his assertion about the cultural specificity of the definition of mental illness.

12. In terms of statutory archival practice, the records should have been destroyed within five years.

13. I have used the Anglicized spelling of 'sangoma' because, in the area in which I worked, there is such a mixing of language and an incorporation of English idiom that 'sangoma' and 'sangomas' are common terms used by my informants.

14. At the time the organisation had about twenty members.

15. At the 1999 conference of the NCGLE, a decision was reached to dissolve the coalition and to establish in its place the Lesbian and Gay Equality Project (LGEP), a new non-governmental organisation (NGO), which would focus on creating and affirming a legislative and legal framework supportive of lesbian, gay, bisexual, transgender and intersex people in South Africa.

16. To 'come out' or 'come out of the closet' means to reveal your sexual orientation.

17. Throughout the book, I discuss some of the unanticipated consequences of my presence in the field. Amongst other things, I focus on my role as a networking resource and also as a potential conduit to access social capital as well as donor funding.

CHAPTER 1

Then and Now

Historical Precedents and Theoretical Concepts

Sexuality and gender: The new South African context

The proliferation of gay spaces I encountered in rural Mpumalanga was clearly related to the deep transformation of South African society over the last two decades, from a social order based on entrenched inequality and discrimination to one in which human rights are sacrosanct to the ideals contained in the Constitution. Yet the ideals of the Constitution do not always reflect the values of ordinary citizens. Nowhere is this paradox between ideals and lived reality more apparent than in the contestations around gender equality and sexual rights. On a formal level – in terms of the Constitution and the law – there has been a shift in a short space of time from a jurisprudence that reflected and reinforced deeply patriarchal and homophobic values to one in which equality on the basis of gender and sexual orientation is a cornerstone of the Constitution. But legal changes have not been matched by a fundamental shift in values amongst the general population. At a social level, patriarchal and homophobic attitudes still have considerable currency.

Deborah Posel (2005b) has argued that sexuality has unexpectedly become one of South Africa's principal sites of political contestation. One of the indicators of the extreme tensions surrounding gender equality is the high level of gender-based violence (Posel 2005b; Niehaus 2005; Walker 2005; Sideris

2005). Incidence of rape in South Africa is amongst the highest in the world and is characterised by high levels of under-reporting and low rates of conviction. According to official police statistics, there was a total of 66 079 sexual offences, including rape, reported in 2003–4 and a similar figure in 2010–11 (66 196).[1] Lesbians, and to a lesser extent gay men, have also experienced this wave of violence, as their public visibility has increased. Research shows that rape of lesbians is on the increase, while effeminate gay men are also targeted (Reid and Dirsuweit 2002). A recent study by Human Rights Watch shows that lesbians living in townships are particularly vulnerable to violence and abuse.[2] However, despite these sobering statistics and the high level of violence, the picture is not altogether bleak. Zethu Matebeni's (2011) ethnographic study of black lesbians living in Johannesburg shows how lesbians remain resilient. The lives she depicts are ones of innovation, creativity and pleasure, despite being lived in the shadow of violence and fear. As Edwin Cameron has persuasively argued, the principle of equality, which emerged from under the shadow of the apartheid era, is one that has widespread support.[3] The idea that no one will be subject to discrimination on the basis of social status or 'natural characteristics' (which includes sexual orientation) resonates strongly with the majority of South African citizens who have experienced racial discrimination in the recent past. Equality is thus a principle that enjoys a high level of consensus.

But, paradoxically, this is also why gender features so strongly as one of the fault lines between constitutional democracy and traditional norms, values and practices. Of course, this situation is not unique to South Africa. As Jeffrey Weeks has pointed out in general terms: 'I want to suggest that sex has long been a transmission belt for wider social anxieties and a focus for struggles over power, one of the prime sites in truth where domination and subordination are defined and expressed' (1985: 17).

In South Africa these fault lines are evident in public discourse about homosexuality. Is sexual orientation a 'natural

characteristic', as was forcefully argued in the various sub-
missions made to the Constitutional Assembly by representatives
of the gay and lesbian movement in South Africa? Or is sexual
orientation a choice, a perversion imported from the West, or
simply a 'fashion'? Is gender equality natural or, conversely, a
disruption of the natural order of things? Since the Constitution
was ratified in 1996 gay and lesbian issues (more than any other
single issue) have been the subject of Constitutional Court
deliberations. Through this process, gay and lesbian equality,
precisely because it is 'unpopular', has taken on the status of a
litmus test for the success of constitutional democracy in South
Africa. The logic of this argument is that a good measure of
human rights values in a given society is to be found in the
treatment of the 'weakest and the worst', as articulated by the
Chief Justice of the Constitutional Court, Arthur Chaskalson,
who wrote the main judgment in the first case to come before
the newly established Constitutional Court in 1995. Ruling
against the death penalty, he wrote:

> The very reason for establishing the new legal order,
> and for vesting the power of judicial review of all
> legislation in the courts, was to protect the rights of
> minorities and others who cannot protect their rights
> adequately through the democratic process. Those who
> are entitled to claim this protection include the social
> outcasts and marginalised people of our society. It is only
> if there is a willingness to protect the worst and the
> weakest amongst us that all of us can be secure that our
> own rights will be protected.[4]

The protection afforded to gays and lesbians as marginal and
vulnerable members of society ('the weakest') is thus a measure
of the success of a social order based on principles of human
rights and equality before the law. During the apartheid era, the
South African state became the foremost example, inter-
nationally, of an obsession with identifying and categorising

people on the basis of race and ethnicity, as well as in terms of gender and sexual orientation. What effect does this fundamental change in the symbolic power wielded by the state have on the forms of self-identification amongst gays and the possibilities for organising as a social movement?[5] And conversely, what do forms of identification tell us about changing social dynamics in South Africa as a whole? Inevitably these became leading questions in my research and in the present book.

Gay and lesbian issues are also used as a measure of the gap between constitutional ideals and lived reality. A survey on public attitudes conducted by the Human Sciences Research Council (HSRC) in 2006 (Rule and Mncwango 2006) found, unsurprisingly, that there was a significant discrepancy between the ideals enshrined in the Constitution and the moral values of ordinary citizens. This disparity was particularly apparent in attitudes towards the death penalty, abortion and same-sex relationships – three key 'moral barometers' used to gauge levels of moral discomfort. Significantly, these arguments revolve around cultural values. One side of the argument is that homosexuality is a recent import from the West, intrinsically un-African and also irreconcilable with Christian morality. The other side suggests that there is ample historical evidence of same-sex practices in Africa and that Christianity is compatible with being gay. Unlike elsewhere in the southern African region these ideas, which run contrary to the spirit of the Constitution and against government policy, are, for the most part, muted. However, widely publicised hearings on same-sex marriage brought these ideas to the forefront of public debate in 2006 (see Judge, Manion and De Waal 2008).

The broader national context of contemporary South Africa thus presents an ambiguous space. On the one hand, there are the Constitution and the positive pronouncements on homosexuality made by well-known and highly respected leaders, including Nelson Mandela and Desmond Tutu and, on the other hand, there is the familiar rhetoric that periodically resurfaces and denounces homosexuality both as a symptom of moral decay and as the embodiment of a fundamental threat to the 'natural order of things' in terms of gender relations.[6]

An obvious question is: To what extent is this emergence of gay spaces in the South African countryside a new phenomenon? Is it to be seen as one of the consequences of the general liberalisation after apartheid and, in particular, of the new and highly liberal Constitution of 1996? A recurring theme in the following chapters will be the complex balance in various domains between older elements and the new opportunities of the 1990s – the specific effects of South African history. Therefore a brief overview might be useful here of the antecedents of the gay spaces I stumbled upon in Mpumalanga.

Moffies and hair salons[7]
As a cultural trope, the gay hairstylist is ubiquitous. Hairstyling is a profession that appears to draw a disproportionate number of gay men into its ranks, in various cultural and historical contexts (Johnson 1997; Prieur 1998; Murray 2000: 217).[8] Hairstyling is also an instantly recognisable niche profession for gay men in a South African setting. One informant remarked that being a hairstylist was 'one of the symptoms of being gay'. An influential proponent of a more sympathetic approach to the range of human sexuality and more positive perspectives on homosexuality, Havelock Ellis, was not immune to this stereotype: 'Some professions show a higher proportion of inverts than others. Inversion is not specially prevalent amongst scientific and medical men; it is more frequent among literary and artistic people, and in the dramatic profession it is often found. It is also specially common among hairdressers, waiters and waitresses' (1948 [1933]: 190).[9]

During the 1950s and 1960s, images of District Six moffies were widely circulated through the popular magazines *Drum* and *Golden City Post*, which provided readers with a staple diet of beauty pageants and hairdressers.[10] A large collection of personal photographs housed at the Gay and Lesbian Archives of South Africa in Johannesburg (GALA) provides an intimate portrait of daily working-class life in District Six and attests to the integration of moffies within the wider community. The photographs belonged to hairstylist and minor celebrity, Kewpie – also known as Kewpie Doll and Capucine. 'Her' celebrity status was established through public performances and the ensuing media attention. The annual Moffie Queen competition held in the Cape Town suburb of Athlone was one of the premier drag performances organised by and well publicised in *Golden City Post*. *Drum* magazine also featured several articles on the Cape moffie scene, and the celebrities of the moffie revues and drag balls were also the mainstay of the city's hairstyling industry. According to Dhianaraj Chetty:

> In the 1950s and 1960s, the Hanover Street area of District Six had a whole cluster of hairdressing salons around which gay life revolved. 'Salon crawls', in which one would while away the day visiting the various establishments, were popular social outings. In other ways, the beauty business gave gays the opportunity and means to create for themselves a world of femininity (1995: 123).

After the destruction of District Six, Chetty notes, these salons were dispersed across the Cape Flats. In relation to moffie culture, documentary film-maker Jack Lewis is struck by the persistence of the patterns of District Six, repeated across the Cape Flats, even in contemporary times.[11] The figure of the moffie thus remains a primary role model for gay Coloured youth growing up in the Cape Flats. So, historically, hairstylists have had an influential place as one of the most visible faces of homosexuality in the South African public domain.[12]

Furthermore, hair was (and remains) intimately connected with racial politics in South Africa. In a special message to the eleventh Out in Africa South African Gay and Lesbian Film Festival, former Anglican Archbishop Desmond Tutu, while affirming gay rights, reflected back on the apartheid past: 'The biological differences between us as South Africans at one time enslaved us all. We were defined by our hair, our lips, our language and the colour of our skin. These days are mercifully behind us.'

At the 2003 Venice Biennale, South African performance artist Johan Thom took up the theme of hair as one of the tools of racial classification during the apartheid era. In his performance entitled 'Pencil Test' he used pencils as hair extensions and divided his body into a white torso and black head. His point of reference for this piece was the apartheid practice of determining racial classification, in what would have been regarded by the authorities as borderline cases, by inserting a pencil into the hair. According to the artist: 'This is due to the fact that "indigenous" Africans' hair was seen as being particularly curly – what is called "kroeshare" in Afrikaans ("frizzy, woolly, crinkly hair")'.[13] This was one of the ways that minor apartheid officials would attempt to determine whether someone should be classified as Coloured or black, or Coloured or white in terms of the Population Registration Act. Through these complex and arbitrary techniques of classification members of the same family sometimes found themselves with different racial classifications.

The practice of hairstyling remains, to a large extent, racially differentiated in terms of training academies, workspaces and stylists. During the course of my fieldwork, in 2003, Jody Kollapen, the head of the South African Human Rights Commission, was refused a haircut in a Pretoria salon on the grounds that he did not have white hair. The case went before the Equality Court (at the Pretoria Magistrate's Court) and the respondent, Jacobus Herklaas du Preez, apologised to all those who had been turned away, agreed to pay R10 000 in damages to charity and to use the services of a professional hairstyling instructor, one Peggy Kane, who would train the staff in his several salons to cut all types of hair, including 'hair types classified as ethnic or African'.[14] Following the agreement, Kollapen was invited for a haircut at any one of Du Preez's salons.

The effects of the case were felt far beyond the respondent's own salons. In fact, all hairstyling academies would, in future, be required to teach techniques of cutting and grooming the various types of hair likely to be encountered in South Africa. The case was especially intriguing to me because throughout my fieldwork, there was only one black stylist who said that he would be willing to cut my hair, but the others all said that they did not work with my kind of hair. At the conclusion of the hearing, Kollapen remarked, 'This is not only about hairdressing but a case about dignity'. The intersections between race and hairstyling are not the focus of this book. But, in the light of the history of hair as a marker of racial classification, the link between gays and hairstyling, and especially the niche that gays seemed to enjoy within the burgeoning black hairstyling industry, are of particular interest to me.

As can be seen from the above examples from history and contemporary controversies over hair and race in South Africa, hair and hairstyling constitutes, to borrow from Mary Douglas and Baron Isherwood, a 'live information system' (1979: 5). Gays' engagement in the hairstyling industry takes place on an everyday, practical level in terms of the routines of hairstyling in salons that range from casual backyard enterprises to more formal establishments. But in terms of a 'live information system', the role of gay stylists is particularly interesting. The proliferation of black hairstyles as 'techniques of the self' (Foucault 1992 [1984]: 10–11) can be seen as registering both African authenticity and cosmopolitanism: Gay hairstylists play a mediating role between African styles (read 'traditional') and cosmopolitan aspirations (read 'modern'). The close association between gays and fashion, which can be broadly extended to include modernity, is a key public perception of gays in the countryside and hence a central preoccupation of this book.

Mines: 'Situational homosexuality' or desire?

Through his social history of sexuality on the mine compounds, Dunbar Moodie (1989) shows how male 'mine marriages' are deeply embedded in both patriarchal and gerontocratic forms of social organisation that characterised the rural communities from which mine labourers migrated and to which (prior to proletarianisation) they aspired to return. His analysis shows how the familiar dichotomies between role-segregated marriage partners (husband and wife); hierarchical authority structures (senior and junior); differential masculine social statuses (man and boy); and gender-defined sexual practices (active and passive) are played out in a male same-sex context. He thus shows how

> mature men with authority in their social and economic sphere are entitled to regular sexual activity. The gender of their partner seems of less import than the overriding right to sexual congress. Furthermore sexuality involves more than the physical act. It also involves a range of personal services that more senior men are extremely reluctant to be without (1989: 254).

The practice of mine marriage is also predicated on the assumption of boys becoming men. The practice of giving gifts and cash to mine 'wives' helped junior contract workers to save up enough money to take a wife and to establish an independent homestead: 'So men became "wives" on the mines in order to become husbands and therefore full "men" more rapidly at home' (1989: 240).

Zackie Achmat (1993) has criticised Moodie (1989), as well as Patrick Harries (1990) and Charles van Onselen (1984), for being too functionalist in their approach, as they tend to over-emphasise continuity with village life. Instead, he argues that the migrant labour system represented a rupture in the lives of rural peasantry, which had the unanticipated consequence of new social arrangements and sexual possibilities. He introduces desire into the discussion about 'situational homosexuality', most dramatically by demonstrating that Van Onselen had elided a small segment from a key historical source – the transcript of an interview with Jan Note.[15] The fragment contradicted Van Onselen's basic argument that the preference for same-sex relations was born out of a fear amongst miners that venereal diseases could easily be contracted from urban women. The full text of the excluded fragment reads: 'Even when we were free on the hills south of Johannesburg some of us had women and others had young men for sexual purposes' (Achmat 1993: 99). Achmat's insights about the place of desire and pleasure are confirmed by oral history interviews, which indicate that men with homosexual inclinations gravitated to spaces around mine compounds in active pursuit of sexual liaisons (see McLean and Ncgobo 1995).[16]

Two elements that are supportive rather than central to Moodie's argument, namely the practices of mine 'wives' in cultivating a feminine appearance and a deferential bearing in relation to their 'husbands', are aspects of his research that I will focus on because of the strong resonance that this has with the construction of masculine and feminine selves in this book. As Ronald Louw (2001) reported from Mkhumbane, in the Durban area, young men would dress up as Zulu maidens in the celebrations associated with same-sex marriage. This practice has a historical precedent. In 1927, the Swiss missionary Henri Junod decried what he saw as evidence of decline amongst the vulnerable Tsonga, exposed to the negative influences of city life, particularly through the system of migrant labour:

> In January 1915 one of my colleagues passing near one of the Johannesburg Compounds, saw a big company of Natives singing and walking in the direction of another Compound where a great dance was taking place. Amongst them there were a number of women. My colleague asked his Native evangelist how it was possible that so many women should be walking about in that part of the world, where the feminine element is very small. The man told him: 'They are not women! They are tinkhontshana, boys who have placed on their chests the breasts of women carved in wood, and who are going to the dance in order to play the part of women' (1927: 492).

On the one hand, Junod notes that 'the sexual life of the Bantus especially shocks our moral feelings' (7) yet, on the other hand, he writes about 'two vices which are prevalent amongst certain civilised nations, onanism and sodomy', suggesting that 'these immoral customs were entirely unknown in the Thonga [sic] tribe before the coming of civilisation' (98). Both Moodie (1989) and Marc Epprecht (2004) refer to the report from a Boksburg mine manager dated 1916, in which he testifies to being witness to a dance in which perfumed young Mozambicans wore 'imitation breasts'. Moodie provides a detailed informant's description of the 'techniques of the self' that were employed in order to ensure that distinctive boundaries were maintained between 'husband' and 'wife' in a same-sex marriage, of which appearance was an important component:

> 'Wives' were also expected to 'look feminine', [according to Philemon]. They would get pieces of clothing material and they would sew it together so that it appeared like real breasts. They would then attach it to other strings that make it look almost like a bra so that at the evening dancing 'she' would dance with the husband. I mean it would appear very real. Don't forget that guys used to play guitars there . . . [Another] thing that a nkonkana had to do was either to cover his beard with a clothing material or had to cut it completely off. He was now so-and-so's wife. How would it sound if a 'couple' looked identical! There had to be differences and for a nkonkana to stay clean shaven was one of them. Once the nkonkana became a grown-up he could then keep his beard to indicate his maturity, which would be demonstrated by him acquiring a boy (1989: 235).

Moodie also commented on the behaviour of mine 'wives', showing that it was not only in physical appearance that they embraced a feminine style. In their various interactions with their 'husbands', 'wives' were expected to maintain appropriate wifely decorum and 'husbands' were also the subject of gossip amongst the 'wives'. The younger men in these partnerships were expected to be sexually passive and receptive. Indeed, mine 'wives' took on the behaviour of women or servants in their relations with their 'spouses'. Thus among the Tsonga 'the boy [would] tell his "hubby" if ever he was going away, say home or to the shops . . . and, if the "hubby" had time, he would also come along'. Furthermore, 'he would not just stand up and say it. He had to say goodbye or any other thing when in a kneeling position'. The boys would 'gossip, just like women . . . perhaps discussing things like "my husband bought me this" or "my husband is good for this and that . . .". And if a husband was stingy he would also come under discussion' (Moodie 1989: 235).

What is striking about this description is the extent to which the performance of gender is so thorough and comprehensive, especially if these young 'wives' are subsequently elevated in social status to a position of masculine seniority. Clearly the emphasis on hyper-femininity, so crucial for my informants to their trajectories of desire, has a long and established history in South Africa.

Bars and gay activism

Other facets of recent gay history in South Africa concern the apartheid context of intensified repression and surveillance that, in a well-known paradox, triggered new forms of activism. Homosexuality and public scandal have been linked through dramatic court cases, some of which date back to sodomy trials, which took place in the Cape in the seventeenth century, and both the 1930s and 1960s saw courtroom dramas and sensationalist media coverage on homosexuality. The 1930s indecency trials, for example, involved male prostitutes and prominent Johannesburg businessmen. The 1960s marked a period of increased public visibility – a nascent gay subculture in the form of bars and clubs frequented by gay men and lesbians.[17] While the public scandals tended to focus on the white middle classes and – in the case of the indecency trials – their working-class cohorts, there was a parallel clampdown on homosexuality amongst black men evident in the dramatic increase in sodomy convictions amongst black Africans (Botha and Cameron 1997). A massive police raid on an all-male party in the affluent Johannesburg suburb of Forest Town received wide media coverage and became the fodder for a moral panic. Justice Minister, P.C. Pelser, proposed draconian measures to curb 'this viper in our midst'[18] and set up a select committee that published a report on the question of homosexuality in 1968.[19]

This period was one of increased repression of homosexuality, but it also marked the beginning of a formal gay movement in the form of the Legal Reform Fund set up, as the name implies, to lobby for change and to represent gay interests at the commission of enquiry. However, this was a white affair. For black gays – as oral testimony reveals – the spaces for self-expression were also curtailed by a myriad race laws. Black men would meet through social networks and, in Johannesburg, at the only multiracial restaurant, situated at the railway station. Public visibility for whites was severely curtailed, especially after the Forest Town party; for black men it was almost non-existent. In the 1970s a small bar scene emerged, but again the Separate Amenities Act ensured that this was for whites only. It was only in the 1980s when the Group Areas Act came under increasing pressure, especially in 'grey areas' such as Hillbrow, that black gay men were able to start frequenting gay bars and clubs.

Many of these issues have important implications for my research. There is a long history of gay activism that, like everything else in South Africa, was shaped by the racial policies of the South African state. The highly publicised 'homosexual scandals' involved the white middle classes, thus reinforcing the prevailing public perception that homosexuality was associated with whiteness and affluence. However, beginning in the late 1980s black gay activists who were highly visible in anti-apartheid politics provided new role models for black gays and lesbians in

South Africa. These various strands of South African gay history have shaped contemporary forms of gay self-identification. In the ambit of my fieldwork this was particularly apparent in the strong racial divisions that exist amongst gays in the countryside, as well as in the popular perception (as a result of less visibility) that black gays are a recent phenomenon – a product of the Constitution.

Analytical aspects: Gays, fashion and the tenacity of gender oppositions

In this book I show how gays develop innovative ways of managing their marginal status and vulnerable social position.[20] The primary focus is on the subtle confrontations and contestations between the global gay movement and local experiences of gender and sexuality that have proved to be remarkably resilient. Two sub themes emerge from this central focus – the one has to do with public perceptions of gays in the countryside, specifically a close association between gays and fashion, which is (as I will show) conceptually interchangeable with modernity. The other sub theme is the apparent insistence amongst gays of a stark gender opposition and the performance of a hyper-femininity as a precondition for erotic desire.

Despite considerable innovation in the making of identities and the creation of gay public spaces, it is striking that gender norms and values remain quite fixed in male same-sex relationships – in contrast to conceptions spread by the global gay movement, which emphasise an egalitarian ideal. Gays conform to a set of deeply internalised gender norms and values that are experienced subjectively as part of the natural gender order. Thus relationships are organised along gender lines that reinforce, rather than subvert gender stereotypes.[21] The norm is that one partner is masculine (a *gent*) and the other feminine (a *lady*). While these categories of *ladies* and *gents* are imaginative ideals, they are also powerful categories that shape individual identities and determine the possibilities for interpersonal relationships.[22] They are further fundamental to social acceptability. By respecting gender norms, effeminate gays become the social equivalent of women who can enjoy solidarity and a degree of protection, but at the same time also experience the vulnerability of women. Their feminine self-presentation and their social designation as women enable their boyfriends to have sexual relations with them, as straight men. After all, in terms of gender, there is always a masculine and feminine partner involved. Initially, my data on *gents* tended to be more scant than the material that I gathered on *ladies*. *Gents* were more elusive and I was more at home in the world of *ladies*. However, over time (and my physical location within the gay palace was indispensable here) I was able to interview several *gents* and also spend social time with them.

In this book, I focus on different strategies that are deployed, including modes of self-styling, forms of activism and ideological interventions – in other words, the way people dress and behave, the jobs they do, the community activities they organise and the discussions and debates they have. Through a detailed ethnography of hairstylists, I show how a particular form of hyper-feminine self-styling is used to gays' strategic advantage in the burgeoning black hairstyling industry. In this way, the moral opprobrium implied in the dismissal of gay lifestyles as 'just a fashion' is inverted and takes on the positive connotations of fashion appealing to clients and hair salon proprietors alike. Fashion suggests 'sophisticated', 'worldly' and 'modern', as opposed to 'traditional' and 'unfashionable'. As is clear from the outline given earlier in this chapter, there are historical antecedents to the deployment of highly feminised gay identities in South Africa and political change has expanded the possibilities for overt and visible forms of self-styling.

One example of how these themes converge is clear from a series of workshops on 'how to be a real gay', facilitated by gays with an activist agenda, which served to critique aspects of hyper-feminine self-presentation associated with style and to question some aspects of prevailing gender norms (see Chapter 5). This approach is directly linked to the changing legal status of gays and lesbians. The workshops, organised by and aimed at *ladies*, focused on a diverse range of topics, including appropriate self-presentation for securing a job, legal rights and Christian ethics. The workshops were organised and run by a small group of well-networked gays who wanted to establish the hegemony of their vision of gay identity over those wedded to style. The workshops suggested alternative ways of being, stressed the importance of coming out as gay and engaged in extensive dialogue about various terms of classification drawn from sexology's lexicon. The forms of self-identification encouraged in the workshops resonate strongly with the ideals of human rights embodied in the Constitution and promoted by the activist programmes of gay and lesbian non-governmental organisations (NGOs). Yet, even in the workshops, being a 'real gay' required adherence to familiar gender roles and norms, which bears testimony to the resilience of these categories as fundamental organising principles.[23]

Another example of the intersection of local and global dynamics is the symbolic importance that gays place on the figure of the sangoma as an important cultural trope in a context in which homosexuality is highly contested. While style and activism are strategies for the management of day-to-day lives, there are also ideological contestations that people have to address. The argument that homosexuality is un-Christian led gays in the region to attempt to launch their own church community. And in a context where the predominant anti-gay rhetoric centres on homosexuality as un-African, the figure of the gay sangoma takes on a symbolic significance. The sangoma, operating under the moral guidance of the ancestors, is quintessentially African and an indisputable part of African culture.[24] If many sangomas are gay (and it appears to be the second most popular form of work for gays, second only to hairstyling) they have a strong ideological value in discussions about homosexuality and African culture. Similarly, in order to demonstrate that homosexuality is not something new and recent, that it is not 'just a fashion', gays place great importance on a sense of history, as can be seen through the lengthy discussions about a Zulu gay dialect and an abiding interest in historical anecdotes, both real and imagined (see Chapters 6 and 7).

In this book I show how a group of people who occupy a vulnerable social position are able to create gay public spaces and, in so doing, engage in counternarratives to the dominant discourses around homosexuality. Michael Warner's notion of publics and counterpublics is pertinent here:

> Dominant publics are by definition those that can take their discourse pragmatics and their lifeworlds for granted, misrecognizing the indefinite scope of their expansive address as universality or normalcy. Counter-publics are spaces of circulation in which it is hoped that the poesis of scene making will be transformative, not replicative merely (2002: 122).

In my research context, 'spaces of circulation' manifest both in terms of self-styling and activism, which, as I will show, are strategies that overlap. The gay beauty pageant, for example, shows how style and activism are brought together in a public performance of gay identity that also has a political aim. Yet, in spite of all these innovations, gender norms and practices remain highly resistant to change and are reproduced in male same-sex relationships. Gay rights movements often set themselves up in opposition to hegemonic sexual and gender practices, creating instead alternative identities and ways of being. The development of gay organisations and homophile spaces in the West has been synonymous with the city and the loosening of social bonds made possible in the anonymity of urban spaces. What is striking about small-town Mpumalanga, where gays are both vulnerable and subject to close public scrutiny, is that the various forms of self-expression, the activism and the community activities, the strict adherence to gender norms and values and the engagement with arguments about Christianity and African culture are all strategies of inclusion that tend to emphasise similarity with non-gays, rather than difference.[25] And yet, amongst men who engage in same-sex relationships, there is a strong emphasis on gender difference that distinguishes between gays (*ladies*) and *gents*. Gender difference is the basis for erotic activity in male same-sex relationships.

All of the above suggests a series of questions that serve as guidelines throughout the following chapters: The central question is what happens when local, strongly gendered versions of same-sex relations are increasingly confronted with the 'global' version of gay identity, introduced at the local level by gay activists in the wake of the new Constitution? Other important questions in this vein are: how can one explain the tenacity of gendered models of same-sex relations? How do people use both models in their everyday life? And to what extent can the activists' ideas provide a counterbalance against the dangers of sexual violence implied by the gendered model of same-sex relations?

Related to this central concern are a series of additional questions: how do people succeed in creating gay spaces in what seems to be a highly adverse context? How do local gays try to invert the general opprobrium on same-sex relations? Important aspects in this context are the tendency to adapt same-sex relations to the prevailing highly gendered version of intimate relations and, on the other hand, the common association of gays with fashion and modernity. Both aspects have highly ambivalent implications in everyday life.

The association of gays with fashion and modernity creates new economic opportunities, notably in the hairstyling industry. What are the conditions for success (or failure) for gays in this business and in related activities? Advertising themselves as 'modern' makes gays vulnerable to the accusation of behaving in an 'un-African' way. How does the debate, now very topical in South Africa in general, on homosexuality as 'un-African' affect the activities of gays in settings such as Ermelo, Mpumalanga?

Two other analytical aspects – already touched upon in the
questions above – might need further elaboration. They can also
serve to show how my argument relates to broader debates on
changing interpretations of sexuality. The first has to do with
fashion and self-styling and how gays living in the countryside
in post-apartheid South Africa have come to occupy a special
niche that is closely associated with modernity. The debate about
homosexuality in South Africa has tended to focus rather
narrowly on homophobia where human rights are often pitted
against traditional customs and norms – this is evident in popular
perception, activist interventions and academic discourse. What
this book does is to broaden the scope of the debate by focusing
on the symbolic aspects of homosexuality – both positive and
negative – and to relate these to ambivalence towards rapid social
change, as experienced in the South African countryside.

The second aspect is the tenacity, already illustrated above,
of gender roles and norms being quite strictly adhered to in
male same-sex relationships. It is necessary to take a critical look
at the 'global sex' hypothesis, which suggests that with
globalisation, increasingly homogenised modern forms of gay
identities are likely to emerge. In this scenario, the emergence of
gay subcultures is both a measure and reflection of globalisation
– 'part of the rapid globalization of lifestyle and identity politics'
(Altman 1996: 78). As should now be clear, my data suggests
quite a different interpretation.

Fashion and self-styling
Through a study of the commodification of hygiene in a sub-
Saharan colonial context, Timothy Burke (1996) demonstrates
the deep ambivalence of consumers towards recently introduced
products in Zimbabwe. On the one hand, certain consumer items
(in this case, 'foreign' items) were closely associated with power
and privilege – initially that of the colonial authority and subsequently of the ruling elite. The introduction of certain
commodities served to engender new needs and desires amongst

the consuming public. Consumer items, in this case soap and personal hygiene products, thus came to represent aspirations for social mobility and desire for power within the context of colonial and independent Zimbabwe. However, given the colonial setting, there were inevitably also strong negative associations with Western-style consumption patterns, as illustrated in the vignette drawn from the autobiography of a Zimbabwean nurse. In this incident, a town woman is criticised for her modern ways: 'They call it *chimanjemanje* – modern way of living. We are losing fast – losing everything' (Burke 1996: 191). Thus the conspicuous consumption of consumer items (and here 'fashions' would equally apply) embody both the promise of the new order and the demise of the old, engendering anxieties about the erosion of tradition and desire for the modern.

Drawing on Judith Butler (1990), James Ferguson (1999) shows how 'cultural style' can usefully be understood as a form of 'performative competence'. Butler argues that gender is constituted through repetitive everyday performances of masculine and feminine roles. Ferguson applies this insight to questions of cultural style, arguing that the performance of a particular style does not imply some deeper cultural essence that is waiting to be excavated. Rather, what he suggests is that cultural style (like Butler's gender) is constituted through performance. Using this model, he shows how divisions between urban and rural, traditional and modern are part of a narration of self, a performance of style. And, furthermore, shared stylistic performances do not automatically imply a common set of shared 'values, beliefs, worldview, or cognitive orientation' (Ferguson 1999: 97).

If, following Ferguson, cultural style is quintessentially about performance and performative competence, gay men in the ambit of my fieldwork are well placed to be seen by the wider community as the embodiment of a particular form of style, or fashion. The idea that gay lifestyles themselves are 'a fashion' reinforces this idea. Gay men are seen to be at the forefront of fashion, as exemplified in the popular beauty pageant. And, in a context in which they are often spoken about as being outside of tradition and culture (un-African/un-Christian) they are by implication seen to be particularly modern, even their lifestyles can be described as 'just a fashion'. In this respect, there are strong parallels between my findings and the transgendered beauty pageants in Tausug, described by Mark Johnson (1997) and in Tonga, described by Niko Besnier (2002). In the former the interplay between 'own' and 'other' worlds and in the latter the negotiation of 'locality' and 'non-locality' are strongly reminiscent of the ambiguous associations of homosexuality with fashion in South Africa. Public rhetoric about homosexuality as un-African and a perversion imported from the West coincides with the emergence of more public and visible gay spaces in rural areas and small towns – a development that is unmistakably linked in the popular imagination with South Africa's transition to democracy.

Don Donham (1998, 2005) links subjective changes in gay men's sense of self and self-presentation with the emergence of a modern nation state, based on the ideals of individual rights and responsibilities. It is in this politically liberal context that the term 'fashion' has become a common way of referring to contemporary gay lifestyles. What can be made of this link? Beauty pageants and hairstyling can be seen as techniques of subjectification, enabling individuals to express aspirations, a particular sense of self and a style, within the constraints and uncertainties of social and political transformation. Fashion is notoriously capricious and ephemeral, but it is also closely associated with the aspirations and desires of a modern consumer society. Elizabeth Wilson regards fashion as an integral part of modernity, its emergence in the West coinciding with the demise of feudal life. She expresses this in terms of 'the restless desire for change characteristic of cultural life in industrial capitalism, the desire for the new that fashion expresses so well' (1985: 63). It is this allusion to 'change' that Wilson sees as both sympto-matic of modernity and exemplified in fashion: 'Fashion is dress in which the key feature is rapid and continual changing of styles. Fashion, in a sense, *is* change, and in modern Western societies no clothes are outside fashion; fashion sets the terms for *all* sartorial behaviour' (3).

She also sees fashion as a public expression of a deep ambivalence towards capitalism, in terms of exploitation and possibilities of social mobility (1985: 14). In an environment such as South Africa, which offers new and previously unimagined possibilities and yet often thwarts aspirations, technologies of the self, such as hairstyling, represent a particularly important way in which individuals are able to act upon the world in a manner that reinforces, rather than detracts from, a sense of individual agency. Fashion is seen to embody the anticipation of new possibilities generated by rapid and continuous social change (Entwistle 2000: 74). In fact, social change is seen as a precondition for the emergence of fashion: 'The key to the emergence and development of fashion seems to be social change: fashion emerges in societies, which have some social mobility rather than a fixed and stable class structure' (82).

Political change in South Africa has meant that homo-sexuality, until recently clandestine, hidden and curtailed by a myriad laws suddenly enjoyed unprecedented legal equality and prominence in the public sphere. The association of gays and fashion invites questions about the role of this association in the making of gay spaces. What role has the new Constitution played in the association between gays and fashion? Another issue will be how does this openness to the modern relate to the continuing social embeddedness of self-conscious gays and their adamant insistence on clear gender differences as a precondition to homo-sexual desire (which means, of course, that the term 'homosexual' is of limited use here).

The practice and performance of gender
As Michel Foucault's treatise on the origins of the modern sexual subject (1978) demonstrates, the emergence of the mutually constitutive homo-hetero binary in Western psycho-medical discourse is a recent phenomenon, which he dates to the late

nineteenth century. Similarly Weeks (1977) has traced the historical emergence of a distinction between homosexual behaviour and homosexual identity. Foucault's now famous dictum, 'the sodomite had been a temporary aberration; the homosexual was now a species' (1978: 43), captured the transition from homosexual behaviour into a recognisable personality type. In other words, before classification within a psycho-medical discourse, a homosexual identity, as an identity (rather than as a set of illegal or immoral practices), was not possible.[26] Dennis Altman succinctly captures the implications of this shift: 'The idea of "gay/lesbian" as a sociological category is only about one hundred years old, and its survival even in Western developed countries cannot be taken for granted' (1996: 79).

There has been considerable disagreement amongst historians about the significance of the existence of homophile subcultures prior to the moment of naming the 'homosexual' as identified by Foucault (his primary interest being a discursive one).[27] Randolph Trumbach (1998), for example, argues that the figure of the sodomite, far from a 'temporary aberration' was a recognisable figure in a system of three genders (men, women and sodomite) that produced the modern heterosexual. Theo van der Meer (2006) concurs, suggesting that the effeminate 'molly' of eighteenth-century Holland was becoming a recognisable type, with all the negative connotations attached to 'sodomite', which endured until the mid-twentieth century. Therefore he placed the invention of the homosexual 150 years before the date set by Foucault. Stephen Murray writes polemically: 'I consider it incredibly arrogant – specifically chronocentric and ethnocentric – to proclaim that no one recognised homosexual desires before late-nineteenth-century forensic psychiatrists wrote about it' (2000: 8). However, despite these disagreements about genealogy and an overemphasis on medical discourse – see, for example, Donham (2005) and Chauncey (1994) – Foucault's basic premise, namely that the idea of sexuality as intrinsic to individual identity has been a peculiar product of recent times, is a foundational axiom for the

'social construction' approach to understanding sexuality: 'What
we so confidently know as sexuality is, then, a product of many
influences and social interventions. It does not exist outside
history but is a historical product. This is what we mean by
historical making, the cultural construction, and social
organization of sexuality' (Weeks 2003b: 28).

Foucault's work has been influential in a rich series of studies
that have shown 'homosexualities' to be both historically
contingent and culturally specific. As Micaela di Leonardo notes:
'The new historians of sexuality, for example, have charted the
coming into being of the social labels "heterosexual" and "homosexual" in Europe and the United States over the nineteenth
century, and the widely varying possibilities for female and male
sexual expression across time and space' (1991: 28–9).

Closely related to the emergence of the homo-hetero binary
is the idea that sexual identity is inevitably linked to object choice.
In fact, these two aspects of sexuality are quintessential aspects
of sexual modernity in the West and intimately linked to an
economic system that gives rise to particular patterns of desire
and consumption (D'Emelio 1993). And yet these developments
have been uneven and irregular across time and in different
cultures. Historian George Chauncey, for example, shows how
in New York this process was a gradual and uneven one: 'The
ascendancy of *gay* reflected, then, a reorganisation of sexual
categories and the transition from an early twentieth-century
culture divided into "queers" and "men" on the basis of gender
status to a late-twentieth-century culture divided into "homosexuals" and "heterosexuals" on the basis of sexual object choice'
(1994: 22).

David Valentine (2002) notes that 'gay' has come to imply
gender normativity, which had its early roots as a reaction against
popular perceptions (and psycho-medical discourse) that tended
to cast homosexuality and effeminacy as synonymous. He also
identifies an emphasis on 'sexuality', rather than gender, as a
central tenet of the gay and lesbian political movement in the
United States (and elsewhere in the Western world). This is also

the basis for legal and social equality – in which sameness is stressed, both in terms of gender normativity in same-sex relationships and in relation to heterosexual counterparts, where the only substantive difference is seen to exist in the realm of sexual object choice.

Butler's (1993) use of performance, as an analytical concept in understanding the production of gender as a necessary fiction,[28] continues to exert a strong theoretical influence. However, criticism of her work has centred on the tendency of performance theory to reify the body, so that it all but disappears beyond the realm of language: 'Such a perspective leaves little space for a "real" or "material" world which might intervene in cultural reality otherwise than through the institutions and structures of language' (Busby 2000: 15).

Theorists such as Grotz, Haraway and Gatens (cited in Busby 2000: 17) have reinstated the agency of the material – both in terms of the body's interactions with the material world and the capacity of the world to mould the body. The influence of Pierre Bourdieu (2001) is evident in the attention to 'practice' as a way of understanding how gender is both produced and naturalised.

Alan Sinfield provides a succinct overview of various cultural and historical accounts of homosexual identities. His book *On Sexuality and Power* (2004) refers to the two general modes of conceptualising homosexuality in different historical and cultural contexts. The first is in terms of gender, focusing on signs of 'inversion': femininity in men and masculinity in women. The second is the Western model in which sexual object choice defines identity, or 'sexual orientation'. According to Gayle Rubin: 'Since the mid-nineteenth century there has been a slowly evolving distinction between homosexual object choice and cross-gender or trans-gender behaviour' (Altman 1996: 82) – which suggests a gradual shift towards a more homogenous model of sexual identity.

The imagined homogeneity of a 'Western model' is a power-ful idiom for imagining 'own' and 'other' in relation to sexual identity (Valentine 2007). In the classic contemporary Western model of homosexuality both partners in a same-sex relationship would automatically be classified as homosexual, based on sexual object choice. Sinfield (2004), echoing Anthony Giddens (1992), shows how the transformation of heterosexual intimacy – of gender roles, norms and ideals exemplified in the culturally sanctioned ideal of 'companionate marriage' – is reflected in the 'egalitarian model' as the ideal of same-sex relationships in the West. But the same author traces also a genealogy of difference – showing how differences in age, race, gender and class have historically been eroticised in gay male relationships.[29] One can wonder, indeed, whether the supposed generalisation of the equality model as the modern form of being gay does not undermine the continuing importance of difference for erotic desire, even in the 'modern' West.

With regard to my informants being gay, or not gay, this was defined in terms of gendered social and sexual roles and not in terms of sexual object choice. This is familiar and common-place terrain in other cultural and historical settings – as anthropologists such as Besnier (1997), Don Kulick (1998), Roger Lancaster (1988) and Evelyn Blackwood (2005), and historians including Moodie (1994) and Chauncey (1994) have shown in different contexts. Annick Prieur's study of *jotas* in Mexico City shows a similar conflation where 'Femininity and homosexuality refer to each other and confirm each other in a closed circle' (1998: 173).[30] Lancaster (1988) argues that while Western terminology has been incorporated into the Nicaraguan landscape, the terms do not necessarily imply a conceptual change in the active/passive notion of homosexual relationships. This is evident in Hugh McLean and Linda Ncgobo's (1995) investigation into gay life in South African townships, where the term 'gay' is incorporated into an existing lexicon of *skesana*, *injonga* and *imbube* – all of which are gendered terms that refer to a division between active and passive roles.[31] In this scenario, it is quite possible for a man to have ongoing sexual relations with a member of the same sex and yet still retain an unquestionably masculine gender identity and, most importantly, a heterosexual orientation.[32] If we take the idea that the construction of the 'homosexual other' was a necessary precondition to producing the 'heterosexual' (Foucault 1978), the policing of boundaries between heterosexuality and homosexuality is also a process of constructing acceptable and unacceptable, or 'normal' and 'abnormal' behaviour.[33] As Chauncey has shown in his compelling history of gay New York – the making of the gay world was also about defining the parameters of 'normal' heterosexual behaviour. He shows how 'the normal world constituted itself and established its boundaries by creating the gay world as the stigmatized other . . . For the erotic behaviour allowed "normal" men three generations ago simply would not be allowed "heterosexual" men today' (1994: 26).

This division between 'normal' and 'abnormal' is emphatically stated by Diana Fuss as inside/outside, in which she equates 'inside' with a heterosexual norm and 'outside' with sexual subalterns: 'How do outsides and insides come about? What philosophical and critical operations or modes produce the specious distinction between a pure and natural heterosexual inside and an impure and unnatural homosexual outside?' (1991a: 2) Fuss's formulation echoes Rubin's 'the sex hierarchy' (1993), with its 'charmed circle' of 'heterosexual, marital, monogamous, reproductive and non-commercial' sex and 'the outer limits' measured in degrees of perceived sexual deviance from the ideals of the 'charmed circle'.

Yet in my research these categories of 'homo' and 'hetero' are not distinct – neither as identities nor as moral categories. Rubin's evocation of the 'charmed circle' of monogamous, heterosexual reproductive sex and the 'outer limits' of socially unacceptable sexual acts is not easily applied in a context where transgression of moral and social norms appeared to be determined not so much by sexual acts, but rather through the respect or transgression of gender boundaries. In other words, a heterosexual man could have sex with an effeminate gay without ruffling many feathers in the ambit of social decorum or jeopardising his status as heterosexual. What does this say about the boundaries between (in Fuss's formulation) the heterosexual 'inside' and the homosexual 'outside'? Homosexual acts, per se, do not constitute homosexuality and same-sex practices can and do form part of heterosexual experience.

The clear distinction between a heterosexual 'inside' and a homosexual 'outside' is blurred. And, in an Ermelo lexicon, amongst gays themselves the presence of an at least nominally heterosexual man seemed to be essential to erotic desire and sexual congress. For gays, heterosexuality was intimately bound up with their experience as homosexuals. Such sexual norms and values, gender roles and sexual practices serve to blur the borders of the homo/hetero binary in fundamental ways. The inside/outside model along the lines suggested by Fuss and Rubin can only be sustained in a cultural context in which the boundaries of the homo/hetero binary remain intact.

What is interesting about my research is that my informants draw heavily on an activist model of gay identity, but also emphasise gender difference as the basic erotic underpinning in same-sex relationships. As long as gay remains synonymous with being effeminate, it seems that 'normal' heterosexual behaviour continues to include the possibility of same-sex liaisons. Becoming gay and creating gay spaces in this context does not necessarily involve making clearer boundaries between heterosexuality and homosexuality.

Hyper-femininity versus the 'global sex' hypothesis
When one of the gays in Ermelo reassured an organiser of the Out in Africa Film Festival, 'Our people are modern, they can't break plates', it was a humorous, throwaway remark, understandable as a joke because the person was playing on a well-recognised trope – that gays are seen to be particularly 'modern' and also see themselves as 'modern'. As mentioned previously, the downside of this is the pervasive un-African and un-

traditional qualification that shadows contemporary forms of gay self-identification, but the ambiguous associations with modernity can be worked to the advantage of gays. This sense of ambiguity is no stranger to modernity: 'Yet, people often regard "modernity" as an abomination as much as a blessing, and yearn nostalgically for a vanished past (in a typically modern way)' (Geschiere, Meyer and Pels 2008: 1). Through a close association with modernity, gays come to exemplify this ambivalence towards both 'modernity's evils and attractions'.

Gay hairstylists, through hyper-feminine performance, for example, play with the idea of gays as synonymous with fashion. This is an advantage in an arena where clients go specifically to get fashionable, trendy and modern hairstyles. Interestingly these hairstyles, the latest fashions are seen to come from 'upper Africa', and hair comes to embody social and political change, a form of identification as Africans. Gays are seen to be at the forefront of fashion. But in another context, gays are also seen to embody modernity in the form of the ideals contained in the Constitution and the values of constitutional democracy. As Peter Geschiere, Birgit Meyer and Peter Pels note: 'Even if grand narratives of modernization and development have lost credibility, among Africans as well as among those who study Africa, notions of being or becoming modern continue to wield tremendous power in everyday African life' (2008: 1). Thus, forms of self-identification that draw on a national and transnational (global) discourse of gay and lesbian identity are increasingly evoked. Gay activism is also an avant-garde practice in this context – a form of self-styling and presentation of a particular 'modern gay identity' that is also necessary in establishing important networks and even in securing resources. Both are aspects of modernity as imagined in local worlds.

As I will show, modes of self-styling and performance are equally applicable to the hyper-feminine hairstylist and to the more sober, normative self-presentation, as exemplified by the activist figure. Both are ways of conceiving and performing the self as 'modern', with the incumbent advantages and disadvantages – the positive and negative associations with fashion and the ambivalent place that homosexuality occupies as both a measure of the success of constitutional democracy and as a barometer of social decay.

One of the debates in sexuality studies is the relationship between sexuality and globalising processes. Parallel with the 'grand narratives of modernisation and development' (Geschiere, Meyer and Pels 2008) is one of sexual globalisation and increased homogeneity. In historical and cross-cultural accounts of homosexuality, various forms of same-sex relations have been identified as analytical categories – typically these are age-structured, gender-structured and gay or egalitarian (Murray 2000). This form of analytical categorisation is one that is also widely used in historical studies of homosexuality. As Gert Hekma notes: 'Gay history often works with three models of same-sex relations: age-structured as in ancient Greek pederasty, gender-structured with effeminate and masculine males as in the Latino maricone-macho dichotomy and the equal and reversible relations of modern gays' (2009: 168).

While Murray points out that these categorisations are 'ideal types' (2000: 267), nevertheless implicit in these categories is a 'hierarchy of modernity' in which the social organisation of homosexuality along egalitarian lines (which is closely associated with the West) is placed at the apex of an evolutionary progression from other more archaic forms of sexual and social arrangements.[34]

In their analysis of female same-sex practices in Africa, Ruth Morgan and Saskia Wieringa emphasise that contemporary forms of identity and social networking have historical roots:

In Africa, local movements and networks of self-identified lesbian women develop in relation to global movements, creating new visions and spaces for living non-normative social and sexual practices. But they do not arise in a vacuum. Communities of women having sex with women, who identify differently, exist side-by-side and pre-date these new emerging lesbian groups (2005: 310).

To what extent were the developments in Ermelo and similar towns related to transnational flows and to what extent were they drawing on local cultural norms? This relates to an ongoing debate in sexuality studies that suggests, on the one hand, that globalisation will see an increase in the homogenisation of sexual identities and a proliferation of 'Western' concepts of sexual identity in the rest of the world. On the other hand, the resilience of local forms of sexual self-understanding is emphasised – see, for example, Johnson (1997), Sinnott (2004) and Wekker (2006). Altman sees the changes evident in local sexual cultures as a litmus test for globalisation:

> Homosexuality becomes a particularly obvious measure of globalization, for the transformation of local regimes of sexuality and gender is often most apparent in the emergence of new sorts of apparently 'gay' and 'lesbian', even 'queer', identities. Yet we must be aware of reading too much into these scripts. What is happening in Bangkok, Rio, and Nairobi is the creation of new forms of understanding and regulating the sexual self, but it is unlikely that they will merely repeat those forms which were developed in the Atlantic world (2001: 100).[35]

In her critique of Altman, Gloria Wekker articulates a fairly widespread discomfort with the cultural homogenisation thesis in the realm of sexuality: 'Unfortunately, in the literature there is still a significant trope that foregrounds cultural homogenization. The direction of cultural flows has generally been seen to emanate from "the West to the Rest", with the Rest supposedly swallowing Western sexual constructions wholesale and adopting Western labels like *gay*, *lesbian* and *homosexual*' (2006: 224).

Neville Hoad suggests that 'the South African case is both typical and exceptional in thinking through the place of sexual politics in the shift from a Cold War era to neo-liberal globalisation' (2005: 14). What is unique about the South African situation is that in a very short period of time vigilant repression of homosexuality has given way to an era of sexual liberalisation that has set an international legal precedent.

Notes

1. See http://www.saps.gov.za/statistics/reports/crimestats/2011/categories.htm.
2. See http://www.hrw.org/reports/2011/12/05/we-ll-show-you-you-re-woman.
3. Inaugural address delivered at the University of the Witwatersrand, entitled 'Sexual Orientation and the Constitution: A Test Case for Human Rights' (1992). See also Botha and Cameron (1997).
4. *State v. Makwanyane* (para 88). See http://www.constitutional court.org.za/site/thecourt/history.htm#cases.
5. I am taking my cue here from Rogers Brubaker and Fred Cooper (2000) who take issue with the term 'identity' as an analytical category (which they argue is too diffuse to be useful), offering instead a delineation of 'identity' into more discrete and precise analytical concepts, such as 'identification', 'self-understanding' and 'categorisation'.
6. Elizabeth Povinelli captures this paradox succinctly: 'Along with the emergence of the identity of heterosexuality and homosexuality as a thing one can be and can be independent of kinship has come homophobia as a thing one can also be, creating a separation between people' (2006: 72).
7. The term 'moffie' originated in the Western Cape. Initially a pejorative term for homosexuals and transgender people, it has been reclaimed as a term of self-identification.
8. There are various explanations for this trend. On the one hand, it is suggested that in contexts where gay identity is linked to effeminacy or gender inversion, hairstyling is an acceptably feminine occupation (Prieur 1998); other studies suggest that work

in the beauty industry must be understood in terms of broader cultural transformations and the liminal, in-between space that transvestites occupy (Johnson 1997); while Rosalind Morris suggests that in Thailand *kathoeys* are seen to display 'superior knowledge of feminine fashion and comportment' (1994: 24). All these explanations apply to my study.

9. Ellis based many of his 'inversion' observations on his associates in scientific and literary circles, thereby breaking with a prior focus on homosexuality as pathology. He made some other curious observations, including the observation that 'male inverts are sometimes unable to whistle' (1948 [1933]: 200).

10. District Six was situated in the city of Cape Town. In 1966, the neighbourhood was declared a white area under the *Group Areas Act* of 1950. By 1982, the 60 000 residents had been forcibly removed to barren outlying areas aptly known as the Cape Flats, and their houses in District Six were flattened by bulldozers (for more information, see http://www.districtsix.co.za).

11. Personal communication, 3 January 2007.

12. It is important to point out that moffies were from so-called Coloured communities in the Cape. The popular perception that homosexuality was not part of African culture was thus not dispelled by the moffie figure, as the following remark from my field journal, heard at a public hearing on homosexuality held in KwaZulu-Natal, indicates: 'Gays were not in existence amongst the Zulus. Gays were prevalent amongst whites and Coloureds. They are the ones who are gay. They walk around in tight pants.'

13. From text at http://www.art.co.za (go to: Thom, Johan: *Pencil Test*).

14. See http://152.111.1.87/argief/berigte/citypress/2005/04/03/C1/22A/02.html.

15. Also known as Nongoloza (1867–1948), a famous gangster, credited with the establishment of the notorious Ninevites or 28s, who included ritualised homosexuality in their prison gang culture.

16. See also Gay and Lesbian Archives, Oral History Project, UWL, AM 2709, University of the Witwatersrand Libraries, Johannesburg.

17. For a fuller account of this period, see Gevisser and Cameron (1995) and Epprecht (2004).

18. 21 April 1967 (*House of Assembly Debates*, Cols 1405–6).

19. For a more detailed account, see Retief (1994).

20. The markers of this ambiguity are the apparent increase in homophobic incidents and attacks, an increase in gay and lesbian visibility and the proliferation of gay public spaces.

21. Gayatri Reddy (2005) explores the ways in which subversion and reinscription operate simultaneously amongst *hijras* in India. Similarly, Morris notes how the transvestite figure is often co-opted as an icon of gender subversion. Instead, like Reddy, she insists on situating gendered performances within the cultural context in which they take place. In fact, she suggests that Butler's approach to performativity, located as it is within a Western gender binary, may well serve to 'shore up the absolutist claims for genetic or morphological duality' (1994: 22). David Valentine makes a similar point when he suggests that his informants' auto-biographical stories are only rendered ambiguous in a context of 'a binary system where primary "gender" or "sexual" identity must be conceived as two distinct arenas of one's experience' (2007: 136).

22. The idea of gender as a hyperbolic ideal culturally constructed through repeated acts of stylised, everyday performance is developed by Judith Butler (1990).

23. Drawing on Mary Douglas (1966), Valentine (2007) couches the policing of boundaries between 'gay' and 'transgender' as an instance of 'category crisis'. Intense debate about authenticity, about what constitutes a 'real gay', can be understood in similar terms. Discussions about authenticity are ubiquitous in ethnographies of gender and sexuality, whether in China (Rofel 2007), India (Reddy 2005), Thailand (Sinnott 2004), or Indonesia (Boellstorff 2005). Invariably these debates are symptomatic of processes of self-making in a context of flux and change.

24. The deployment of 'tradition' in the processes of self-making in a globalising world is a theme that has been extensively explored in transnational and cross-cultural studies of gender and sexuality. Some recent examples include works by Martin Manalansan (2003) in his analysis of Filipino gay men living in New York City; Tom Boellstorff (2005) in relation to gay and lesbian subjectivities in Indonesia; and Lisa Rofel who contends that desire for 'cultural belonging' means that 'Chinese gay men index neither another exemplar of a global gay identity nor mere local particularity' (2007: 89).

25. In other words, gay self-making must be understood beyond the parameters of sexual identity, also in relation to issues of gender norms, traditional values, religious beliefs, family ties and kinship networks.

26. Eve Sedgwick (1990) is wary about narratives of rupture and provides a caveat to Foucault's thesis by emphasising 'the unrationalized coexistence of different models'. This approach has a receptive audience amongst ethnographers sceptical of the unmediated universal applicability of Michel Foucault's model (see Donham 1998, 2005 and Morris 1994), and historians who note the partial and uneven ways in which ideas about sexual identity permeate society and who question the top-down influence of medical discourse (see Chauncey 1994 and Meyerowitz 2002).

27. According to Foucault: 'We must not forget that the psychological, psychiatric, medical category of homosexuality was constituted from the moment it was characterized – Westphal's famous article of 1870 on "contrary sexual sensations" can stand as its date of birth – less by a type of sexual relations than by a certain quality of sexual sensibility, a certain way of inverting the masculine and the feminine in oneself' (1978: 43).

28. See also Jeffrey Weeks (2003a) on identity categories as 'necessary fictions'.

29. As Alan Sinfield (2004) shows, the idea of a homogenous gay identity in the West is an imagined construct that refers to hegemonic ideals of what it means to be gay. Nevertheless 'the West' is often situated in comparison to 'the rest' in a way that suggests homogeneity and other associated dichotomies of 'tradition' and 'modernity'. Manalansan warns against 'the danger of focusing on a monolithic or global gay culture' (2003: 190), while Rofel cautions against the 'invocation of an already global gay world' (2007: 110) – see also Altman (1996) and Valentine (2007).

30. See also Carrier (1995).

31. Similar terminological disparities are evident in Edward MacRae's discussion of 'homosexual' identities in contemporary Brazil, where he notes a move away from the definition of 'active/passive (bofe/bicha)' to a more 'egalitarian' view of homosexual relationships (1992: 189).

32. Valentine addresses a key question in his ethnography/genealogy of the category 'transgender', asking 'how might the claim that gender and sexuality are distinct be *productive* of that distinction rather than simply a description of the way things are?' (2007: 31) In this way, he invites us to relook at the ways in which gender and sexuality have been 'conceptualized and institutionalized as separate experiences' (243). This book also begs that question, by contesting the notion that, as Valentine puts it, 'the separation of gender and sexuality is a universal truth which has finally been revealed' (170).

33. As David Halperin argues: ' "The homosexual" is an imaginary "Other", whose flamboyant "difference" deflects attention from the construction of heterosexuality' (1995: 43).

34. This is what Valentine refers to as 'a modernist progress narrative' (2007: 62), the kind of 'colonial constructions of "Third World" sexualities as anterior, pre-modern, and in need of Western political development' that Gayatri Gopinath seeks to critique (2005: 12). Similarly, Sinfield notes: 'Anthropologists and social historians have tracked this development among lesbians and gay men, looking for the emergence of egalitarian relations as a sign of progress' (2004: 59).

35. In her study of female same-sex desire in modern China, Tze-lan Sang cautions against an uncritical reading of similarities, pointing out that when lesbians in China compare themselves to their counterparts in the West, 'the equivalence is phantasmatic because the Taiwanese or Chinese interpretations of what it means to be lesbian may well diverge from common Euro-American beliefs, (2003: 32).

CHAPTER 2

Ladies and Gents
Gender Classification and Self-Identification

A man is a man completely and a wife is a wife completely.

— Clive

This chapter focuses on the ways in which dichotomies were imagined and invoked in relation to processes of self-identification. One of the most immediate and striking features in my fieldwork experience was the pivotal role that gender played, both in expressing individual identities as masculine or feminine and in the ways that this dichotomy manifested itself in interpersonal relationships structured along gender lines. The primacy of gender roles in same-sex interactions was already apparent from my prefatory research and the video documentary that arose from it (*Dark and Lovely, Soft and Free*). Paulo Alberton, the Brazilian filmmaker with whom I worked, despaired of finding 'masculine gays' to appear in the documentary and wherever we went, he sought them out. It soon became apparent, however, that his quest would be forever frustrated. In the small towns, urban peripheries and rural areas that we visited masculine gays were an oxymoron: to be gay was to be effeminate. It was the boyfriends of gays who were masculine, but because they rarely regarded themselves as gay and social and sexual norms conspired to keep them 'straight', the boyfriends were quite an elusive group, difficult to locate along the spectrum of identity categories. Would it be appropriate to call these men 'gay' (they did not think so); or 'straight' (they and their partners said so); or 'bisexual' (when this term was rarely used and only in very specific circumstances)? A gendered ordering of same-sex relationships is commonplace worldwide as ethnographic research in Tonga, Philippines, Thailand and Latin America shows (Johnson 1997; Besnier 1997; Sinnott 2004; Lancaster 1988; Prieur 1998). It is the egalitarian ideal of Western Europe and North America that remains the exception. At the time of my research, the Mpumalanga province, like other parts of rural South Africa, was marked by quite an abrupt confrontation of local models by this quite different global vision of gay identities through various interventions of activists in the wake of the new Constitution.

While making the documentary, we interviewed a couple in the Eastern Cape province – Mthetho, the reigning Miss Gay Queenstown 2000 and his boyfriend, Vusumuzi. In a few words, Vusumuzi expressed a rather stark division of gender roles, norms and practices. When asked who had made the first move, Vusumuzi replied, 'Obviously it was me' and went on to describe Mthetho thus: 'She is a she, not a he. No, to me, she is a she and I love her the way she is.' 'The way she is' was, of course, self-evident to Vusumuzi, whereas to me the statement begged substantial questions about sex, gender and sexuality, questions that prompted an extended period of further research. It was also apparent that even if Vusumuzi had not made this declaration, his demeanour, mannerisms, dress, deportment and hairstyle announced 'masculine', whereas everything about Mthetho said 'feminine'.

In an initial conversation with Nhlanhla, who lived on a farm in a district close to Standerton, he spoke about his relationship with his boyfriend. He showed me a photograph of a handsome and muscular young man, a farm worker, taken against a backdrop of grain silos. In the interview, he said that this man, whom he loved very much, was 'very jealous and likes beating me'. Nhlanhla presented this as one of the drawbacks in an otherwise satisfactory relationship and he said it in a matter-of-fact way that spoke volumes about the normalisation of domestic violence as a routine experience for many people in South Africa and, in particular, for women (Simpson and Kraak 1998). This harsh reality is backed up by police statistics, feminist research and masculinity studies (see Bhana 2005; Wood and Jewkes 2001; Posel 2005a; Niehaus 2005; Sideris 2005; Walker 2005). But the point was that in a same-sex relationship involving Nhlanhla and his boyfriend, it was the boyfriend who did the beating and Nhlanhla who was beaten. Whether in the protocols surrounding the declarations of love or in domestic violence, gender divisions played an indispensable role – in this instance, a determining role, both in the matter of liaison (who was proposed to) and in the matter of control (who was beaten). While physiologically there were two men engaged in these interactions, socially it was clear that a man and a woman were involved.

And yet these roles were not intrinsically disadvantageous to gays. Within these apparently rather confining gender roles, *ladies* often found imaginative ways of inventing themselves. In the mining town of Virginia, in the Free State, for example, Pule described himself as the town wife of his migrant labourer boyfriend who, like many others in a similar situation, retained a rural homestead. In his self-narrative, Pule emerged as the wage-earning contributor to an extended family, in which he played the role of second wife and mother figure to his husband's children who were at school in the town, a role he seemed to relish. In an interview with one of his informally adopted children, it was a role that appeared to be relatively unremarkable: 'It is just like having a mother and a father, normal ones,' he said.

A sharp distinction between 'masculine' and 'feminine' was also very apparent when I began my intensive fieldwork in Ermelo. It was here that I was introduced to the terms *ladies* and *gents*.[1] I initially heard these terms in the context of 'jolly-talk', the local gay slang, and they were used pervasively in the region. *Ladies* and *gents*, it seemed, were fundamental to the sexual and social organisation of relationships. I came to discover that difference (in this case articulated along gender lines) was fundamental to the domestic structuring and social ordering of relationships and was also essential to erotic tension and sexual charge.

I was also drawn into this world in ways that I had not anticipated. For example, I was soon accepted as one of the gays, which meant one of the *ladies* and my personal life was seen and interpreted in these terms. So when I arrived in Wesselton with my eclectic selection of furniture – including a bed, a desk, a couch and a washbasin – Nathi, a slim figure, at once fragile and resolute, shy and composed, popped into my room dressed in his Zionist church uniform, the one worn by women members of his congregation and, with his gold tooth flashing in the glare of my single bare light bulb, he asked, 'Graeme, how can your husband let you come here with all your things?' I soon realised that by being embraced into the coterie of *ladies*, I was also rendered vulnerable, in the same way that *ladies* were vulnerable in certain situations and especially in relation to men. At a party held at Bhuti's place, for example, I was cornered in his back yard by a man who forcefully declared his love for me:

> I love you. I love you so much. Let us go and talk where no one can see us. I know I am a black man and you are white, but just give me a chance to show you how much I love you. I want you to be my girlfriend.

I was a bit taken aback, having never laid eyes on him before and while I had no intention of going 'where no one can see us', I did not read the situation as immediately threatening or dangerous. But the *ladies* knew him and were keeping an eye out for me. So I soon found myself extracted from the ambit of his attentions and promptly escorted to a house nearby where I would be spending the night. To this day I don't know exactly what the threat was, beyond veiled allusions to 'thugs' and the dangers of rape and robbery. In another incident, when I was dropping Nathi off at his home, a young man who was mowing the grass on the verge came over to my stationary car and grabbed my arm through the window. 'I love you,' he said. 'I have never met you,' I responded. He tightened his grip, no longer flirtatious, but openly aggressive. 'I love you,' he continued as I began to drive away and eventually he was compelled to let go. Tsepo, who was with me in the car at the time, said, 'I hate it when people say "I love you" when they don't even know you'.

So pervasive was this dichotomy between *ladies* and *gents* that I soon found myself drawn into it in ways that initially prevented me from seeing them for what they were – ideal types and categories of the imagination, rather than real (in the sense of rigid, unyielding and impermeable) divisions between masculine and feminine in personal relationships. Indeed, within the framework of this dichotomy, the terrain of gender was as infinitely varied and complex as the people involved. While the categories themselves were quite clear-cut and unambiguous, within those parameters, there was a wide range of possibilities in terms of self-styling and relationships.

As my fieldwork progressed, these neat categories were revealed as messy, complex and nuanced, but they remained foundational to what Gayle Rubin has referred to as the 'sex/gender system' (1975: 159).[2] *Ladies* and *gents* might be categories of the imagination, but they were fundamental in shaping and understanding the intersections between sex, gender and sexuality amongst my informants. As ideals they wielded a symbolic power that could be felt in the nooks and crannies of everyday life.

These gender ideals – *ladies* and *gents* – offered me the possibility of exploring the dynamics of gender and sexual identity without the assumptions contained in preordained categories such as 'gay', 'straight' or 'bisexual', although, as I will discuss in Chapter 5, these terms were also used. Thus in this context, as elsewhere, terms such as 'gay' and 'straight' are 'borrowed' from standard English and recast as categories of gendering, rather than categories of sexual orientation. While a similar point has been made in a wide range of ethnographic studies, I refer here to Megan Sinnott's work in Thailand that provides a useful comparative perspective. In her study of transgender identity and female same-sex relationships, the terms *toms* (derived from tomboys) and *dees* (derived from ladies) similarly denote the gendered basis of relationships between women. Sinnott outlines her approach as follows: 'Rather than assuming commonality between *toms* and *dees* as "homosexuals", this book explores constructed and contested meanings deployed by *toms* and *dees* in the creation of their identities, relationships, and communities' (2004: 17). Like *toms* and *dees*, *ladies* and *gents*, taken on their own terms, offered a route to follow in exploring the particularity of gender dynamics in a local context.

An emphasis on performance in relation to gender, exemplified by the work of Judith Butler (1990), has conceded its limits and given way to a closer scrutiny on everyday practice as constitutive of gender (see, for example, Bourdieu 2001). Henrietta Moore argues for an ethnographic approach to the complex interplay between individual (gendered) activities and practices that take place in a context of broader social relationships: 'Ethnographic accounts often give a very vivid sense of people's perceptions of their "lived anatomies", and of how understandings of bodies, gender identities and sexual differences are given substance through involvement in repetitive daily tasks and through the concrete nature of social relationships' (1994: 24).

'The concrete nature of social relationships' requires an awareness of 'intersectionality', the way in which markers of difference (such as race, class, gender and sexuality) and the forms of social constraint that go with these are interrelated and need to be understood as such (Di Leonardo 1991). Similarly, in masculinity studies, the social position of men in relation to 'hegemonic masculinity' needs to be understood in relation to questions of race, class and sexuality (Connell 1995).

Questions of sex, gender and sexual difference were of immediate and compelling interest to the *ladies* and *gents* of

Ermelo. They came up frequently in conversations, they were the focus of a series of workshops (see Chapter 5) and they were raised in religious meetings. They were performed in day-to-day interactions, enacted in ritual ceremonies and displayed in beauty pageants. They were also a site of speculation and contestation. One of the first gay events that I attended in Ermelo was an engagement ceremony that took place in December 2003 in a dilapidated and secluded spot on the outskirts of the town, overlooking a small, picturesque dam. This was one of the occasions where gender ideals were enacted in a very stark way, thus creating the impression of a world in which gender norms and practices were rigidly enforced and adhered to. These divisions were embodied in the figures of the prospective bride and groom and those people who circulated in their respective orbits.

There is an implicit assumption in gay studies of a universal trend towards a modern gay identity. A key feature of this dominant thread is the construction of discrete categories of sexual identity, namely heterosexual and homosexual. In this scenario, where sexual object choice is pivotal to sexual identity, both partners in a same-sex relationship would be considered gay. Furthermore, a classificatory and ideological ideal of these relationships is egalitarian (as opposed to age-structured or gender-structured, which are seen to be evolving towards a more modern and egalitarian ideal). This modern gay identity is certainly present in South Africa and is given powerful symbolic expression through the inclusion of sexual orientation in the Constitution. It is evident in the robust gay and lesbian movement and in gay and lesbian organisations and it is even reaching the countryside now through NGOs and other activist interventions. It is also apparent in the urban bar, club and party circuit scene. Various factors, including the history of gay and lesbian political activism, media representations, the sexual orientation clause in the Constitution and the legal changes that have ensued, serve to privilege modern gay identities in the South

African public domain. On a local level, aspirations towards a modern gay identity are evident in the rhetoric and practices of activism, aspirations towards cosmopolitanism, in social life and in rights-based claims to equality. Yet, as my fieldwork in Ermelo shows, despite this innovation in the making of contemporary gay identities, modern gay identities are pushed aside in favour of a model in which a strong emphasis is placed on gender classification. In this model a rigid conceptual separation is maintained between *ladies* and *gents*. In this chapter I explore the factors that affirm this dichotomy and thereby reinforce a gender-based model in which sexual identity is linked to gender classification, rather than object choice. What are the specific circumstances that account for this strong tendency towards gender classification, despite a context in which modern gay identities are privileged in the Constitution and promoted on a local level through a set of practices that appear to champion modern gay identities?

The engagement party
The following description, based on my field notes, serves as an introduction to the nuances of gender in Ermelo.

On 12 December 2003, in the early evening, a group of *ladies* find themselves outside the local supermarket in Ermelo surrounded by shopping bags, looking tired, a trifle stressed, primarily exuberant. These *ladies* are, in fact, young men. I arrive and my car is soon loaded with as many *ladies* and groceries as can fit in. I drive to Wesselton township, situated on the outskirts of Ermelo and park the car outside Bhuti's place. Bhuti stays in a room next to a busy, noisy shebeen 'full of thieves', remarks Henry, a visitor from Standerton and he is perhaps right – later tonight Bhuti will throw three unwelcome male guests from his room, accused of theft and attempted rape of one of the ladies. But that is later. For now arrangements are still in full swing for the engagement that is to take place in Ermelo tomorrow afternoon. Once the groceries are offloaded, I again drive back towards town. A symphony of cell phone ring tones and snippets of conversation – 'Hello sweetheart!' 'Thank you, darling!' *'intombazane!'* – accompanies the jolly-talk in the car.[3]

Word has reached Andrew, the bride-to-be, that Bruce from Durban has arrived and is waiting at the taxi rank in town. Andrew has invited Bruce to the engagement as a blind date for Tsepo. As we travel towards the taxi rank, all attention is focused on Tsepo, who is animated with anticipation. He touches up his hair playfully in the mirror and briefly brushes a piece of imaginary fluff from his shirt pocket. Andrew alights to find Bruce and, once out of earshot, someone exclaims in the spirit of jolly-talk, 'You can see that the bride is a bitch, he knows all these men'. There are a few tense, speculative moments as we wait to see the elusive Bruce, who travels light, a bag slung over his shoulder. He is handsome and aware of his good looks. A beret sits askance on his head in a gesture of masculine bravado. This blind date is to end in heartbreak, a discussion on the nature of betrayal, with Tsepo resolving to find a white boyfriend. But we don't know that yet and in the meantime we share with Tsepo his sense of initial excitement and his dreams of romance kindled at this moment by a frisson of lust.

Meanwhile the groom, Thabo, is hungry. He calls Andrew several times on his cell phone, demanding to know when supper will be ready. In the car there is talk of divorce before marriage because the groom is already hungry and wondering where his bride-to-be is. Andrew pacifies him over the phone until we get back to Bhuti's place. At Bhuti's place the groom and his friends are sitting separately from the ladies, smoking, drinking Hunter's Gold and waiting for supper. It is a very masculine space. It is in this room that the groom tells his friends that he is only doing it for the money. In the next room, the kitchen is a hive of activity as groceries are unpacked and supper is prepared by the ladies amidst laughter and chatter. Bhuti leaves his guests to get on with preparations while he steals some time to have his hair plaited by a neighbour in readiness for the big day. 'Is the groom still angry?' he asks grimacing as his hair is tugged and deftly woven by a young woman who keeps an eye on the *The Bold and the Beautiful*, a popular television soap opera, while working with his hair.

Wandile, who has traveled from Standerton, is relieved to have made it to Ermelo at all. His boyfriend did not want him to come and had argued with him before he left. Wandile told him that the bride-to-be was 'not just anybody, he is my friend'. The boyfriend eventually relented on condition that Wandile ironed his clothes and made him supper before he left. The boyfriend reminded Wandile, 'When we are married, then you will have to obey me'. However, Wandile is not so keen on marriage as he does not trust his boyfriend completely. He explains that his boyfriend is 'straight' and he suspects that he also has a girlfriend because he sometimes comes home very late at night or even early in the morning without a plausible explanation.

That night I am accommodated in a nearby house, sharing a small room and large bed with Henry, who in Ermelo is seen as a *lady* and who has recently moved from Soweto to Standerton. Henry is struck by differences and similarities between gay life in his Soweto home and in Mpumalanga and is keen to share these insights with me so we talk late into the night. 'Most Zulus are gay,' Henry observes, having lived in Standerton, a predominantly Zulu-speaking area, for little over a month and receiving many propositions from men. However, he explains that 'here it is unlike in Johannesburg or Cape Town where you find a gay partner who does not have a girlfriend. Here maybe he is gay, but he has a girlfriend. You start to ask, "Is this person gay, or what?"'

The next day, several hours later than planned, the engagement ceremony takes place on the outskirts of Ermelo. Thulani starts the formal proceedings by welcoming the guests and asserting that the engagement gives expression to 'something that is within us. We are not faking it.' He introduces Pastor Nokuthula from a gay Pentecostal-style church community in Johannesburg who officiates at the ceremony. She grew up in the town of Volksrust, not far from here, so the ceremony has special resonance for her, even though she has conducted several similar services in her Johannesburg congregation. She expresses regret that the bride's and groom's family members are not present: 'Part of me feels so disappointed when I don't see the family. It kills me somehow.' She bewails the fact that marriage is not yet legal, but says that she hopes and prays that one day God will make it possible. She gives advice to the assembled guests on the nature of true love and the obstacles and pitfalls in its path. A speaker explains that he was there when the couple met while shopping at the local Shoprite supermarket. 'From now on I'm going to shop until I drop until I find the one,' he declares. Engagement rings are exchanged and to end the day's formal proceedings a bouquet of flowers is thrown to the single ladies present and much pleasure and enjoyment is derived from the fact that Emmanuel, who caught the bouquet, is ignorant of its meaning and significance. Unwittingly he has placed himself next in line for engagement and, possibly, marriage.

The engagement ceremony was a performance in which gender ideals were centre stage. There was a neat division of labour between *ladies* and *gents*. The activities that surrounded the event thus constituted forms of practice or 'repetitive daily tasks' that constituted 'gender identities and sexual differences' (Moore 1994: 24). Like its historical antecedents (see Chapter 7), the ceremony was both innovative and derivative: innovative in that it involved a same-sex couple; derivative in that it drew on a heterosexual wedding between a bride and a groom. The event was both public and concealed. It took place in a peripheral setting, witnessed only by invited guests. At the time that the engagement ceremony took place, same-sex marriages were not legal, but the possibility of legally sanctioned marriages loomed large and fuelled the aspirations of the participants.[4]

The gender hierarchy

A striking feature of the engagement was the extent to which there is a sharp distinction between masculine and feminine, with a marked hierarchical aspect that resonates with a heterosexual model. It was these kinds of events and my interactions with gays and their boyfriends that both produced and confirmed (and convinced me) that there were clear divisions between masculine and feminine, between *ladies* and *gents*. What follows is a brief summary of the ideal characteristics of *ladies* and *gents* and then an examination of some individual complexities and contradictions through thumbnail portraits of two men that serve to add specificity to the generic category *gents*. Forms of femininity and contestations about gay identities will be explored more fully in subsequent chapters.

While I came across many manifestations of gay identity during the course of my fieldwork that were quite particular, there are some generalisations that can be made about the way in which gay identity is conceived, practised and performed in the context of Ermelo and surrounding towns. The most pervasive is that being gay in these environs is almost invariably synonymous with being effeminate or, in local parlance, a *lady* or *sisButi*. According to jolly-talk, 'straight' men can be 'somehow bended'. Bhuti explained to me that in 'location language', the phrase 'somehow bended' refers to 'straight' men known or suspected of being available as sexual partners to gays. Those who are 'somehow bended' are also referred to as *gents*. These are important categories, as 'straight' men remain the primary object of sexual desire for gays. *Injonga* also refers to a 'gay butch', someone who is attracted to and involved with gays, but who maintains a male social and sexual role in a same-sex relationship. This term is almost the same as a *gent*, but the subtle distinction is that the term suggests a primary, albeit not exclusive, attraction or sexual involvement with gays, whereas a *gent* is primarily heterosexual, in orientation, if not always in practice. A *lady* is a femme, who ideally maintains a female social and sexual role in relation to a *gent*, a 'somehow bended' or a butch.[5] This gender binary is respected and adhered to by both *ladies* and *gents*. It is an orthodoxy that was constantly confirmed and reinforced in daily practice and through gossip, banter and rumour. People were characterised and allocated a gender role according to this gender binary and usually the allocation seemed so self-evident that it was not worthy of comment: a *lady* was obviously a *lady*; a *gent* clearly a *gent*.

Nevertheless, there was room for ambiguity. The term 'Greek salad' was coined to describe anyone who remained confused or ambivalent about his or her sexual identity. This term would have applied to Clive (whose story is outlined later in this chapter) who felt able to be either a 'husband' or a 'wife' in a same-sex relationship. This dilemma arises where, as George Chauncey has pointed out in a different cultural and historical context, men in same-sex relationships are defined by their differences (gender roles) rather than their similarities (homosexuality) (1994: 96). In other words, Clive is unable to identify with a term such as 'gay' and allow for a range of social and sexual roles within that generic category. What is most striking about Clive's dilemma is his urgent need to decide on one gendered identity and then stick to it.

To be a *lady* does not mean that you want to be a woman, although some passed quite successfully at that. Hairstylist Nathi, for example, was so successful that he had been able to compete professionally against women in beauty pageants and once was even placed in the top five of the Miss Ermelo competition. In Ermelo, to be a *lady* is to be gay and to be gay is to be socially effeminate and sexually receptive.[6]

Ladies tended to occupy traditional feminine spheres, both at work and at home. Many *ladies* were drawn to hairstyling where they are often highly regarded, sought after and very successful. *Ladies* were seen as relatively affluent and were often the victims of muggings, bag snatchings and cell phone theft. *Ladies* organised social functions; they took care of the detailed planning of events (such as the engagement ceremony); they did the catering and housework; they cooked, cleaned and ironed. At the pre-engagement party, the *gents* waited impatiently to be served. A *gent* explained to me how household duties and responsibilities would be delegated in the household, if he lived with his lover: 'I would expect him to do the cooking. I would expect him to do the washing and the cleaning of the house . . . Just to give him his role as the lover.' For this informant, acknowledging his partner's feminine role and creating the space for him to fulfil that role was conceptualised and expressed in terms of his responsibilities as 'the man'. He felt that it was important to have distinct masculine and feminine spheres in the home and for each partner to have an area of primary responsibility. However, a *lady* complained to me: 'I am doing multitasks, even my husband's tasks, because he is often away. When my husband is back he is glued to the TV. He is tired from his job.'

Amongst themselves, *ladies* gossiped about each other and about their men in the form of jolly-talk. They often provided materially for the *gents*. For example, it was Andrew who paid for the engagement party, thereby incurring significant debt. Andrew worked in a government-run paralegal agency. Amongst those *ladies* who had regular work, some worked in local government departments, or they were hairstylists, or traditional healers (sangomas).[7] As breadwinners, *ladies* were thus understandably wary of 'gold-diggers', a frequent topic in jolly-talk. 'They are using us,' hairstylist Nathi told me. 'Most boys are around because they are after something,' another informant told me. Certainly the idea that *gents* are exploitative was pervasive amongst *ladies*. Sipho, who was invited by Andrew to be the photographer at the engagement ceremony, was included in the inner circle of *gents* at the pre-engagement party when they assumed that he was 'one of them'.[8] In this setting he heard the groom say that he was only doing it for the money. Sipho said it was to get money to support his child. 'Andrew has to give him money every month,' he told me. In a discussion with a group of *ladies* prior to the engagement, there was heated debate about 'straight' men who have sex with gays for money or other material goods, which was described as a form of 'high-class prostitution'.

Gents, on the other hand, are not gay in local parlance. To the extent that masculinity is a relational concept, defined in terms of what is 'not feminine' or 'not female', in this context it must also be seen as 'not gay' (Connell 1995; Whitehead and Barrett 2001). During the preparations for the engagement, the *gents* kept themselves separate from the *ladies*, opened bottles of Hunter's Gold with their teeth, smoked cigarettes held between thumb and forefinger, talked in low, subdued tones, listened to music and generally did what *gents* do. *Gents* were boyfriends to gays and their lives were not atypical compared to other men from working-class backgrounds living in Wesselton. *Gents* typically had irregular, poorly paid manual work. Drinking alcohol was an important part of entertainment. They tended to exercise a form of masculine domination over their *lady* partners, such as monitoring and restricting their movements, demanding domestic services and meting out forms of discipline and punishment, which, not infrequently, manifested in violence.[9]

As described above, Wandile was nearly prevented from attending the engagement ceremony by his irate boyfriend who insisted that domestic duties came before independent travel. Even Bhuti, who was hosting the party and was assertive about his independence, was, for a short while, subject to a form of punishment when his boyfriend, jealous of his wide network of friends and associates, confiscated his cell phone and then monitored all his calls. His boyfriend also attempted to restrict his movements by insisting that he no longer visited friends after work, but rather 'report to him', as it were, on his way home. During this period Bhuti also had to get permission from his boyfriend to go anywhere. During the course of my fieldwork, I was aware of at least six instances in which *gents* attempted to assert authority and control over *ladies* through violence.

The social norm was that a *lady* should be faithful to one *gent*, although this seldom happened in practice. *Ladies* might have 'roll-ons',[10] but they needed to exercise discretion or run the risk of being beaten. When I asked a *gent* how he had responded when he learned that his partner, Msizi, had had an affair, he explained: 'Obviously if you are a man you have to prove your powers. I had to beat Msizi.' *Gents*, on the other hand, frequently had multiple sexual partners, both *ladies* and women. And they were quite open about it, not always to their girlfriends, but their *ladies* usually knew. Multi-partner sexual arrangements were justified as an expression of male sexual needs (including the 'bisexual' needs of a 'straight' man) and were sometimes arranged in a quasi-formal model of a polygamous marriage, as evident in the domestic arrangement that Brian entered into.

Brian was deeply moved by the birth of his first child: 'In February 2000 when my child was born, I realised that maybe God was telling me something about that. Maybe he showed me that I am a real man. So I have to stick to my family.' Brian told me that his wife was pregnant with their second child: 'Our first child is a boy and he is so cute, like his dad. Well, I am just trying to avoid having a lot of children with her because I am not going to marry her.' Sibusiso has two children with different women and stays involved in their lives: 'I play with them. I talk to them. I want them to feel that I am their father, so that they know what I like and don't like in life.'

Brian's girlfriend discovered that he was seeing someone else when she found condoms in his room at his home in Richards Bay on the KwaZulu-Natal coast. She confronted him about it. At first he told her it was another woman, but she was already suspicious. She took their child and left him, telling his mother that her son was gay. His mother denied this, saying, 'No, I know Brian is a boy'.[11] But later she told Brian that he would have to 'pack his things and go' if he did not change his ways. Brian said that with the exception of his younger sister (whose husband also had sex with gays) his family did not accept him and spoke badly about gay people. However, after a short separation, Brian's girlfriend returned. Brian said, 'The mother of my child said no, she wants to go on with me because she loves me. So we are back together and we are still lovers. And right now she is pregnant with our second child.' He remained involved with his girlfriend, but he moved to Ermelo to put some distance between himself and his family. In Ermelo he had a primary gay partner, known amongst other gays as his 'senior wife', as well as various other gay partners. While his girlfriend knew that he had male lovers, she did not want to see them. His gay partners knew about each other. The protocol observed was that the 'senior wife', Zithembe, would grant Brian permission before he took another gay lover. Zithembe was deferential to Brian, declining to be interviewed, for example, until he had received permission from his 'husband', Brian.

In some instances, *gents* saw themselves in the role of protector: 'A man always gives protection to the lover,' Sibusiso told me. He said that in a relationship between a man and a gay, both parties were entrusted with different practical and symbolic roles:

> I have got the protection and he has got my dignity. I have got no dignity without Tsepo and he has got no protection. If you are a man, it is obvious that you have to get a lover, someone to love you, someone to take care of you. That is why I am saying that I have no dignity without him.

Sibusiso's sense of *gents* as protectors is perhaps borne out in certain instances – Nathi's policeman boyfriend certainly offered him both protection and a sense of justice when the men who had mugged Nathi were arrested and subsequently sentenced to lengthy jail terms. But 'protection' was complex and closely tied up with subjective ideas about masculinity and control, as Tsepo discovered when he resisted Sibusiso's protection. Sibusiso, in his self-styled role as protector, did not want Tsepo to walk home unaccompanied. So when Sibusiso wanted to leave a party and Tsepo refused, they argued and Sibusiso grabbed Tsepo and dragged him outside where he beat him. In the aftermath of the beating, when Tsepo returned to the party visibly upset and with his shirt torn, the *ladies* present were divided in their opinions. Some said that Tsepo should leave his boyfriend, while others were more conciliatory. A *gent* who had witnessed the event explained to me that Tsepo had been in the wrong. There were four factors to consider, he told me. First, alcohol was partially to blame; second, Tsepo had been disrespectful by not listening to his man; third, there were other men present so it was understandable that Sibusiso did not want Tsepo to stay behind and thereby risk being cuckolded; and fourth, 'If a man is on [aroused] it is not easy to wait,' he told me.

It seems to be that erotic dynamics are critical to the creation and maintenance of gender classifications. Theo van der Meer draws similar conclusions from a vastly different context – seventeenth-century Holland. He reflects that a shift from a hierarchical culture in which differences (in class, age, sex) were emphasised, to a more egalitarian one, brought about profound changes in the nature of desire: 'Whereas at first hierarchy itself had been eroticized, the new egalitarian culture also brought along a new economy of desires, in which gender became the central focus of subject and object choice' (2006: 63). Amidst the innovation and creativity in the realm of gender, one thing appears to remain constant – the erotic necessity of *gents* and *ladies*. As Alan Sinfield has suggested:

> Fantasies of dominance and subjection should be regarded as unsurprising transmutations of prevailing social relations of domination and subordination. Hierarchy is neither an aberration nor a misfortune in desire, but integral with it. Indeed, it may well be that power difference is the ground of the erotic; that it is sexy (2004: 58).

In terms of this conceptual model, sex can't happen between two *ladies* or two *gents*.[12] This was clearly articulated in a discussion about a marriage. Lucky was talking about the impending marriage of his boyfriend to a woman. He still hoped that even at the eleventh hour, his *gent* would choose him over her. When Sipho, my research assistant, asked why he and his close and intimate friend, Henry, did not form a relationship, rather than hoping for the enduring affections of a 'straight' man, he replied, 'Oh, I love him very much, but I am not a lesbian!'[13]

The idea of two *ladies* having an affair was met with thigh-slapping hilarity in a discussion on gender and sexuality amongst a small group of friends in Bhuti's room.[14] 'If I am a gay and I sleep with a gay does that mean that I am a lesbian? Yes, because we are both *ladies*. Jolly-talking, it is lesbianism,' I was told. To be desirable to the *ladies*, a *gent* needs to conform to norms of hegemonic masculinity, including heterosexuality. Power and desire are inextricably linked: 'Power and sexual desire are deeply, perhaps intrinsically connected in ways we do not fully understand and just can't abolish' (Newton and Walton in Sinfield 2004: 73).

A *gent* might drink too much occasionally and sometimes he may beat his *lady*. He might have a wife or other partners. These forms of masculine behaviour provoke ambiguous responses amongst *ladies*. On the one hand, they are disapproved of – 'Men are filthy, disgusting pigs', a *lady* blurted out during a discussion on boyfriends – but as forms of behaviour that are indicative of 'hegemonic masculinity' (Connell 1995), in other words, typical of 'real men', they can also be eroticised. In a context in which gender difference is the basis for erotic exchange 'real men', even if they are 'filthy disgusting pigs', are objects of desire for *ladies*. Ideally, a *gent* should be 'straight', which presents its own difficulties in relation to wives and girlfriends, a point to which I will return later.

Town and country: A related opposition

The city, as a prerequisite for the emergence of gay identities and sociability has 'become a cultural and academic common-place over the past century' (Houlbrook 2005: 3). According to Henning Bech, the city is 'the social world proper of the homosexual . . . to be homosexual he must get into the city' (Houlbrook 2005: 5). These observations are borne out in historical and cultural studies in which the city features as the quintessential setting for the making of gay spaces (Ingram, Bouthillette and Retter 1997; Chauncey 1994; D'Emilio 1993; Hallam 1993; Eribon 2004). According to John Howard, this dominant narrative of rural to urban migration has particular salience for gays because it is often intertwined with another gay rite of passage, namely coming out: 'The stories of physical migration from rural to urban spaces employ the same metaphors as those describing the individual ideological shift of the coming-out narrative' (1999: 27).

Didier Eribon provides an insightful summary of some of the reasons for the migration to the city and the possibilities for self-realisation that exist there. He points to the well-documented effects of city life on family and social bonds that translate into less control over individual behaviour. He also points to the possibilities of the city for the creation of specifically gay worlds – emerging from a common experience of stigma and marginalisation. And in the city, individuals can more easily adopt multiple identities – for work and leisure, for example. Referring to Erving Goffman's work on stigma (1986), Eribon points out that the move to the city does not represent a desire to live elsewhere in order to search for anonymity, but rather a rupture of biography in the sense that 'it also creates the possibility of redefining one's own subjectivity, reinventing one's personal identity' (2004: 24). He quotes Eve Kosofsky Sedgwick's formulation of the move from small town to big city as the 'more than Balzacian founding narrative of modern identity of numerous American and European gays' (1992: ix), citing it as an evocation of the psychological trajectory of this geographical relocation.

In the smaller towns where my research was based, conservative values, particularly in relation to gender and sexuality, hold sway. Townships located on the peripheries of small towns, such as Wesselton township in Ermelo, certainly did not offer the anonymity of urban life. Instead, gays tended to be visible and, of necessity, negotiated their identities under scrutiny from the broader community. The possibilities of organising as a discrete gay subculture were limited. In this small-town environment, gay spaces were evident in varied spheres – the niche profession of hairstyling attracted gays who tended to be quite flamboyant in their self-presentation, while traditional healing appeared to be an unremarkable, albeit less explicit, option for those displaying gender ambiguity. Beauty pageants were also relatively commonplace, held in community halls and shebeens of small provincial towns. Gay spaces thus tended to be nested within a broader social world. Interestingly, in prior research, some of these features – namely an emphasis on social integration and acceptance within the family – were evident even amongst urban township dwellers (see Reid 2010). The specifics of apartheid planning, which aimed to keep black people out of the cities, except as temporary sojourners, meant that even in urban-based township environments, gays were seldom afforded the anonymity of the central city, and gay community groups responded accordingly – by emphasising the need for social embeddedness.

My informants often expressed different habits and styles relating to sex and gender in terms of the dichotomy between town and country. Following an incident in which I walked through some muddy and marshy terrain in a quest to meet the sangoma Nhlanhla (see Chapter 6) I became known as the 'country girl', later christened Thembi,[15] 'with a city style'. 'City style' was invoked whenever I took a perceived risk while driving, or made some minor infringement of traffic regulations, or showed impatience on the road. It was also invoked when I wore something seen as fashionable, such as Ray-Ban sunglasses, for example, or bought a new cell phone. If my actions, tastes and temperaments could be categorised into 'city' and 'country', so too were those of my informants and this was particularly evident in terms of gender and sexual identity. This meant that these two dichotomies, between *ladies/gents* and town/country, were conceptually linked in very interesting ways.

Similarly to my initial thinking about *ladies* and *gents*, the division between town and country was so pervasive in the language and imagery used by my informants, that I too found myself thinking in terms of metropole and hinterland, as if they existed as distinct entities. In some ways, this was backed up by my prior experience and the evidence that I would subsequently gather in the field. I had, for example, done extensive research in an urban community where dichotomies between *skesana* (the equivalent of *lady*) and *injonga* (the equivalent of *gent*) were certainly present, but they were not nearly as starkly apparent as my experience in the countryside would suggest. In the mid-1990s, I had conducted research for my Master's degree in an African, Pentecostal-style, gay church community in Hillbrow, Johannesburg called the Hope and Unity Metropolitan Community Church (HUMCC) and in this church the interplay between sex and gender was never far from the rhetoric and activities of the community.[16] For example, a visitor from Durban once suggested that the church should facilitate *umama* (literally, 'mother') classes for effeminate gays to teach them how to be dutiful partners, as may be expected of respectable church women. This proposal was met with much mirth by the rest of the congregation, who conveyed a sense of Johannesburg sophistication when it came to gender roles and norms. Yet, when the HUMCC decided to host a beauty pageant in which the church ambassadors, Mister and Miss, had to be a man and a woman respectively, there were few contenders. A choreographer was brought in to train the male contestant to walk and behave 'like men', while the women received most of their tips from the gays in the church, who were old hands at walking and performing 'as women'. So while the *umama* classes were seen as unsophisticated, perhaps some of the laughter expressed discomfort, rather than ridicule, since gender was clearly a contested terrain. The church was actively promoting a gay identity in which sexual object choice, rather than gender, determined sexual identity. Thus the ideals of masculinity and femininity, embodied in Mister and Miss HUMCC, were ideals where 'gay' and 'lesbian' transcended these gender dichotomies. In this model, unlike the dominant one presented to me in

Ermelo, both partners in a same-sex relationship would be seen as gay. Thus to be gay was not synonymous with effeminacy, as the masculine bravado of traditional wear, the rippling muscles displayed in swimwear and the suave sophistication of formal wear would demonstrate.

These competing and overlapping discourses of gay identity and their complex intersections with gender were presented to me in terms of different styles. I was, in local terms, a 'country girl' with a 'city style'. Clearly I was seen to straddle two worlds and to bring to the country something of the city and to the city something of the country. Implicit within this division between town and country was a set of expectations in relation to gender roles and sexual norms and this was made explicit, often by other 'outsiders', as the following anecdotes will demonstrate. Sipho grew up in the country (Driefontein) and migrated to the city (Johannesburg) where he lived and worked. In his frequent visits to Mpumalanga, he sometimes engaged playfully with local ideals of gender and their associated norms and practices, which could humour, offend or scandalise. There were distinctive urban and rural styles, as Sipho put it: 'In Johannesburg everyone is into this gay thing,' he told me, 'whereas outside of the big cities you must be a little bit "too much", even if you don't wear girl things'. In other words, a certain flamboyant style is expected amongst gays in the countryside.

Sipho was well known in the district and regarded as a *gent*, both in appearance and reputation. In fact, his rumoured sexual prowess as an active partner was a common source of gossip amongst the *ladies*. So when he referred to himself as 'gay', it sparked confusion and disbelief amongst some gays, such as Nathi, who abandoned a client in the Professional Hair Salon to discuss this matter privately with Sipho and me on the pavement outside. He said that people were saying that Sipho was gay. 'Yes, I am gay,' answered Sipho, which left Nathi exclaiming in disbelief, hands cupped over his mouth.[17] Similarly, Sipho expressed the desire to 'do Phumlani', a well-known *gent* in Wesselton, which astounded and amused the *ladies* present: 'No, he is a boy'. To which Sipho responded, 'That does not mean anything to me. When you get into bed you can talk. We do the same things. He can be surprised, he can do these things.' This discussion highlighted the fact that there were competing and coexisting understandings of what it meant to be gay. In Sipho's view, sexual object choice, rather than gender, determined sexual identity.[18] His argument was that if a man had sex with another man, regardless of their respective gender identities or their sexual practices (be they penetrative, receptive or reciprocal), he was still 'gay' in desire and practice. For *ladies* and *gents*, on the other hand, gender and sexual roles (penetrative/ receptive) determined sexual identity. It was, after all, quite possible for a man to be 'straight' and to have ongoing sexual relations with other men, provided of course that the men were *ladies*. In Sipho's view, this distinction was closely linked to a city/country divide:

> If you take Phumlani to Johannesburg, he can forget about girls. Take him to the clubs, introduce him to other people who you would never think are gay and say, 'No, this is the life'. Because he lives out of the big city, he thinks that he is doing girls and boys.

When the South African Broadcasting Corporation aired a documentary entitled *Four Rent Boys and a Sangoma* (Muller 2004), it prompted a discussion between Tsepo and Bhuti about the dangers of gold-diggers. Rural gays, the discussion suggested, would be more vulnerable after this film because men may think that they can easily exploit gays.

These stories and others like them are both reinforcing and undermining of their framing device – the separation between city and countryside. They tell something about the dangers of the city, the different gender norms and expectations of the city and the sophistication and the sexual practices of the city, but they also show how the boundaries between city and country are permeable, artificial and easily crossed, both literally and figuratively. After all, the stories are told by people who travel between Ermelo and Johannesburg, or Ermelo and Durban. Or they refer to the way in which a documentary television programme set in Johannesburg may be received and interpreted in Ermelo. The country/city divide was thus constantly being traversed. Hairstylists tended to do their bulk shopping in Johannesburg. Born in Standerton, Bhuti went to primary school and received medical treatment for polio in Soweto. Tsepo's blind date from Durban, who arrived during the engagement weekend, was not an unusual arrangement – the road between Johannesburg and Durban was often an avenue for romantic and sexual exchanges. There was also engagement with political and cultural organisations based in cities. Representatives from gay and lesbian organisations in Pretoria and Johannesburg, for example, attended events in Ermelo. The Lesbian and Gay Equality Project (LGEP) facilitated a workshop on the legal position of gays and lesbians in 2004, while the Out in Africa South African Gay and Lesbian Film Festival first staged a mini satellite festival in Ermelo in 2005. Country and city were certainly not distinct entities, but subtle differences in gender norms and sexual practices were expressed in these terms. As Sipho points out, 'masculine' style in one context would be inappropriate in another; a *gent* in Ermelo can be a gay in Johannesburg. Sipho teased country *ladies* by disrupting the categories and flaunting the gender norms conceptualised and expressed in terms of rural and urban styles.

When an acquaintance of mine from Johannesburg embarked on an affair with someone from Ermelo, Bhuti said something to me about 'the wife must ask the husband' and I asked him, half jokingly, 'And who is the husband and who is the wife in this case?' Bhuti laughed and said to me, 'Oh, I don't know, Graeme. That is your job; you'll have to make it up!' We both laughed a lot and it seemed like an important moment of recognition, both of the arbitrary nature of these categories ('husband' and 'wife') as well as an ironic reflection on the observer/informant relationship.

So there was some truth and some fiction in the rigid dichotomies between *ladies* and *gents* and similarly with regard to the separation of city and country. I came to realise that the clue to understanding *ladies* and *gents*, city and country, was to look at them as ideals, which gave expression to a set of values and norms and practices. In the same way that the division between metropole and hinterland was being constantly traversed through real, imaginative or technological means, so were the boundaries between *ladies* and *gents* constantly being transgressed. In fact travel, crossing boundaries and transgression were as essential to the maintenance of these categories as was the policing of their borders. Sipho could be seen to be a *gent* in the country and a gay in the city and he could assert that if Phumlani were to move to Johannesburg 'he can forget about girls'. That may be so, but 'country', as an imaginative ideal, required a particular set of norms, values and behaviours that were seen to be appropriate, as did 'the city', and both represented cultural resources that could be drawn on in different ways. It was regarded as desirable to have a pastor from the city (although happily she had grown up in the nearby town of Volksrust) to officiate at a gay engagement. It was also seen as necessary to have judges from the city to select Miss Gay Ten Years of Democracy and her princesses. There were ways to behave in the country and ways to behave in the city. These borders could be traversed, but 'country' and 'city', as distinct conceptual categories, remained intact. Similarly, there were appropriate ways to be a *lady* or a *gent* and, while these borders could be crossed and transgressed, *ladies* and *gents* as conceptual categories continued to wield a strong symbolic power and had an important influence in setting the parameters for appropriate behaviour for both *ladies* and *gents*. I draw here on James Ferguson's evocation of 'performative competence': 'The idea of style as a cultivated competence implies an active process, spread across historical and biographical time, situated both within a political-economic context and within an individual life course' (1999: 101).

There are many ways to be a man

Thabo, the prospective groom in the engagement party described above, had many characteristics of a typical *gent*. The *ladies* regarded him as 'straight' and indeed he had a girlfriend. He was also viewed as an opportunist (a gold-digger) and he expected his bride-to-be to fulfil traditional feminine roles and responsibilities. Two months after the engagement ceremony, a group of *ladies* joked with Andrew about Thabo's anticipated infidelities. One of the *ladies* pointed to Andrew's ring and reassured him: 'He is yours while he is here. Once he is out the door it's a different story. But you will always have a special place as his wife. So don't be worried about how many "roll-ons" he has.'

Sipho, who had a different view on these matters, was adamant that Thabo was gay. He told me, 'Thabo says that he is not gay. I asked Andrew, "Do you mean that he is doing you a favour? No, he is gay because he is sleeping with you and you are a boy, not a girl."' Prior to the engagement, in a discussion about the meaning of the term 'gay', Bhuti and Andrew also argued about Thabo. Andrew was emphatic. He said that Thabo was not gay; he was straight. Bhuti responded by saying, 'I am sorry to tell you this, but I tell you looking straight into your eyes that he is gay.' And Tsepo and Bhuti agreed that it was better for gays to have a relationship with each other because then 'they have something in common'. Yet, in a private conversation about his boyfriend, who was eight years his junior, Bhuti told me: 'He is a straight man, so to say. I can't say he is different.' In another conversation, he observed about his lover, '[He] is not a saint. I don't push him to get rid of his girlfriend.' Tsepo's boyfriend, already the father of two children, continued to have relationships with women and defended gays as 'normal people': 'They are just like us. That is why I protect them,' he told me. The term 'somehow bended', I was told, referred to a 'straight' man, 'but they [gays] bent him to be a gay butch'.

'Straight', 'somehow bended', 'a man', 'a gay butch', 'a *gent*', 'the groom' – all these terms designated masculine gender roles constructed in contrast to 'gays' and *'ladies'* or *'sisButis'*. These categorical labels were difficult to elude. For example, however much Sipho's worldview may differ from these local categories, he was unquestionably a *gent* in Ermelo and although he may wish to 'do Phumlani', Phumlani was highly unlikely to agree to 'be done'. Similarly, when teased by Bhuti (in a different context) about his designation as *lady*, Henry was upset, saying that people should not 'talk about things they don't know'. He said, 'I can be a man'. But, in this particular social and sexual landscape, it was a complaint that fell on deaf ears. Whatever you called yourself, it was important to be one thing or another, either a *lady* or a *gent*.

Achieving masculinity: Thando's story
In 1996, Thando was something of a hero in the small gay community situated in the township of Sakhile on the outskirts of Standerton. Five years later, he was a pariah. The story behind his fall from grace and his subsequent life choices provides insight into the ways in which *gents* attempt to achieve successful masculinity and reconcile the tensions that exist between multiple social expectations and conflicting individual desires.

I first met Thando in 1995, when he found himself in trouble with his church and with the law. He was a short, stocky man with a confident manner about him. He stayed with his parents in Sakhile. His father was clearly very proud of his son, despite the difficulties he faced at the time and clearly had high hopes for him. Not only had Thando been evicted from the Apostolic Faith Mission seminary school, but his lover's family had laid charges against him under sodomy laws contained in the soon-to-be-abolished Sexual Offences Act. In a predicament, he had contacted the Centre for Applied Legal Studies at the University of the Witwatersrand. As a result of this contact, gay activism came to his rescue in the form of legal counsel, political advice and moral support. The charges were dropped and he told me that he had lied his way back into seminary school by renouncing homosexuality.[19] I also met Thando's young partner who was very effeminate, quietly spoken and diffident. He explained to me that his family had pressurised him into laying charges against Thando, but he was still in love with him.

Thando was a masculine gay and, as such, the only *gent* to belong to Gays and Lesbians of Sakhile (GLOSA), a nascent gay organisation founded with the assistance of two concerned women ('supporters of gays') and dominated by *ladies*. The organisation's members congregated in a corrugated iron shack, usually on a Sunday and combined consciousness-raising with prayer and social conversations. Thando's presence was unusual. *Gents* would not normally belong to a gay organisation, but Thando regarded himself as gay, but unquestionably masculine.[20] He was popular with the *ladies*, many of whom he had 'promoted' (introduced to gay life through sexual debut).

In 2001, a story about Thando appeared in the popular *Bona* magazine, in which he denounced homosexuality and announced his impending marriage to a young woman. 'I fell in love with her on April 27th 2001,' he told me. At the time she was fourteen years old and, in terms of legislation regarding underage marriage, they submitted an application to the Department of Home Affairs. They married the following year when she was fifteen, ten years his junior. At the time that the article appeared in *Bona*, Thando called me in Johannesburg to tell me that the journalist had got it all wrong and that he never said the things that he was alleged to have said. However, he was getting married and the article was richly illustrated with photographs.

Thando received a calling and went for training as a sangoma, as his father had done before him, while continuing to act as a pastor at the St John's Apostolic Faith Mission, which he shared with his father. His engagement coincided with increased domestic responsibilities when his uncle died and Thando, as the only son, had to take over the house. In the local government elections held on 5 December 2000 he had been elected to the Standerton town council as a representative of the Inkatha Freedom Party (IFP) – a political affiliation that confirmed his alienation from the gays of Standerton who almost uniformly support the African National Congress (ANC). Things started to unravel when he was suspended from the council on suspicion of fraud. He struggled unsuccessfully to find work and at this time took in a male homeless teenager who was a distant relative of his wife's. He subsequently fell in love with the fifteen-year-old youth and the three of them continued to live together under one roof until his wife moved out on 9 August 2003 and returned to her parents' home, followed by the teenager. Subsequently Thando had found another *lady* partner, but resolved to keep the relationship a secret so that he could successfully negotiate the return of his wife. When I spoke to him in June 2004, he thought that that he would be able to manage if he had one regular guy in addition to his wife, 'like polygamy', he said. He also had a child, but not from his wife. Thando's mother had taken on the responsibility of raising his child. Shortly after my last interview with him, he was arrested for armed robbery, although it turned out he was carrying a toy gun. His father told me, 'There is something wrong with Thando. I don't know what happened. I think that it is since he lost his job.' Certainly in the ten years that I had been acquainted with him, he had changed from an optimistic young man to someone with an air of defeat.

Thando's story shows that it is not always easy being a *gent* when there are conflicting social obligations, family duties and personal desires at play. While he feels that his parents have tried to accept his homosexuality, he also senses a deep ambivalence, 'as if they are seemingly giving me permission, but turning against me'. His church does not condemn homosexuality outright, as other fundamentalist churches do. In his church homosexuality is regarded as a sickness, which can be healed through prayer. Thando felt that he was more sexually attracted to gays than to women: 'In a month, maybe I can go for about one and a half weeks with a woman; with a gay I can go for the whole month.' All these aspects of his life exercised competing claims on what it meant to be a man. It is significant that he got married when he was required to take over his uncle's house and assume a more responsible role in the family. Prior to his marriage to a young bride, Thando had become a father and in this way fulfilled another important male social role. In church he gained acceptance and respect as a responsible, married man.

The image of the 'traditional man' is signified in his role as a sangoma and also as a member of the IFP, where his Zulu ethnicity would be emphasised. The image of the Zulu warrior promoted in IFP cultural propaganda and political practice is an archetypal masculine trope in this particular context. The figure of the married man attracted to men, and especially young men, added another dimension to this palette of competing masculine identities. He was also under pressure to provide financially. His father had become ill and was put on early retirement. The family, whose meagre income had dwindled, turned to Thando for support. He also had to sustain his wife as well as his boyfriend, who became increasingly impatient with him when he was suspended from work and was no longer able to provide according to his expectations. Thando thus turned to armed robbery, although the image of the toy gun, in a country saturated with real guns and where 'masculinity and violence have been yoked together' (Morrell 2001: 12), strikes a strange note of poignancy and impotence that somehow echoes Thando's many failed attempts to achieve successful masculinity. Even in his violent response to circumstances, as an armed robber, Thando had failed. It is through this example that some of the social, cultural and material expectations associated with masculinity become evident. In Thando's case, the complications arising from his domestic relationships with his wife and boyfriend were only one factor in a complex set of dynamics that eventually led to a desperate bid to fulfil the role of provider.

'Will I be the husband or the wife?'

Clive was the second-last child born in his family. He had nine siblings and grew up on a farm near the town of Piet Retief. Both his parents were farm workers. Initially he attended the local farm school, but as he grew older his parents sent him to relatives living in Gauteng where he continued his secondary education. He spent his youth living in urban townships, including KwaThema situated to the east of Johannesburg.

I met him when he was in his late twenties, although he seemed older than he was, perhaps because his expressive face was lined in a way that was unusual for someone of his age. We had both been to a party at Bhuti's place. He was tall and very dark-skinned. Clive, Sipho and I had left the party together and returned to rented rooms in Ermelo where we spent that night. Later one of the *ladies* complained to me that Sipho was unfair taking Clive away from the party, as there was a shortage of *gents*.

Clive was first introduced to gay life in KwaThema, although he was no stranger to having sex with men. Since he was twelve he had had thigh sex with older male farm workers who brought him gifts or small amounts of cash. 'We never kissed,' he told me and they never spoke about it. Sometimes Clive dressed up a bit, in 'ladies things'.

When visiting his cousin in KwaThema, he noticed that there was a young woman sleeping in his bed, her body covered with a blanket. 'Oh, you have got a lady today,' he remarked. 'No, he is a man,' his cousin told him. Clive said, 'When he woke up, I saw something different about him. I thought that he had double organs.' He subsequently befriended the 'lady', Mpumi, and accompanied him to the gay shebeens of KwaThema,[21] still believing that he was a *stabane* (hermaphrodite). He recalled dancing at shebeens: 'I used to dance as a gentleman, but others had different, feminine styles.' It was at Club 31 that he was approached by a man:

He kissed me . . . I was so shocked because how are we going to make sex? He said that he loves me, unlike the other thing on the farm. Now it was like a man and a lady. But then I thought maybe it would be the same sex, like the other one on the farm.

Clive was too afraid to meet the man the next day, as arranged. Instead he proposed to Mpumi because, he explained, 'in my mind I thought he had a vagina'. Mpumi said that sex was out of the question because they were friends. Clive protested, 'But you are a lady and I am a man.' Clive remembered what Mpumi told him: 'He said that he is not a girl; he is also a man. He just looked like a girl.' Clive tried to get Mpumi to explain how two men had sex, but Mpumi was not willing to go into details and he told Clive, 'You have seen that I am a man. Just try it and you will see.' So Clive took his advice and he found the sex very different from the 'old system' on the farm: 'We had anal sex and there was touching all over. I said to myself: "It is happening." It was amazing.'

When he was nineteen he met a younger man, Hope, in Soweto. Hope was sixteen at the time and had also grown up in a rural area not far from Driefontein. They embarked on an affair and Hope was to be the love of Clive's life. When Clive's brother, a taxi driver, was murdered in a spate of taxi violence, Clive returned home to Driefontein. Fortuitously Hope's family also returned to the rural areas to establish a business there. Clive told me that Hope came from a 'rich family, a known family of business people'. They were meticulously discreet about their affair until the day when Hope left his bedroom door unlatched and his mother walked in on the two young men: 'She found us naked, busy kissing and fondling each other.' Clive described the scene vividly, as if it was still fresh in his mind. He remembered the exact time of day, how they had reacted, how scared they were. He remembered how she had 'just stood in the doorway, looking amazed'. Hope's mother, recovering from her initial shock, turned around, shut the door behind her and never mentioned the incident again. In 2000 Hope died tragically in a car accident. Clive fought back tears as he told me the story four years later. Wracked by grief, Clive went to stay with friends in Escourt where he was surprised at the vibrant gay community he found there: 'I was surprised because most people in KwaZulu-Natal are strong believers in culture, where there is supposed to be no such thing [as homosexuality]. So I was so shocked to see that so many people were gay.' On Friday nights the gays would meet in a hair salon, which was an important place for gays to meet each other and 'the straight guys who came to socialise with the *ladies*'.

Clive had a girlfriend. Andrew, the bride-to-be, asked Clive who he preferred as a sexual partner. Clive answered: 'I prefer the boys, but the most preferable is a homosexual.' He also said that he loved his girlfriend, 'but I don't have a final decision right now'. His main concern was role switching in his sexual relationships with men:

> I am confused about that. I have got a guy that I am in love with. With that guy, I act as a man. On the other side, there is another one and we act 50/50. That is the problem . . . Mostly in the black community there is a man and a woman. A man is a man completely and a wife is a wife completely. Myself, I do perform both sides completely. But I think that there must be a final decision. If I am a man, I must be a man . . . I am confused about that, whether to be a man or a wife. I have tried several times to make a choice.

His main concern was that he would ideally like to be involved with one person, but felt it was impossible to make a choice until he had decided whether he was a *lady* or a *gent*: 'I want to give my all, 100 per cent, if I fall in love with someone, so I need to know.'

Clive had gradually told his family, starting with his younger brother. When one of his siblings called him a *stabane* during an argument, he was strongly reprimanded by their mother, who said that it was none of the brother's business. Clive said that his mother used to allude to his sexuality, but never directly. She would say things like, 'You have a lot of friends that are looking like girls.' Once, he told me, he asked her a hypothetical question: 'What if I am gay, what would you say?' To which his mother responded, 'Well you are. Your sister told me seven years ago.'

Clive was not aware of others who shared his dilemma and asked me, 'Have you ever met someone with the same problem?' It was a dilemma born from the *ladies* and *gents* dichotomy and while Clive clearly did not fit neatly into these categories, they had a powerful influence on his sense of self.

Clive's dilemma was not unique. Thando told me when he was promoted by a fellow delegate at a church convention in Durban, he was 'a femme', but his promoter advised him, 'You won't pass to be a femme. You are too energetic.' Brian once tried a different sexual role. He told this story about it:

> I tried it once. I tried to be a woman. On the first day when we made love, that thing is painful. It is only the pain. I enjoyed nothing. I told him, 'I am not going to be a girlfriend of you.' He became a girlfriend of me. But he kept it as a secret. Since then I did not try to be a woman. I enjoy to be a man.

While Sibusiso had no doubt about his social or sexual role 'as a man', he did feel the need to make a choice at some point between 'spending my life with a gay, or spending my life with a woman, or spending my life running [between] the two . . . So I have to decide. I still have that homework on my mind. I'm still doing that research'. All these examples show how the gender dichotomy is a central framing device in the construction of interpersonal relationships. To be unsure in a context where ideally 'a man is a man completely and a wife is a wife completely' is a source of intense personal discomfort for men like Clive because it is completely at odds with social norms and practices.

Sexual practices and HIV/AIDS

Clearly, as Brian's testimony shows, sexual roles here, as anywhere else, are interchangeable. However, the symbolic power of the gender dichotomy as the basis for sexual relationships means that these transgressions are both unusual and, where they do occur, must be kept a secret.[22]

Who then are the *gents* having sex with? Public health discourse has popularised the phrase 'men who have sex with men' to target those, like the *gents*, who do not regard themselves as gay, but who have sex with other men. This understanding assumes a neat division between sex and gender. In Ermelo, while the *gents* certainly see themselves as men, they do not see the *ladies* as men. Similarly *ladies* make a gendered distinction between themselves as feminine and their boyfriends as masculine.

The categories *ladies* and *gents* give rise to a specific set of sexual practices, which have implications for the transmission of HIV. This is an urgent question in a country where it was estimated by the Joint United Nations Programme on HIV/AIDS (UNAIDS) that 5.5 million people were living with HIV in 2005, a figure which has remained comparatively stable since then with an estimated 5.6 million people living with HIV in 2010.[23] There was a strong awareness of HIV in the region where I carried out my fieldwork. Burials of young men and women who died of mysterious ailments took place on a weekly basis. There was a way of speaking about certain deaths that suggested that HIV/AIDS was the underlying cause. It was certainly one that I recognised when I was told that a young man, otherwise healthy, had died from a mysterious ailment or as a result of malevolent forces. Some of the reasons given to me for the cause of death were 'influenza' or 'a boil on the neck' or 'bewitched by relatives'. However, there were exceptions to these euphemisms. An outspoken *lady* from Ermelo who was HIV-positive and spoke out about the dangers posed by the transmission of the virus had died. *Ladies* included information and discussion about HIV in workshops, where many misconceptions about HIV-transmission were expressed (see Chapter

5). Some hair salons distributed free condoms, although the supply, like safer sexual practices, was well intentioned, but erratic. Rumours did the rounds about who was ill and what it signified. The fear of dying was pervasive and many spoke with a sense of resignation about the prospect of a short life. There were stories of tests taken and results never collected. One young stylist, who had been ill for some time, pointed to witchcraft as the source of his ailments. Intentions to practice safer sex were sometimes thwarted by alcohol and a sense of sexual urgency. One well-informed *lady* thought that it was okay to have anal sex with a *gent* 'as long as he doesn't come inside'. A *gent* said that he felt the need to protect his young lover from HIV, but he was 'one of those people who don't like condoms'. Although he had lost his brother to AIDS in 1998, his approach to safer sex remained situational and provisional, based on subjective perceptions of safety and risk: 'Sometimes I used to use some condoms if I don't trust that person.' The dangers of HIV-infection were sometimes also included in a rural/urban framework, in which the perils of city life are highlighted. As Bhuti, who was often in the role of confidant, told me:

> Condoms are not always in the picture. There was one incident last week when three friends went to Johannesburg. They went to a dark room and they just enjoyed themselves. I asked them, 'Did you use condoms?' and they looked at each other and laughed and said, 'Yes, we did use a condom.' But I know for a fact that they did not.

Another interviewee who lived in a township near Johannesburg for a few years suggested that his exposure to information about HIV and awareness of AIDS-related deaths in an urban context contributed to his commitment to safer sex practices and a confidence in how to prevent HIV-transmission through the regular use of condoms: 'AIDS won't get me.' However, he regarded his approach as exceptional: 'Most of the gay people that I know, I think most they don't use protection. They just do it. Myself luckily I have been in different places, seen different things, that is why I use it.' Sadly, his prediction that 'AIDS won't get me' was not accurate and he died two year later.

According to another informant, there is also some perception, especially amongst the *gents* that having sex with a *lady* poses less of a health risk than having sex with a woman. This is apparently because of the fact that the AIDS pandemic in southern Africa is driven primarily by heterosexual transmission: 'People here say they want to be in love with a gay. Even though statistics show that straights are more infected, we are at high risk.'[24] There is also a historical precedent for this idea, originating in men's hostels accommodating migrant labourers on the mines. A common rationale for male same-sex relationships was the dangers of contracting venereal diseases from urban women or female prostitutes (Moodie 1989; Van Onselen 1984).

Gender inequality has been identified as one of the main reasons for women's particular vulnerability to HIV-infection in the South African context. Research shows that women are less able to negotiate safer sex and, generally speaking, men exercise the prerogative about whether or not to use condoms. Violence and coercion in sexual exchanges place women at further risk of HIV-infection. Aside from these sociological factors, women are also physically more vulnerable to infection (Walker, Reid and Cornell 2004). All these factors can equally be applied to *ladies*. *Gents*, generally but not invariably, decided on condom use, rendering *ladies* less able to negotiate safer sex. As the receptive partners in anal sex, *ladies* were physically more vulnerable to infection than *gents*. *Ladies* were also frequently subject to violence and sexual coercion. Myths and misconceptions flourished in which sex between men was regarded as less risky than sex between a man and a woman. The situation was exacerbated by the fact that same-sex practices were virtually absent from public health messaging (Berger 2004).

Marriage and authenticity

The Constitution raised hopes amongst my informants that same-sex marriage would become a reality. While the South African Law Reform Commission entered into lengthy deliberations, gays nevertheless went ahead and got married or engaged. While these marriages drew on historical antecedent (see Chapters 1 and 7), for the first time the prospect of legal recognition of these unions became a plausible reality. Marriage and engagement ceremonies thus reflected the interplay between older traditions of same-sex marriage and the options opened up by the Constitution.

Same-sex engagement and marriage ceremonies that took place were events where traditions were both evoked and reinvented. They constituted significant social occasions where the performance of gender was enacted in a particular, ritualised way. These events were also topics for seemingly endless speculation, rumour, gossip and fantasy. For example, during the course of my fieldwork there was a rumour that the British Broadcasting Corporation (BBC) was looking to make a documentary on 'an African gay wedding'. The story was that the BBC had approached the HUMCC (the gay Pentecostal church in Johannesburg) and the news had spread from there. Most importantly, the BBC would 'sponsor everything'. Andrew (who was already engaged at this point) suggested that he should fast-track his marriage when he heard about it and said as much to Bhuti, who was sceptical: 'Can you meet someone and get married in the same year?' Meanwhile Bhuti elaborated on his own extravagant wedding fantasy located, somewhat modestly, on the banks of the Vaal River in Standerton and peopled with a chaotic throng of well-wishers from his home base in Sakhile township. In the glare of the television cameras he would marry his one and only love who, at the time, had recently shifted in status from secret admirer to lover. He told me that if that were not possible, he would throw his 'love heart' in the water and never love again. The image of the television cameras created an imaginary setting in which Bhuti could invent a playful and extravagant soap opera script of romantic love, community acceptance and social recognition.

To a certain extent, marriage could be seen as a path towards respectability. Yet it was an aspiration undermined by rumour and gossip. In Bhuti's fantasy, the chaotic throngs of well-wishers are a powerful reminder of the strength and importance of social institutions such as marriage and also why, of all rights secured by constitutional equality, this was the one most frequently spoken about and discussed. At the time of my fieldwork the South African Law Commission continued to prevaricate in a mire of legislation concerning the regulation of traditional marriage, religious marriage and same-sex marriage, yet some gays simply went ahead and got married, in form, if not in legal substance. Tobi and Lwasi were one such couple. However, if gossip was to be believed, it was extraordinary that their relationship had survived the troubles and turbulence that beset their marriage. The gossip revolved around familiar themes. Lwasi, the husband, was regarded as a gold-digger, who used Tobi to finance liaisons with women and, most outrageously, to throw a party for his girlfriend. Then Tobi, the *lady* wife was accused of brazen infidelity. It was an indiscretion that was said to have taken place at Andrew's pre-engagement party with the fiancé's best man. As Andrew remarked, 'Shameless, and with the ring on!' However, similar stories plagued Andrew's engagement. Andrew's fiancé lived in Witbank, which, travelling by minibus taxi, was about an hour away from Ermelo and over two hours from Driefontein, a rural enclave where Andrew actually lived and worked. Whenever the fiancé visited Andrew (they usually met in Ermelo) it was rumoured that they always stayed in a guesthouse, which was seen as an act of secrecy and concealment, a setting apart that suggested that there was something wrong and something to hide. It was also common knowledge that Andrew was struggling to pay off the engagement, let alone the added financial burden of a fiancé whom he seldom saw and who apparently had heavy financial demands.

Another factor that detracted from aspirations towards respectability and social integration implicit in Bhuti's wedding fantasy was the absence of important family members, evident at both the wedding and engagement ceremonies I witnessed. In some cases, the secrecy seemed to be misplaced. For example, when Tobi's mother discovered that he had got married in secret and without her knowledge or involvement, she insisted on a subsequent ceremony to bless the marriage. Tobi and his husband then moved into her home and shared the house with several other relatives. Andrew, who continued to live with his mother, hid his engagement photographs and concealed his ring. But his mother was privy to the increasingly persistent rumours circulating in Driefontein and she eventually confronted him about it. Pastor Nokuthula made this point strongly at the engagement ceremony when she said about the absence of family members, 'it kills me somehow'.

While Bhuti may have fantasised about a white wedding and honeymoon, Bongani of Bethal aspired towards a more traditionally African engagement and wedding ceremony, which included *ilobola* negotiations between the respective families.[25] He described the engagement or *umhlambiso*, suggesting that the groom's family would come with a cloak, a shawl and a 'don't-touch scarf', which would be tied around the bride's neck: 'Like a ring in an African way', this signals that 'this is a wife not to be proposed to by anyone else'. Seen from this perspective, Andrew's engagement was 'too much Westernised' and I was told, 'Usually we have an *umhlambiso* followed by a white wedding, a traditional engagement with a white touch.' Bongani explained that while protocol does not allow for a discussion of the actual bride-price, which is a private matter, he is confident that because he has his own home (albeit a makeshift corrugated iron house with a mud floor subject to periodic flooding) and has 'adopted' a niece (and there is a strong value placed on children) he should fetch in the region of about R5 000.[26] Another advantage for a prospective husband was that Bongani was independently employed. While he had largely given up hairstyling (after being bewitched by jealous rivals), except for occasional braiding work, he subsequently established a relatively busy shebeen in his home, conveniently situated on a main thoroughfare in the township. While the details of his imminent engagement were presented to me almost as fait accompli, it was difficult to separate the facts from the fantasy – what the engagement ceremony would look like if or when it actually takes place. Which members of the respective families would participate and how much *ilobola* would be paid? Andrew assured everyone that his mother would be present and actively involved in his engagement ceremony, but she only found out about it later through the reliable community grapevine.

Family members can play an important role in domestic disputes. When Wandile's boyfriend assaulted him, his family intervened and his boyfriend vowed never to beat him again. Bhuti found that his boyfriend's family supported him and tried to mediate in disputes that took place between them. A sangoma who lives in Bethal was able to call on his and his partner's families to mediate in a domestic row that threatened to end in court.

On the one hand, marriage signals a pinnacle of social acceptance and equality before the law. The fact that individuals were getting married in spite of the law suggests that social acceptance was a primary motivating factor. The fact that the law was poised to change and that marriage would then have legal substance was bound to have a profound impact on the meaning and significance of the ceremonies, transforming them from symbolic alliances into ones with legal status and hence different social consequences. Yet a constant stream of rumour and gossip undermined these aspirations, not only for those who were already married or on the path towards marriage, but for those who apparently aspired towards marriage. The gossip that plagued the engagement and wedding ceremonies is perhaps symptomatic of the impossibility of keeping a 'straight' man indefinitely. It is accepted as a truism that 'straight' men in-evitably end up with women. It is also the case that in both the

engagement and the marriage, it is the *ladies* who bring money
and a degree of affluence to the relationships. However, it seems
that the rumours of gold-diggers (and the constant warnings to
be alert to this in any relationship) are also about the discrepancy
in emotional investment. In a relationship between a *lady* and a
gent, a gay and a 'straight', the emotional costs are perhaps
inevitably somewhat one-sided. The negative, undermining
gossip that runs parallel to the aspiration of marriage also seems
to represent a disbelief in the possibility of marriage, beyond
the realm of fantasy and soap operas. It is a context in which
'love hearts' must inevitably end in the Vaal River, or as Henry
explained to me, 'Another thing that I have noticed is that gays
here are struggling to get the right partners. The community
understands, but gay people are so lonely, they don't have dates
and all those things.'

Thus, while engagements and marriages are performed and
have tangible results in the form of enhanced social status,
acceptance within the family or as a kind of integration into a
wider social network, the gossip highlights the innovative and
tentative nature of the events themselves and emphasises the
precarious social position of the *ladies* in these relationships.
It seems that underlying the rumour and gossip and the
simultaneous idealising and undermining of marriage are also
related to the question of authenticity. Is a gay wedding in this
context real or is it play: does it involve form as well as substance?
Can institutions such as marriage really be adapted to meet the
needs of *ladies* and *gents* in Ermelo? These concerns were
expressed during the preparations for the engagement ceremony,
where organisers were anxious that the event should start on
time and that there should be a pastor officiating. Otherwise, I
was told, the community would not take them seriously, or as
Thulani put it in his introductory remarks, 'We are not faking
it'. One organiser told me that people wanted to be the first to
get engaged or married to enhance their social status. He
complained that in gay weddings there was far too much
emphasis placed on superficial things such as rings, food and

especially clothing, at the expense of more substantial issues, such as the quality of relationships.

His observation points to an important dimension of engagement and marriage ceremonies. One cannot ignore the highly performative aspect of the events – the strong emphasis on style, the constant interplay between sincerity and camp humour, the solemn vows and prayers and the irreverent gossip. These are performances of the gendered ideals explored in this chapter, an evocation of ideals of romantic love and a celebration of an erotic sensibility based on gender difference. *Ladies* and *gents* become husbands and wives in a ritual that dramatises difference and inequality. Think of the groom waiting to be served and Wandile's remark: 'When we are married, you will have to obey me.'

Historical antecedents, such as same-sex marriage on the mines, could be partially explained in economic terms. Patriarchal and gerontocratic social arrangements were reflected and perpetuated through marriages between older and younger men, senior and junior partners, economically secure and vulnerable men, which coincided neatly with masculine/feminine social and sexual roles (see Chapters 1 and 7). In this instance, however, while *ladies* are undoubtedly vulnerable (in a similar way that women are vulnerable), they also tend to be better off economically (see Chapter 4). Andrew was expected to support the groom and pay for the ceremony. Similarly, Bhuti was the breadwinner and older than his *gent* and many gay hairstylists supported their boyfriends.

Henry's unheard protest, 'I can be a man', is of course true – gender roles and norms are not fixed and stable. Country style and city style are not mutually exclusive or immutable. When Tsepo asked Sipho if he could accompany him to Johannesburg, he told him, half-jokingly, that he would not do so until he had learned to walk and dress more like a boy. The eroticisation of gender difference is part of 'country style' – a sensibility, a way of doing things. The engagement produced and celebrated stereotypes of masculine *gents* and effeminate *ladies*. These could be read as symptoms of self-oppression or false consciousness, a willing submission to gender norms and the inequalities they perpetuate. Or, based on the universalising assumptions of a hegemonic Western model in which egalitarian relationships are venerated, this model may be seen as a form of 'arrested (gay) development' that will ultimately evolve towards the egalitarian ideal as sexual object choice replaces gender as the basis for self-identification. According to Pierre Bourdieu:

> If the sexual relation appears as a social relation of domination, this is because it is constructed through the fundamental principle of division between the active male and the passive female and because this principle creates, organizes, expresses and directs desire – male desire as the desire for possession, eroticized domination, and female desire as the desire for masculine domination, as eroticized subordination or even, in the limiting case, as the eroticized recognition of domination (2001: 21).

However, while there may be elements of truth in both these arguments, the engagement ceremony is pre-eminently a dramatic enactment and celebration of gender difference as the basis of sexual charge and erotic life for *ladies* and *gents* opting for a 'country style'. In this context, equality is certainly not seen as an ideal form; in fact, it is gender inequality that is imbued with sexual meaning and erotic potential.

Historical evidence suggests that the gendered model has been the most pervasive in organising same-sex relationships in a South African context (Epprecht 2004). This is the case in most social contexts outside of Western Europe and North America. As Sinfield has argued, even where the 'egalitarian' model is sanctified, there is a gap between ideals of equality and lived reality (2004). What is unique in the South African context is that the persistence of a gender-based model coexists with a Constitution that recognises sexual orientation as a freedom and emphasises gender equality. It is this combination of a rights-based Constitution and deeply traditional gender norms and practices that requires further consideration. In order to understand the tenacity of the gender-based model, we need to look at the interplay between power and desire.

Notes

1. *Ladies* and *gents* were used interchangeably with the terms 'gay' and 'straight'. However, the use of *ladies* and *gents* tended to be in the light bantering form of jolly-talk and, as such, came across as one of many ways in which gender was engaged with in a humorous and sometimes self-depreciating way. The terms 'gay' and 'straight' would be used in the context of more serious discussions, when engaging with outsiders, for example, and in more formal contexts, such as workshops (see Chapter 5).
2. According to Rubin, the sex/gender system is 'the set of arrangements by which society transforms biological sexuality into products of human activity, and in which these transformed sexual needs are satisfied' (1975: 159).
3. *Intombazane* means 'girl' in Zulu.
4. Same-sex marriage became legal in terms of the *Civil Union Act* on 30 November 2006.
5. 'Lady' is also used amongst my informants as a term to refer to women.
6. I use both these terms as they were used by my informants – i.e. *gay* and *lady* are synonymous – although, as I show in Chapter 5, these categories are becoming more and more differentiated (through the introduction of the term 'transgendered', for example).
7. I elaborate on this in Chapters 3 and 6.
8. I met Sipho at the engagement party and he subsequently became my research assistant and photographer.
9. This takes place in a broader social context in which domestic violence between men and women in heterosexual relationships is also rife.
10. 'Roll-ons' are secret lovers who can be turned to for uncomplicated sex, especially when things are not going well between a *lady* and his boyfriend.

11. The mother is alluding here to the term 'stabane' (literally translated as 'two organs' or hermaphrodite), a common and usually pejorative term for gays. By asserting that her son is 'a boy' she is dismissing the idea that he is 'gay'.

12. Whether this is always the case in practice is a moot point (see note 22). Nevertheless, it is normatively unthinkable.

13. It is questionable whether the exclamation 'I am not a lesbian!' would be self-evident to someone like Sizane (a lesbian from Bethal), for example, who envisaged herself paying ilobola for two wives and establishing a polygamous household, drawing on models of Zulu masculinity. Her girlfriend told me that Sizane had approached her in an 'African way, as a guy approaching a girl'. In this context, a female same-sex relationship, like a male same-sex relationship, was likely to include 'a guy' and 'a girl'.

14. This is typical of an environment in which gender plays such a prominent role. For example, Mark Johnson writes of gays in the southern Philippines: 'In regard to two gays having sex, most find repulsive the idea that one would have sex with their "own kind"' (1997: 90).

15. Thembi is a common girl's name.

16. For a full account, see Reid (2010).

17. Again, the term 'gay' has different meanings. I am using it here as it would be used amongst my informants, but because it is a contested term, it has subtly different meanings depending on who is using it.

18. Similarly Nokuthula, from the Johannesburg-based HUMCC, who officiated at the engagement ceremony, was asked whether she was a pastor or a pastoress and responded, 'What kind of a question is that? I am a no-name brand, which means no stress.' She said that a butch could fall in love with a butch and a femme with a femme. The lesbian who asked the question was sceptical. She said that she would not like to be approached by a femme: 'I am a lady. I would have to tell a femme that I can't do them.'

19. Ultimately the charges were dropped because of an incomplete charge sheet and unclear accusations. Thando was always grateful to the activists and lawyers from Johannesburg who had taken the time and trouble to intervene on his behalf.

20. Similarly Sibusiso, a 'supporter of gays', attended gay functions in Ermelo.

21. These were Club 31 and MaThoko's Place at 32 Legodi Street.

22. This is necessarily speculative, but in interviews, conversations, joking exchanges and even in a private diary of sexual encounters, sex roles appear to be quite fixed. It is understandable that *gents* might not want to compromise their masculine status by admitting to a passive role, but *ladies*, who would not experience a loss of status, also confirm this. Of course, as one of my informants put it, 'There are things that happen behind closed doors'. But the power of gender categories, as masculine and feminine styles, is implicit in the maintenance of active and passive roles, so that transgressions, where these do occur, must be relegated to the realm of secrets and taboos, as in the case of Brian. The most common sexual practices between *ladies* and *gents* were anal or intercrural sex.

23. See http://www.unaids.org/.

24. For a wide-ranging study on the impact of the silence in relation to homosexual transmission in South Africa, see Reddy, Sandfort and Rispel (2009).

25. The meaning of *ilobola* is bride-price.

26. This was about $750 at the time. The exchange rate in July 2012 was R1 = $0.122118 ($1 = R8.41).

CHAPTER 3

Hairstyling

Being Feminine and Fashionable

Many gays appeared to enjoy a high level of social integration and acceptance within local communities. During my fieldwork, this was especially true of individuals who were obviously gay and who performed in highly feminine ways. Not only were gays very visible, but they also participated in ordinary and everyday community activities. For example, some gays attended church services and participated in ritual activities as female members, dressed in the women's uniform. Their 'dressing up' made them both distinctive and unremarkable; distinctive because the congregation knew that they were gays and un-remarkable because the uniform grouped them together with other females and gave them a clear set of roles, functions and responsibilities.

One of the spaces in which gays were very present was within the ubiquitous township hair salon. Flamboyant forms of self-styling often meant that gays were very visible and well known. This was particularly apparent amongst gay hairstylists who tended to perform hyper-feminine identities. Locally famous hairstylists were sometimes referred to as 'celebrities', a term that alluded to the interplay between style, public visibility, femininity and social status. 'Celebrity' implied a degree of veneration and respect and, in this context, it was linked to an overt form of feminine self-expression and a hyperbolic dramat-isation of feminine gender norms and roles.

One Sunday in April 2006, I sat with hairstylist Nathi in his room while he changed out of his church uniform and into the clothes that he was going to wear to a party that afternoon. Within a short space of time he had taken off a uniform that signified demure feminine respectability (a bottle-green dress and a white shirt, headscarf and matching belt) and put on clothing that announced stylish femininity (a pair of 28-waist, tight-fitting, white pants, stylish boots, earrings that were long enough to brush his shoulders and a delicate pink blouse that cascaded down his left thigh, offset with an orange jacket). There would be nothing remarkable about women church members changing from formal to informal wear, but because Nathi was not a woman, but a *lady*, his clothing was part of an ongoing and self-conscious performance of femininity. In both churches and hair salons, gays frequently presented themselves as feminine, but in these two different spaces there were, of course, completely different styles. This chapter is concerned with the forms of femininity performed in the ambit of the hair salon, the kinds of hyper-feminine performances that gave rise to the notion of 'celebrity'.

Hairstyling was a common occupation for gays in my fieldwork. In December 2003, when Bhuti compiled a list of ten of his closest gay associates in Ermelo, four worked with hair. Amongst those on the list were Dumisani, who at the time was self-employed, and Nathi who worked at the Professional Hair Salon. Also on the list were Manti, who helped Dumisani from time to time, and S'thembele who was in his penultimate year in high school and was at the same time earning money by plaiting hair from his parents' home.[1] Bhuti's list did not include some of the best-known stylists who had moved away from Ermelo – Siyanda and Ayanda who lived and worked in eMbalenhle, and Mondli who had settled in Witbank (both townships situated about an hour away).

Gay hairstylists were quite successful in this highly competitive informal industry. Independently run gay salons tended to be busy establishments with a lot of clients, the vast majority of whom were women. Gays who worked as employees in hair salons enjoyed a special status as highly skilled practitioners.

Importantly, the hair salons served as a point of interaction with the broader community – perhaps the main site of engagement and exchange between overt gays and a largely heterosexual female client base. The gay stylists thus occupied a strategic position. Their visibility, status, fame and their role as interlocutors meant that they had a large influence on public perceptions of gays in their community.

Histories of homosexuality in Western countries assume that urban spaces are a prerequisite for the emergence of gay social spaces. The anonymity of urban life has meant a weakening of the hold of traditional authority structures, the loosening of family control and the dissipation of intense social surveillance characteristic of small towns or rural communities (Houlbrook 2005; Chauncey 1994; Eribon 2004). In this scenario and in a South African context, gay spaces are more likely to be found in major urban centres, rather than in smaller towns, such as Ermelo or Piet Retief, or in townships on the peripheries of industrial centres, such as eMbalenhle. Well-established gay organisations that address the social, cultural, health and political needs and aspirations of gays and lesbians are to be found in cities such as Durban, Johannesburg and Cape Town. Yet gays who worked as hairstylists in the small towns of my research enjoyed a high social status, were very visible and the hair salon itself became a gay social space. This suggests a different possibility to gay culture as synonymous with the city.

Paradoxically, alongside a high level of visibility, acceptance and integration of gays, was evidence of vulnerability. I was aware of four incidents of violence directed against gay hairstylists during the course of my fieldwork – three muggings and one case of sexual assault. In addition, there was a pervasive public rhetoric that denounced gays as 'un-African', 'un-Christian' or as a manifestation of political corruption and social decay. These kinds of views were, for instance, expressed with passionate conviction by speaker after speaker at a public hearing – organised by the National House of Traditional Leaders (NHTL) in Badplaas, Mpumalanga in February 2005 – on the prospect of legal changes that would accommodate same-sex marriage (for a more detailed account see Chapter 6).

In such a context of violence, sexual assault and anti-gay rhetoric, how do gays become not only accepted in this particular niche profession of hairstyling, 'the profession that accommodates the dragging queens' (as one of my informants put it), but actually celebrated and venerated as highly skilled and sought-after stylists? How do hairstylists create gay spaces in the rough and often dangerous social environments typical of South African townships?

Dumisani (1978–2006)

'This is the funeral of a celebrity,' remarked one of the mourners as Dumisani, a gay hairstylist from Wesselton, was buried on a Saturday morning in February 2006. The elderly preacher, a small red ribbon pinned to his lapel, was concluding the service and the coffin was almost ready to be lowered into the rain-drenched earth. The crowd began to sing a slow, rhythmic and mournful hymn. Standing near the grave, a man unrolled a woven grass mat and, using the sharp edge of a shovel, punched holes into it. At that moment, I was surprised to see another young man remove his jacket and ease himself through the gap between the edge of the grave and the coffin. Once he was in the hole with the coffin suspended above him, the perforated grass mat was rolled up and passed down to him. Out of sight of the mourners, he unravelled it onto the bare soil to serve as a final resting place for the wooden casket. The young man then emerged from underground and the coffin was covered with a floral blanket before being lowered slowly. In the meantime, a group of young men and women collected all funeral pro-grammes from the mourners and later threw these onto the casket.

The men took turns filling the grave with soil; shovels passed from hand to hand. Then a man held a shovel full of earth at waist height, his back slightly bent from the weight of it, and the women filed past, each taking a handful of soil and throwing it into the grave. This was also a signal for the gays and they too joined the queue, taking a symbolic handful of soil and casting it into the grave. This feminine procession thus included a group of church members; a number of Dumisani's relatives; many, many clients, as well as several young men in high-heels and skirts, all showing their last respects to Dumisani. As the grave was filled, their hymns mingled with those sung by other mourners at other funerals taking place on that day and in close proximity. This cemetery, like others all over South Africa, was filling up much more quickly than local government officials had anticipated and, at the entrance, a new space-saving concept in burials was being advertised on a billboard. Dumisani was buried in the traditional way, while in the background workmen built innovative tombs in the form of a mausoleum-type structure of stacked concrete crypts. I wondered at the time how popular they would prove to be, whose idea it was and what such a burial would look like. What, for instance, would happen to the ritual grave-filling, the grass mat, the blanket and the funeral programmes in an internment in a concrete tomb?

When the men had finished their work and Dumisani was buried under a heap of freshly turned earth, an empty bottle of mineral water was placed on top of the grave, half-submerged in the loose soil. This simple plastic container served as a temporary marker to distinguish the otherwise nondescript earth mound of Dumisani's final resting place from those around him. A graveyard official held up a card with a number printed on it so that members of the immediate family, seated under an awning, could see it. It was the number allocated to this particular grave, which would distinguish it from the long row of identical mounds, should the plastic bottle not suffice as an identification marker. The awning reserved for family members, together with individual umbrellas, provided the only shade in the immediate vicinity of a cemetery bordered by blue gums but otherwise treeless. His work done, the elderly preacher moved away from the grave, greeting and chatting to the family and members of his church, a branch of the Apostolic Faith Mission. Dumisani had been an occasional visitor at the St Paul's Apostolic Faith Mission and some of his fellow congregants were there, but it was his sister who had rallied the support of the preacher from her branch of the Apostolic Faith Mission. It was her preacher who had visited Dumisani in his last dying days and who then officiated at his funeral.

The crowds began to disperse from the cemetery, squeezing into whatever transport was available or walking the few kilometres from the grave to the house where Dumisani had lived. In front of the house, the mourners formed a long queue to the table, where gays and young women in aprons dished up a meal from large aluminium pots, consisting of a chicken dish, a lamb dish, various salads, chakalaka, rice and pap. A small group of gays was in charge of the catering and their plan worked efficiently. While Dumisani was being laid to rest, several gays had stayed behind at the house in order to complete the cooking, which had started the night before and continued from the early hours of that morning. The owner of the N.M.B. Hair Saloon, Nobuhle, oversaw the whole enterprise. N.M.B. was the salon where Dumisani had worked for just over a year, before he became too frail to fulfil his duties. Nobuhle was particularly busy on the days leading up to the funeral, making sure that everything went according to plan and that Dumisani had a proper send-off. Fortunately for her, when Dumisani's illness became debilitating, three other gays had stepped in to help her out at N.M.B. Hair Saloon, including Siyanda who had recently returned to Ermelo and saw N.M.B. as a good stop-gap, while he looked for suitable premises in which to open his own salon, which would be 'the biggest saloon in Wesselton', he told me.

It was Siyanda, dressed in white slacks and a blouse, offset with pink shoes and matching accessories – a handbag, scarf, necklace and earrings – who handed out white ceramic plates to people standing in the queue in the hot sun. He saw to it that important people were discreetly picked out of the lines and whisked to the front of the queue or personally served in their cars. He also ensured that there was a rapid circulation of plates being washed and made available to a crowd that was larger than anyone had expected. The queue expanded dramatically when the 48-seater bus arrived from the cemetery and 121 passengers emerged from it onto the street. The unlucky ones who could not squeeze themselves onto the bus and who had failed to find a place in one of the twenty or so vehicles driving back from the cemetery – those who were not even able to hitch a ride on the back of a bakkie – arrived last, having walked the few kilometres from the cemetery. Many carried umbrellas against the harsh midday sun.

I remembered how, during the previous year, Dumisani had sat on the front stoep of this house leaning against the unplastered concrete breezeblocks – the cheap materials from which the house was built. The roof was made of grey asbestos sheeting and the only gestures towards adornment were the door and window frames, which were painted blue. The house number was painted onto the raw concrete using the same blue paint, as was the metal postbox at the rudimentary barbed-wire garden fence. Dumisani sat between the wooden front door and the large, metal-framed window, warming himself in the winter sun, trying to stop his thin, frail body shivering from cold and fever. As we sat on the north-facing stoep that afternoon, the sun had that deeply warming effect that the Highveld sun can have, even in mid-winter. It was at that time of day just before the evening fires were lit in almost every house, for cooking and for warmth; when Wesselton would be choked with smog and Dumisani's fragile frame would once again be racked by fits of coughing. He was determined to get better quickly because he was the hairstylist for a wedding due to take place in the nearby town of Morgenzon that weekend and he planned to use the proceeds from the wedding to buy an outfit for the forthcoming beauty pageant, Miss Gay Ten Years of Democracy. He needed his apprentice, Manti, to help him with the wedding at the weekend. Manti's main jobs would be to work with hair-relaxing chemicals and to do blow-drying, while Dumisani attended to the actual design and styling of the bride's and groom's hair. But the two had recently fallen out, because Dumisani's close friend Nathi told Dumisani that he had overheard Manti saying 'bad words' about him at Bhuti's place, where Manti was staying. Bhuti and Dumisani were not on speaking terms at that time either. Before I left, he asked me to pass a message on to Manti, saying that he really needed to see him about the wedding.

Dumisani's aunt lived in the four-roomed house, while his sparsely furnished room was a backyard shack built of corrugated iron, hot in summer and freezing in winter. At one stage he ran his business from there as well, advertised with a hand-painted sign. Beneath the blue lettering, 'Hair Studio', were two budding leaves, also in blue, a symbol of new possibilities and new growth, perhaps. Dumisani had died young, barely three months into his 28th year. He had been ill for a long time. I asked some of the gays, Dumisani's close friends, what had caused his death. They gave me knowing, evasive looks, as if I were asking a trick question and said things like, 'You know' or 'I am not saying anything'. I asked three of his clients, young women who travelled with me to the cemetery and back. They looked at each other; there was an awkward silence and then one answered for all of them, 'We don't know'. They did know, but no one was saying. It was only the small red ribbon worn on the priest's lapel that even alluded to the unmentionable. Later that day, I learned that members of Dumisani's family had confided in one member of the local gay community, hoping for advice on treatment options for HIV. Unfortunately this intervention was too late to save Dumisani.

During the church service, which took place earlier that day under a tarpaulin erected in front of the house, there was an enlarged, framed photograph of Dumisani placed on his coffin. It was taken at Miss eMbalenhle in September 2000 and showed him in his persona of 'Jacqueline', in high-heels, a black top and skirt, with his midriff exposed. A small group of women from Dumisani's church, accompanied by matronly aunts, all wearing doeks, asked to have one last look at the photograph. They exclaimed how beautiful he was and then left, walking down

the dusty street on their way home. At this point, a small group
of gays also decided to leave, some for 'after tears',[2] others to
make their weary way home. First, they went to say goodbye
to the family. The small group gathered in the stifling room
where family members sat on the few chairs available, while
others sat on the floor. Bhuti spoke, a hymn was sung; the aunt
whose home it was responded, thanking them for being such
good friends and taking care of Dumisani right until the end,
even though by that stage he was in and out of hospital. The
aunt said that their friendship with Dumisani was like a marriage:
inevitably there were quarrels and disagreements, but ultimately
they stuck together. She also said that she had a small hairstyling
business of her own that was not doing particularly well. She
said half-jokingly that she was looking for a suitable stylist and
she made it clear that she would only employ a gay.

Dumisani had elected to work, not with his aunt, but rather
with Nobuhle, perhaps because her business was bigger and more
profitable. A mother of three children, Nobuhle had a matronly
air and an easygoing manner. She was always well dressed and
drove a good car. She was financially independent and an astute
businesswoman. Initially, she was a client of Dumisani's and
when they got talking, as they did while she had her hair styled,
Dumisani suggested that they go into business together. In fact
his business, which at that stage was run from his room, was
not going particularly well. 'I am not satisfied in Ermelo,'
Dumisani told me, 'I would prefer to be in any busy place.'
Nobuhle liked the idea of opening a salon, knew the allure of
gay stylists, especially one with Dumisani's experience and in
July 2004, the N.M.B. opened its doors. It was on one of the
main roads serving Wesselton, a secondary one, admittedly, but
tarred nevertheless, and passing trade was good for business. It
was a modest shop.[3] The two small windows and glass door that
faced onto the street were heavily covered in burglar bars, the
rough, crude variety of many township business establishments,
where security takes precedence over aesthetics.

The N.M.B. Saloon

The following description of the N.M.B. Saloon is a composite of notes and recordings from February 2005 (a year before Dumisani's death).

Directly in front of me, as I walk through the front entrance of the N.M.B. Saloon and onto the white floor tiles, is a long list of available styles and a price list. It is handwritten with black marker pen on orange cardboard [see the Appendix at the end of this chapter]. Directly above this list is a clock. It is 10.00 a.m. and the Saloon has been open for an hour. Since it is a weekday, it will close at 5.30 this evening. On Saturdays, it is open from 9.00 a.m. until 7.00 p.m. or, if business is slow, until 6.00 p.m. On Sundays, the Saloon opens after church, from midday until 5.30 p.m. Everyone works seven days a week, although this sounds more onerous than it is in practice because there are often long periods of inactivity between clients and stylists can always be summoned from elsewhere in the vicinity when they are needed. Salons tend to serve as social hubs, places of relaxation, as well as sites of work.

Hanging beneath the clock, on either side of the hairstyling menu are two posters, both advertising hair products. One of them is advertising products from the company Black Like Me. Towards the back of the shop, a few paces from the front door, are two hairdryers perched on legs and poised above the drying chairs. Near the hairdryers is a three-tiered plastic tray on wheels bearing the most colourful range of plastic hair accessories imaginable, carefully colour-coded and arranged into piles of pink, blue, yellow and green by Xolani, assistant and apprentice to Dumisani. On my left is a set of mirrors hanging on the wall above a row of storage cupboards that, if I sat on one of the styling chairs, would be at eye-level. Between the mirrors is a handmade sign, stuck onto the wall, announcing one of the proprietor's trading principles: 'Strictly No Credit', and above the sign is a poster advertising a Dark and Lovely hair product. This poster, and the one advertising Black Like Me, is one of many distributed free of charge at retail outlets where hair products are bought. Alternatively, certain products and supplies can be bought from travelling sales representatives. There is a bit of commotion when one of the representatives arrives at N.M.B. and Dumisani argues about the prices of the products. Xolani joins in the fray, but it is all play. The prices are set and this is only pretence at bargaining, for the good-humoured fun of it. The representative has a limited range of products from well-known brands – Ladine, Dark and Lovely and Caivil on offer. 'She is our friend,' Xolani tells me.

It is in this part of the shop, facing the mirrors, that Dadi is braiding a woman's hair. There is some communication trouble because Dadi struggles with English. She is a refugee from the Congo and as she tries to express herself in faltering English, she invariably lapses into French. Somehow Dumisani manages to translate from the client's Zulu back into a form of English that is intelligible to Dadi, although there are a few impatient hand gestures and demonstrations thrown in for good measure. According to Dumisani, women from the Congo have a reputation for being excellent at hair braiding and so the client is prepared to put up with this minor inconvenience.[4] Two of the client's friends are in the shop, chatting to help pass the hours while the time-consuming braiding work is done.

On the same side of the shop (as I enter, on my left) is Ephraim. He seems to have only one tool for his craft – electric clippers. He is cutting the hair of a young boy in school uniform. The boy is impatient and almost wriggling under the plastic shawl that directs his clipped hair onto the floor. Ephraim will work all day cutting men's and boys' hair with his electric clippers. He offers a no-nonsense R10 cut. His clipper is plugged into a wall-mounted electric socket. For this, he pays the proprietor extra for electricity, over and above the monthly rental that he pays for the use of this space. Other than that, he pockets the profits. He has a self-sufficient, autonomous air about him, appropriate for someone who effectively works for himself. As he finishes with his young client, he takes out a green plastic brush and pan, carefully sweeps up the hair from the floor and, picking up a half-cigarette from the counter, he leaves the shop to dispose of the hair and finish his cigarette.

On the opposite side of the shop, on my right, is the heart of the Saloon, the washbasins, tools and equipment for styling work. There is a small set of shelves with a limited range of essential hair products. These have been bought en masse at Jumbo Cash and Carry, a retail supply outlet in Crown Mines, Johannesburg, where many stylists go to get their products. Immediately in front of these shelves are a small counter and a stool. Here Dumisani is in charge. When he is not styling hair, like now, he is perched on the stool behind the counter. The financial and stock-control records are kept in a drawer within his easy reach and under his watchful eye. As I go through the books, I notice that there is a recorded profit of R4 590 for this month of February. This is after the rental of R800 has been paid as well as the combined salary bill for Dumisani, Xolani and Dadi of R1 700. Eight months into the Saloon's existence, employees are still on what Dumisani describes as 'start-up' salaries. I notice that Dumisani, in his role 'like a manager', earned a meagre R600,[5] the same basic salary as Dadi, while Xolani, his apprentice, earned R500. While the Saloon opened in July 2004, the books only start in October 2004, so it is not an accurate reflection of all income and expenditure, a practice that is not atypical of many salons. For example, there is no record of the Miss Face of Africa beauty pageant that saw 40 contestants from five local high schools coming through the doors of the Saloon shortly after it opened in July 2004, in order to be prepared for their big night. The books, then, are a record of individual clients, their styles and contact numbers, rather than an accurate record of all income and expenditure. On top of their basic salary, hairstylists like Dumisani usually earn a commission and some take on freelance work, such as home-based braiding when they can get it, thereby supplementing their modest basic salary. Dumisani, in addition to commission, had a special relationship with Nobuhle, the owner of the Saloon, which meant that there were other, additional perks. 'Dumisani,' Bhuti told me, 'is lucky. The owner likes him so much she gives him everything that he wants.' This included additional cash as well as emotional, practical and medical support during his long illness.

Dumisani also controls the small portable radio and CD player. Right now it is tuned into Radio Swazi and you can hear a public interest commercial warning about the ravages of AIDS in the area and urging listeners to use condoms and practice safer sex. At other times it would be more likely that Dumisani would be playing a CD of the indeterminate disco variety. There is also a small television set tuned to SABC 1, the channel that includes popular soap operas such as *Days of Our Lives* and *The Bold and the Beautiful* in its programming schedule.

Xolani says that everyone is family here and I understand something of what he means by the air of intimacy and familiarity in the shop. Nobuhle arrives for a short visit to check up on things, chat to the clients, follow up on some details with Dumisani and see that all the arrangements have been made for Xolani's party tonight. He is turning 24 and a party is being held in his honour. Nobuhle is stylishly dressed, in large-size jeans, a rust-coloured blouse matching her henna-coloured hair, offset with gold bangles and necklaces. Her pointed shoes are a little tight for her feet, so she eases them off as she sits on one of the hairdrying chairs, swivelling slightly as she talks to this person and then that one in a light, bemused and engaging banter. She is planning a beauty pageant and she would like Bhuti to organise it. She says that she wants to see gays and girls competing on the same stage. 'The gays say they are better,' she says, 'I want to see who is the most stylish girl.' A woman appears with a plate of cooked breakfast (fried pink polony, fried eggs and a pile of white bread) and a bottle of Fanta Orange. The plate is first presented to me and then passed around the shop. Everyone helps themselves to a little. She tells me that she is an 'aunt'; Xolani and Dumisani contradict her, saying, 'No, she is a client'. They all laugh about it. Then Nobuhle leaves as quickly as she arrived, driving off in her white sedan, carefully circumnavigating the potholes in the road. As if to confirm the family nature of her enterprise, the name N.M.B. is derived from the first-name initials of Nobuhle's children – Nomfundo, Mpendulo and Baneli.

Dumisani's hairstyling history
Dumisani experienced a precarious career of fluctuating fortunes before securing his place behind the counter at the N.M.B. Saloon. He started doing hair when he was in his penultimate

year of high school, learning skills informally at home from his mentor, Siyanda. His career began in the Professional Hair Salon in Bethal, where he was employed for a year. He then got a summer job, at Moth's Hair Saloon in Wesselton, Extension 2.[6] Dumisani then branched out on his own, taking a risk by opening a salon in a remote one-horse town, Perdekop. He thought that Perdekop would be a good place to introduce style: 'I was thinking that they don't know about our style. I wanted to improve them. People came for new styles, but not enough.' His business failed to thrive due to a lack of customers. So he turned to trade (sex work) and in this venture he found that there was no shortage of clients. He claims that trade thrived as his male clients discovered the pleasures of anal sex: 'I took them to bed to demonstrate. I throw them to my Durban [anus]. Because you know that Durban is too small. They scream and scream and say, "Oh, if I can stay with you, baby, you are hot! You are hotter than women."'

The men also started frequenting his salon as clients, requesting popular styles such as S-curl and waves. Dumisani told me that while they kept their girlfriends, they also continued to enjoy his 'special cake'. Dumisani demonstrated how his deft use of a towel concealed his penis from view and helped to maintain the performance of femininity and masculinity in these sexual exchanges. He felt sorry for, in his terms, 'a gay' that he met in Perdekop. This gay worked as a dance instructor and he was regularly coerced by other men to socialise with them, in order to make him more masculine in his mannerisms and behaviour. In contrast, Dumisani said, 'I was comfortable in Perdekop because they know me as a girl, not a gay'. The successful and sustained performance of femininity was Dumisani's ticket to success in Perdekop.

Dumisani returned to Ermelo in 2001 and worked at the Unisex Hair Saloon, before opening up his own business in Wesselton, the JB Hair Saloon. This did not work out as he was plagued by burglaries. When his styling combs were stolen, he decided to close the shop and started styling at his clients' homes, before he began working from his own room in his aunt's back yard. His loyal clients continued to use his services and it was here that he and Nobuhle had hatched the plan to start the N.M.B. Hair Saloon. Dumisani got on well with his landlady aunt. She had stood between Dumisani and his father when it became apparent that he was gay. Dumisani said that there was in fact no need for him to tell anyone that he was gay since it was perfectly obvious. He had realised it himself when he was fourteen. Although even before that, when he was a young child, he felt that he was different from the other boys. He played with girls and wore dresses: 'I got the feeling, when playing mother, like I can sleep with a man, not a woman'. Initially his father, who worked as a glass-fitter, disowned him, saying that he did not produce *stabane*. Dumisani told me that his aunt had become used to gay people when she lived in Daveyton and had managed to persuade his father 'just to accept me the way I am'.

Dumisani was popular as a gay stylist. Bhuti would have said that Dumisani was accepted as a woman, not a gay. This kind of observation motivated Bhuti to run a series of workshops on the topic (see Chapter 5). When Bhuti observed that 'the gays of Ermelo don't know how to be real gays' and explained that they were accepted as women and not as gays, he was making two observations: first, a number of gays performed femininity in very overt ways and second, a feminine identity was linked in complex and contradictory ways to prospects of social acceptance and integration. Dumisani would concur with Bhuti's assessment. After all, it was his observation that his social acceptance and sexual allure in Perdekop was experienced 'as a girl, not a gay'. Gays who performed in overtly feminine ways could be accepted into society and integrated into local communities as women, but the social position that they accepted as women also came at a price: they were vulnerable in the same way that women were vulnerable. On the level of the mundane, they were generally expected to be deferential to *gents* and required to perform domestic services. They were also vulnerable to gender-based violence. In one year, Dumisani, for instance, was mugged and sexually assaulted in two separate incidents. While I was visiting Nathi in hospital, where he was recovering from a hand wound that was inflicted during the theft of his cell phone, Dumisani arrived. He had been in court, once again, in connection with his rape case, in which one of the accused was his cousin, a young man, still attending high school. The case had been postponed. Dumisani was hoping for a settlement. The pressure was on the accused. Dumisani told Nathi and the group of women visiting, including Nathi's mother, that he had agreed to drop charges in return for a payment of R1 000 per rapist, amounting to a total of R2 000. The women all expressed sympathy and concern as well as indignation against the rapists. There was a strong sense of female solidarity. Later, after Nathi was discharged and I drove him and his mother home from the hospital, together with Dumisani, they filled me in on the full story. Nathi pointed out the place where Dumisani had been abducted and the cemetery where the young men had taken him, sexually assaulted him and left him naked to find his way home. Dumisani told me that the men had masturbated over his naked body, took turns ejaculating in his mouth and then urinated in his mouth, saying that he 'must swallow the sperms'. Dumisani explained that he was willing to drop the charges and accept a cash payment because one of them was a relative. Other family members were shocked and appalled by this assault: 'I don't know what is happening with that boy!' exclaimed an aunt. Dumisani experienced both solidarity and empathy with other women who recognised that, as a *lady*, Dumisani was vulnerable to similar forms of violence that women could be subjected to.

As shown in Chapter 1, if there is domestic violence in a relationship between a *lady* and a *gent*, it is invariably the *lady* at the receiving end of the violence. Similarly *ladies* may be the victims of sexual assault or be seen as easy targets for theft. In fact hairstylists who flaunted their success through dress and other accoutrements were frequently the targets of muggers.

Their gender rendered them vulnerable to attacks from men and their perceived affluence made them especially desirable targets. Yet vulnerability was only half the picture. Femininity, as both Dumisani and Bhuti observed, could also be deployed to strategic advantage.

Femininity and social integration

Dumisani was buried as he had lived, openly gay and remarkably integrated into his social milieu. Bhuti had selected the enlarged photograph that would appear on the coffin and did so with his own agenda – to emphasise the fact that Dumisani was gay, although it would be unlikely that anyone at the funeral would not know. Bhuti, in keeping with his activist role, nevertheless chose an image that foregrounded Dumisani's gay identity. The photo that appeared on the coffin captured something of the essence of Dumisani and his short life. The photograph showed Dumisani in a moment of aspiration, competing for the title of Miss eMbalenhle as 'Jacqueline', wearing a dress that reflected the glamour that inspired and shaped him, but was in stark contrast to the harsh material reality of his daily life. The context of the beauty pageant was also appropriate – after all, it was to beauty that he devoted his working life. These elements – an emphasis on style, feminine forms of self-presentation, aspirations towards rising above circumstances, devotion to beauty and the need to make do with whatever was available – were characteristic features of Dumisani's life and in many respects strongly resonated with the experiences of his gay contemporaries.

Although he was only an occasional visitor to his branch of the Apostolic Faith Mission, Dumisani was afforded all the rites and rituals associated with this church, albeit indirectly through his sister's more devotional participation in another branch of the same umbrella church. His funeral brought diverse social groupings together, from elderly and respectable women members of conservative church communities to gays in full drag. There was full participation in the funeral: the young men preparing the grass mat as a final resting place, for example; the ritual grave-filling; the elderly preacher, as well as the efficient catering for a large crowd. Aside from some criticism from other gays that the preacher from St Paul's, Dumisani's home branch of the Apostolic Faith Mission, did not conduct the service, there was no indication of any tension or animosity. On the contrary, the scale of the funeral was such that it reinforced his status as a 'celebrity'. This was certainly not the funeral of a marginal member of society. There were no attempts to conceal even the most flamboyant aspects of Dumisani's lifestyle. Funerals often provide the opportunity for conflicting viewpoints to be discretely presented – a forum where family tensions can be expressed within certain parameters and social conventions.[7] Yet there were no voices of dissent or criticism in any of the orations.[8]

It seemed that, aside from being considered a less-than-devoted member of his own congregation, Dumisani had found a niche in even the most conservative of communities. His close friend Nathi had certainly found a home within his own church community – one of the many independent African churches that fall under the broad umbrella of Zionist groups. Nathi felt that while Dumisani was referred to by the priest at the funeral as 'he' (which is what Dumisani would have wished and expected) Nathi would prefer to be referred to as 'she', when the inevitable day came. He said he would inform his fellow congregants at Inhlanhla Yezikhova Ezimnqini of his wishes.[9] It was a request that would be unlikely to encounter any argument, given that Nathi was a fully-fledged member of his church, wearing the women's uniform and participating in all the female activities of a church community that was highly differentiated in terms of gender roles and responsibilities. When I asked one of the women congregants why she wore a starched white shawl, which distinguished her and a small group of women from others in the church, she explained, 'If you are married, or a mother, you wear it. You see Nathi is not a mother and is not married, so she just wears without the shawl.' Nathi really is considered a woman, although it is known that he is a gay. When I questioned church members about Nathi's integration as a gay within the church community, my line of questioning was met with incomprehension. People said that she was a good singer, an indispensable part of the choir (where she sang soprano), she was a very devoted church member who attended regularly and she was a personable presence in the church. There did not seem to be any plausible reason as to why she would not be accepted. The issue of her being gay did not come up. She had the status of an unmarried woman in the church. 'They accept me very much, they love me, they take me as a girl,' said Nathi. Nathi said that he chose this particular branch of the church to worship in, because 'the guys there are so cute'.

Mondli was also an active church member. He used to run his own salon in Wesselton, the Optimum Unisex Saloon and had a reputation for being the best producer of cornrows in Ermelo. Before he moved to Witbank to be closer to his boyfriend,[10] he served as the treasurer of his Zionist church group in Wesselton. He wore the women's uniform and participated in the activities that were the preserve of female members.

The Zionist churches have a reputation for being accepting of gays. According to Brendan, a 49-year-old gay man living in Sakhile, Standerton, Zionist-affiliated churches 'don't have any problem with gays'.[11] Not all gay members attended as women. For example, Nhlanhla, who worked as a sangoma (see Chapter 6), wore the male cloak when he attended church and Dingane from Piet Retief, who was a preacher in his church, also went in male uniform. Sipho, who attended a Zionist church in Germiston (a town to the east of Johannesburg) comprised mainly of people from near his home district of Driefontein in Mpumalanga, was very conscious not to be too obviously gay in the way he dressed or in his hairstyle, eventually changing to a different branch, where ideas about gender and appearance were evidently less rigid.[12]

Stylists such as Nathi and Mondli and other gays were able to integrate themselves into their local communities as *ladies* and, in so doing, participate in a broad range of activities, including their local churches. Nathi and Mondli styled themselves as feminine both in their working lives and as members of their respective church communities. Yet, as Bhuti's observation that gays were accepted 'as women' and Dumisani's recollection that he was accepted 'as a girl' emphasise, they are clearly not women or girls, but, rather, like them or similar to them. This points to the pivotal role of performance in creating and sustaining a gay identity. This complex interplay is evident in Dumisani's description of how, in his role as a sex worker, he had to explain the meaning of 'gay' to men who propositioned him:

> It was an awkward situation as a girl. When I was proposed, I told them that I am a gay. They asked, 'What is a gay?' I explained, 'Gays are these people. People who have a big, big . . .' [he gestures to his penis, and laughs]. No, gays are people who feel like them, but we are homosexual. When I said 'homosexual' they wanted to know what that meant. I explained that they are girls, but with no breasts. They took it easy as they were very understanding.

The self-conscious performance of femininity played an important role in the social integration of gays. This played itself out in a very subtle, almost unseen way at the funeral where a number of gays, in a seamless fashion, joined the procession of women who were paying their last respects to Dumisani by casting a symbolic handful of earth into the grave. The ritual offered the possibility of inclusion, through a ritual practice observed by women. Not all mourners participated in the process of filling the grave; some simply sang hymns throughout. Similarly, not all gays joined the queue of women. Some stood on the sidelines, singing. The gays who did participate were those in full or partial drag. While some of the gays joined the women, none joined the men in shovelling soil.

Ladies might be like women, but they occupy a liminal gender position that enables them to integrate in local communities, to sustain a sexual allure amongst straight men and, as I argue in the next chapter, to secure an economic niche for themselves.

Nobuhle's beauty pageant in which 'gays and girls would compete against each other' resonated with the common perception that simultaneously conflated effeminacy and gay identity and yet recognised a distinction between 'gays and girls'. What was unusual about Nobuhle's pageant was that it would see girls (as an assumed 'natural' category) and gays (as a recognised 'performative' category) competing against each other on stage, on the basis of their ability to produce 'style'. Nobuhle's beauty pageant points to two aspects of gays in relation to women. The first is identification with and aspiration towards the effeminate, and the second is rivalry and competition with women. This perception of gays as effeminate and in competition with women came up frequently in my fieldwork. It is a perception that I might have initially dismissed as the understandable misconceptions of outsiders, were it not so strongly echoed by gays themselves. It came up frequently in joking banter, in competition over boyfriends and amongst hairstylists in competing over the symbolic terrain of relative skill and expertise.

In December 2003, Siyanda's boyfriend, whom he described as a 'steady boyfriend for two months', was in hospital after being stabbed in a drunken brawl. Siyanda told me that he had visited him at the same time as his girlfriend, who was upset that Siyanda was there. He told me that his boyfriend had elected to see him, rather than her. Siyanda also said that he was adept at turning straight men into gays: 'I like straight guys. And I also change them. If I used to make love with someone, he follows me. Or, if we break up, he will hunt for another gay. I'm like that.' Dumisani also bragged about his sexual prowess, in competition with women, during his stay in Perdekop: 'Men had other girlfriends, but when I am there they ignored their girlfriends. I am a queen in town and they rushed to their queen.' As these anecdotes suggest, gays are in competition with women in relation to straight men. In Chapter 2, I showed how the desire for straight men as sexual partners can lead to rivalry and competition. As hairstylists, gays often compare themselves to women stylists and promote themselves as better than them. In Nathi's words, 'Among the girls, I am number one.'

The hair salon as a gay space

After school, Simphiwe found welcome respite at the Cynobrey Hair Gallery.[13] At the time, he was sixteen years old and 'a gay', Ayanda told me. He had delicate gestures and moved with a subtle feminine gait, as if his apprenticeship was also to Siyanda's more flamboyant style – Siyanda's way of walking in high-heels, for instance. Simphiwe seemed like an unformed version of Siyanda, someone who was only beginning to develop a charac-teristic repertoire of mannerisms, gestures and postures and a particular sense of style. He spent his afternoons at the Cynobrey Hair Gallery as an informal apprentice. He did bits and pieces of work – the most strenuous activity was collecting the occa-sional bucket of cold water from the bathroom in the main adjoining house. Otherwise he was to be seen behind the make-shift corrugated iron counter playing games on his cell phone. He wore a small plaster on his forehead, hiding an adolescent skin blemish, which also inadvertently accentuated his youthful vulnerability. He told me that his ambitions did not lie in hairstyling – he would rather do catering or fashion design.

Yet, in spite of his aspirations in other spheres of work, he was in a subtle way being inducted into the business, as many other hairstylists had been before him. For Simphiwe this was an informal, almost incidental process of induction, by simply being there and doing various small tasks. Xolani was specifically employed as an apprentice and assistant to Dumisani, thereby learning the hairstyling trade from a seasoned professional. Similarly, Manti had served as an informal apprentice and assistant to Dumisani when he worked from his home-based Hair Studio. This form of apprenticeship is typical and one of the ways in which hairstyling is perpetuated as a niche profession for gays. Ayanda learned his hairstyling techniques from Siyanda, whom he had known since childhood. Dumisani had also learned from Siyanda, who allowed an air of mystery to surround his talents. One client remarked that Siyanda was 'very talented, she can do a thing out her head'. She once told me that Siyanda 'prays at night and God tells her how to do it then. She knows how to do things without going to school to learn it'. While they were still at school, Siyanda and his friends spent a lot of their spare time at the Everest Saloon in Wesselton, run by a woman by the name of Thoko. Siyanda had also worked with another gay stylist before branching out on his own, but being entirely self-taught was part of his mystique. Other gay stylists talk about their natural abilities with hair. Nkosinathi, for example, described himself as self-taught and said that he 'learned naturally'. He told me that while he had never trained formally, he started by styling his twin sister's hair and, when others saw the results, they asked him to style their hair. In this way, he became a stylist. 'I did it naturally,' he reiterated.

Xolani's apprenticeship with Dumisani was a formal paid job and he had a clear set of tasks – most importantly he helped with 'relax', the chemical treatment that precedes most 'wet' styling work. He tidied up, swept, cleaned and arranged things in the shop. He would pass to Dumisani extensions and the bits of wool used to fix them to the clients' natural hair. He thus learned the skills of styling through observation and increasing levels of experience and participation in the actual procedures. Nathi learned from a gay stylist, Pat, in Hammanskraal, north of Pretoria. He worked with and learned from Pat for two years. Pat, he told me, had many gay apprentices. Few gay stylists who participated in this study had any formal training. Almost all had learned through apprenticeship. Nathi, like Simphiwe, did not see hairstyling as his chosen career, though. When he was 23 years old, he said that 'since he has schooling', he would rather be doing something else. However, two years later he was still in the same job and appeared to have settled into the life of a hairstylist. Similarly, Nkosinathi had other ambitions. He planned to branch out into adult basic education, but in the meantime his salon took up all his time. Simphiwe too may find that through apprenticeship and experience, his future lies in hairstyling.

The presence of younger gay apprentices helped to make these hair salons gay enclaves. Importantly, the system of apprenticeship secured hairstyling as a sustained niche profession for gays. Clive, from Driefontein (see Chapter 2) spoke fondly of a gay-run hair salon in Estcourt, KwaZulu-Natal, where he met a number of other gays:

> In Estcourt, I met a lot of gay people . . . They used to meet every Friday at a saloon, at a hair saloon . . . In the saloon there would be music and all the gays would gather from districts around Estcourt and various places in KwaZulu-Natal . . . That stress was a little bit relieved, to be in a group of people and to talk to each other.

The N.M.B. Saloon, Cynobrey Hair Gallery and Ladin'Co. all served as gay social spaces. The latter were businesses owned and run by the gay proprietors, while in the former, Dumisani had a central role in the business. The Professional Hair Salon, where Nathi worked, did not have the same sense of being a gay community space. This was because Nathi was an employee amongst other stylists and the owner of the salon, a large, middle-aged woman, was invariably behind the counter managing the business. The salons where gays had more autonomy tended to be enticing spaces for other gays to stop by and hang out. Importantly, aside from being a social space for other gays, a place where the 'stress was a little bit relieved', the hair salon was also a site of interaction with the broader community, as the following vignette from the Cynobrey Hair Gallery illustrates.

Both stylists at the Cynobrey Hair Gallery, Siyanda and Ayanda, are gay. Ayanda has a matronly air about him. The informal apprentice, Simphiwe, sees himself as a friend of Siyanda, but not Ayanda who, he tells me, 'is too old'. Even though Ayanda is the same age as Siyanda, Siyanda exudes a youthful, trendy style while Ayanda presents himself as the older matron. Siyanda is lithe and slim and pays meticulous attention to both clothes and accoutrements. His favourite outfits tend to be primarily white, offset by scarves, handbags, rings, belts and shoes in striking and colourful contrast. Ayanda, who has an ample figure, tends to wear long skirts and large blouses in plain colours or in colourful print patterns, of the sort that remain popular amongst mature African women in townships such as eMbalenhle.[14]

Ayanda was in a dilemma about applying for a driver's licence and asked me for advice on how to fill in the form. On that day he was wearing a particularly striking outfit, the same one that he had worn to a music concert the previous weekend. It consisted of a brightly coloured skirt, a blouse with puff shoulders and a matching turban. He was recounting to the women clients, as well as to a female friend, who was helping out in the salon that day, how he had met a man at the concert and, when the lights failed in the stadium, had grabbed him and kissed him. Everyone was laughing and enjoying the story. Ayanda said that a photographer had taken pictures of him in his outfit and he expected a photograph to appear in *Drum* or the *Sunday World*. Ayanda wanted to know if it would be okay if he filled his sex in as 'female' on the relevant form for the driver's licence. He wanted to know what would happen if he was stopped at a roadblock. He felt that his rights as a gay were not being championed in Parliament and resolved not to vote in the forthcoming election. He used his driver's licence dilemma to illustrate his point.

On that day Siyanda was in Ermelo planning his birthday party. One of the three women clients in the salon at the time overheard my research assistant referring to Siyanda as 'brother' and said that Siyanda would fight if he heard himself referred to as 'brother'. A red minibus taxi drove by, slowed, then stopped. The driver leaned out and shouted to Ayanda: 'You are a friend of white people!' He laughed and shouted back, 'Yes, I have class!' and the driver went off, but his red minibus kept reappearing. Ayanda explained that the driver was a boyfriend, keeping an eye on him.

In this setting, we see highly visible gays running and managing a salon, interacting with clients, salespeople, occasional visitors, friends, boyfriends, the landlord's family, sales representatives and ordinary people on the street. The salon becomes a gay enclave. It is one of the places where younger gays can learn about gay style and be inducted into the hairstyling profession. It is, for example, a safe space for school-going Simphiwe to interact with other gays and a place in which gays interact, on their own terms, with members of the public. So the immediate physical environment, in the space of the salon, which in this particular case is a transformed single garage, becomes a social space in which gay identities can be expressed in very visible and flamboyant ways.

Journalists reporting on the Miss Gay Disco Queen beauty pageant held in Bonteheuwel remarked: 'No matter that these gorgeous glamour pusses are really local, mostly unemployed, cross-dressing boys. There seems to be a complete acceptance of their femininity, a rejoicing in it even, by their families and by their tough community' (Gordon and Clermont 2006).[15]

In their day-to-day lives, gay hairstylists are able to deploy feminine identities in highly productive and advantageous ways, while simultaneously being subject to the vulnerabilities that come with their feminine gender identities. Local gender norms are fundamental to the ways in which same-sex sexual identities are expressed and performed in public. Gender norms also provide the framework for acceptable and transgressive forms of gay identity. Yet the deployment of an overtly feminine identity by gay men cannot simply be understood in terms of imitating a heterosexual norm, or unwittingly perpetuating gender stereotypes. In other words, a feminine gender identity is not simply imposed or adopted in the face of patriarchal pressure, the unrelenting logic of which would render gays effeminate and thus unthreatening to heterosexual masculinity. Certainly, for gays, a feminine identity can lead to assault and even rape, but it can equally be a source of economic security, social status and sexual allure. Gay hairstylists perform femininity, but it is a self-conscious and mutually recognised performance that tends to be an expression of hyper-femininity. The hyper-feminine performance, associated with clothes, mannerisms and gestures, that are described as 'too much' by those with a more demure presentation of self, is both a claim to similarity, as feminine, and an acknowledgement of difference, as gays. *Ladies* are like women, but they are not women. While gays are accepted as feminine, they occupy a liminal gender position, which can render gays vulnerable, but can also be worked to their social and (as I show in the following chapter) economic advantage. It is this ambiguity that enables gays to become celebrities, excelling in beauty pageants and in traditionally feminine occupations, such as hairstyling. It is this liminality that led the owner of the N.M.B. Saloon to remark, 'They even excel from the girls.'

Notes

1. Of the rest, three worked in government or quasi-government departments. One was a traditional healer, one was a full-time student and another was described as a part-time caterer. In fact, three of Bhuti's friends worked with him as part-time caterers. They were part of a small group of gays who did catering for social functions, although this work was informal and infrequent.

2. One of the mourners, Manti, who had worked with Dumisani as an informal apprentice, used this common term which refers to an 'after tears party', usually following the funeral of a young person. These parties have become features of an era in which HIV/AIDS continues to claim so many young lives.

3. For Nobuhle, the N.M.B. Saloon would be a sideline business, something to supplement a regular income from her work in a local government department in Ermelo.

4. For a comparative perspective on foreignness and hairstyling proficiency, see Rijk van Dijk (2003).

5. To put this into context, the minimum monthly wage for farm workers was set at R650 in 2003.

6. Hairstyling work is subject to seasonal fluctuations, with business being slower in winter and busier during the summer season.

7. The funeral of controversial gay pastor and founder of the Hope and Unity Metropolitan Community Church (HUMCC), Reverend Tsietsi Thandekiso, was a case in point. His funeral also took place in an Apostolic Church near Vereeniging on the Vaal Triangle. Yet his funeral service provided the opportunity for tensions and conflicting views to be expressed in largely indirect, but clear language. His funeral brought together a large Apostolic congregation, members of the gay church of which he was the founder and leader, members of his family and gay activists, all of whom were included in the formal proceedings.

8. The taboo at the funeral was not the fact that Dumisani was gay, nor his strong expression of a feminine self, as exemplified in the photograph. The only unmentionable seemed to be AIDS.

9. Inhlanhla Yezikhova Ezimnqini is the Ethiopian Holy Baptist Church in Zion.

10. The rumour in Wesselton was that his boyfriend had lured him with the offer of R10 000 to open a salon in Witbank.

11. He also said that the Apostolic Faith Mission and Assemblies of God had a reputation for 'casting homosexuals left and right'. Yet Dumisani's funeral was conducted under the auspices of the Apostolic Faith Mission, a church to which other gays also belong.

12. Both Dingane and Nhlanhla had a strongly feminine style of self-presentation in their daily lives, whereas Sipho resisted and challenged the conflation between gayness and femininity, often teasing others about this.

13. The name is partly an incorporation of the name of a previous boyfriend of the owner, Siyanda.

14. This kind of African-print material has also been transformed into a fashionable line of trendy youth wear by the Johannesburg-based fashion house, Stoned Cherrie, for example.

15. Bonteheuwel was established as a township on the outskirts of Cape Town in order to accommodate Coloured families forcibly removed from places such as District Six and Diep River under the Group Areas Act. It is a typical working-class suburb.

Appendix: List of Styles, Treatments and Fees at the N.M.B. Hair Saloon, Wesselton, February 2005

Revlon	R50.00
Restore	R50.00
Soft 'n Free	R40.00
Perfect Choice	R40.00
Ladine	R70.00
Dark and Lovely	R70.00
Precise	R40.00
Sunsilk	R70.00
Treatment	R35.00
Wash 'n Set (Curls)	R15.00
Wash 'n Style (Tongs)	R25.00
Spirals	R40.00
Phondo	R45.00
Straight back	R30.00
Popcorn	R40.00
Waves	R35.00
Singles (long)	R100.00
(short)	R60.00
Ponytail (long)	R100.00
(short)	R60.00
Oil sheen	R30.00
Hair food	R15.00
Hair bands	R1.00
Ponytail Hair pieces (long)	R20.00
(short)	R15.00
Ebony Hair	R7.00

CHAPTER 4

Hairstyling as an Economic Niche

In the previous chapter I showed how a feminine identity renders gays both vulnerable and acceptable. Gays experience vulnerability in similar ways to women in relation to domestic violence, exposure to HIV, muggings and sexual assault. And yet feminine roles also provide a recognised social space for gays to participate in the rituals of community life, such as church services. While gays are accepted as feminine, there is an acknowledged difference: *ladies* are not women. To be a *lady* requires a self-conscious performance of femininity. For outsiders, gay lifestyles are often described in terms of their performative aspect – 'it is just a fashion' being a common refrain – while for some gays, an excessively feminine identity can be seen as unstable or excessive. For example, overt forms of femininity may be discouraged as being 'too much', except at special events such as dress-up parties or beauty pageants (see Chapter 5). The instability of the category '*lady*' is evident in rumours about gays who become straight and, as a result, change their friends, dress code, movements and mannerisms. Because 'being a lady' is a recognised performance of femininity, in certain circumstances these performances tend towards the hyperbolic. In the hairstyling industry gays often adopt a hyper-feminine style and, in several cases, it is precisely this style that helps them to attain a degree of economic success that is vital for maintaining status as a *lady*. How does this very visible form of feminine self-expression help to secure an economic niche for gays in the hairstyling industry?

Failure and success in hairstyling

When one of the mourners at Dumisani's funeral observed that 'this is the funeral of a celebrity', two things came to mind. The first was the scale of the event – the large number of people who attended, the convoy of cars and the bus packed to more than double its capacity. The second was the diverse range of people who participated in the funeral – *ladies*, many of whom were in drag, members of the Apostolic Faith Mission, family, friends and clients. Both these things were indicative of Dumisani's status. He did not come from a prominent family – his mother worked as a hawker, selling fruit in the centre of Ermelo, while his father worked as a glass-fitter – but, in his short life, Dumisani had touched the lives of many people in Wesselton and beyond. He had gained something of a celebrity status as a recognisable gay figure in the township and as a well-known hairstylist. He was a lot less flamboyant than his mentor and contemporary, Siyanda. He was not as famous, nor as successful, but judging from the large turnout at the funeral he was clearly a respected figure in Wesselton. One of my informants observed that Siyanda thought that he was better than all the others and that Dumisani was 'not quite so successful because he is not well educated and speaks only a little English'. A lack of competence in English pointed to a perceived shortcoming in a celebrity status that rested partly on the ability to project an air of sophisticated cosmopolitanism.[1]

Nobuhle had planned her business with Dumisani in mind, recognising that his involvement in her enterprise was integral to attracting customers. In fact, prior to his association with Nobuhle, fortunes at Dumisani's own hair studio were flagging. He struggled with limited equipment, hardly any stock of hair-styling products, a less-than-ideal work-from-home arrangement and an erratic cash flow. When, for example, he was asked to do the styling of the bride and groom at a wedding scheduled to take place in the nearby town of Morgenzon, he had to borrow money to buy the necessary products. He also continued to turn to 'trade' (sex work) to supplement his income, even in

Wesselton. 'I have no boyfriend here in Ermelo, just trade,' he told me.

While Dumisani had tried to run his own business, then opted for a collaboration in which he became an employee, other stylists had successfully managed to launch and maintain their own businesses. Dumisani's hairstyling tutor and mentor, Siyanda, left his own salon in Wesselton in June 2002 in order to open the Cynobrey Hair Gallery in eMbalenhle in April 2003. His loyal friend and colleague, Ayanda, joined him in this new venture. The Cynobrey Hair Gallery, which opened from Monday to Saturday, was located in a rudimentary single garage, with a linoleum floor, sparse furnishings and a makeshift counter made of corrugated iron. On this counter there were three indistinctive white and green plastic flower arrangements and a small radio that played continuously. There was also a framed black and white photograph of Siyanda and two friends, one male and one female, taken in Mamelodi.[2] If you did not know Siyanda and were asked to separate the gays from the girls in the photograph, it would be impossible. The R300 monthly rental that Siyanda paid included not only the salon space, but also access to the toilet in the adjoining house, electricity and, importantly, water which was collected with a plastic bucket from the bathroom in the house. Access to the owner's house was through an interleading door. There was only cold water available and the clients' hair was washed using a bucket and basin. There was an elementary wooden bench for clients and others who might stop by for a visit and a chat.

Siyanda told me that he reviewed his prices every five months. The handwritten list pasted to the wall was updated by simply crossing out old prices with a marker pen and adding in current ones. It could be seen that an S-curl and cut, for example, had increased in price from R50 to R60, while a freeze wave had crept up a modest R5 from R30 to R35. Despite these increases, clients appeared to remain loyal to Siyanda and Ayanda, who told me that it had not taken long to build up a good client base in eMbalenhle. Indeed, when they arrived they already had a few existing clients in eMbalenhle who had previously travelled to their Wesselton salon to have their hair styled. Siyanda told me it had taken a year to become the 'best here in the location . . . the whole location knows me'. Notwithstanding Siyanda's tendency to exaggerate his popularity and success as a stylist (he once told me that he had 800 clients), he was well known within a radius of hundreds of kilometres and his salon was always busy.[3]

Nkosinathi was another popular stylist, although in dress and self-presentation he was much more conventional than Siyanda, dressing up when the occasion warranted it, but otherwise maintaining a stylish, but gender-neutral wardrobe. Waiting in eThandakukhanya, the township adjoining Piet Retief, a South African border town with Swaziland, Nkosinathi's client, Thembi, knew more or less when he would be back from his shopping trip to retail supplier Jumbo Cash and Carry, near Johannesburg. She was going to Durban the following day and determined to look fashionable when she got to her home city. Her husband had been transferred to Piet Retief and she had moved with him, but she did not want her friends and family back home to think that she had become unfashionable in remote Piet Retief. She worked at a clothing retail store and was always tastefully dressed, but hair was the critical marker of fashion and for this she relied on Nkosinathi's expertise and ability to source hair products from Johannesburg.

She was thus anxiously waiting for him and for the human hair extensions that he would bring back. These were more expensive than the synthetic variety, but they were authentic and she could afford it. As it turned out, Jumbo was out of stock of these extensions and Nkosinathi's shopping trip was delayed because he had to look elsewhere. However, it did not take too long since he was an experienced shopper and he knew where to go.[4] With his R1 000 worth of products packed neatly into his suitcase, he boarded a taxi and headed back to Ermelo. Normally he would disembark at the Ermelo taxi rank and catch a connecting taxi to Piet Retief, but that evening I met him at the rank and we travelled there together in my car. Like his anxious client, I had stayed in contact with Nkosinathi until his cell phone battery ran out. About an hour after collecting him, we got to his salon. It was 7.00 p.m. Nkosinathi unpacked his suitcase and found that there had been significant spillage. A large plastic container of a hair-relaxing product had spilt all over the other products – fortunately most of them were covered in plastic, but nevertheless it was slow and irritating work for Nkosinathi at the end of a long journey. He used one of the salon towels to carefully wipe the white viscous substance off the interior of the suitcase as well as the other products and he inspected which posters advertising hair products had been damaged. While he was doing this his client, Thembi, arrived. As soon as she saw the light go on, she made her way to the garage that housed Nkosinathi's salon. Thus shortly after 7.00 p.m., she settled in for her '100 per cent human hair' extensions, a procedure that would take over two and a half hours to complete. She laughed at how long 'these fashions' take.

'Welcome to Ladin'Co.' read the sign on the wall of the salon. Each letter had been clipped from the page of a magazine. Outside there was no advertising and on the rare occasions when the garage door was closed, you would not have recognised this as a hair salon at all. But the door was seldom closed. Behind the roller door was a simple space. Linoleum covered the floor, complemented by a couple of mats woven from recycled plastic. There were two small counters at the back of the shop, one where client and financial records were kept and another with a kettle and a vigorous, large-leafed pot plant. The salon had an air of industriousness and productivity, largely due to Nkosinathi's outgoing personality and energetic presence. He also employed two young women as assistants. Having retired to bed well after 10.00 p.m., Nkosinathi was back at work at 8.00 the next morning.[5] He did not have a choice. A client had collected him at home and brought him to the salon, as she was determined to have her hair done, first thing. Already some of the posters that had escaped the deluge of hair-relaxing substance were up on the walls, alongside an existing collage of handsome men lovingly clipped from various issues of *Drum* and *True Love* magazines. Amongst the hairstylists who participated in this study, a celebrity status is something that was aspired to and, often, self-generated. Nkosinathi, for example, concluded, 'I think that I am the best, the best in town. The best in Piet Retief.' While Siyanda, working in eMbalenhle declared that he was the 'best here in the location . . . the whole location knows me'. Nathi claimed that 'among the girls [stylists] I am number one'. These statements express a certain bragging bravado, but the claims are not simply self-aggrandising and are backed up by proprietors as well as clients. The woman in charge of the Black Like Me hairstyling academy in central Johannesburg confirmed that in her view, gay stylists were particularly skilled and hence popular with women clients. Dumisani's aunt wanted a gay stylist to work in her salon. Lindiwe, who is intimately familiar with her mother's business, the Professional Hair Salon, said that clients like gay stylists and hence they tend to 'draw customers'. Sharon, a 37-year-old woman from Soweto who was enrolled in a six-week beginner's course at the Black Like Me academy, spoke with enthusiasm as she offered the following explanation for the success of gay hairstylists in the burgeoning black hairstyling industry in South Africa:

Gay men have an identity crisis. Men who are gay are striving for perfection. They are perfectionists and this helps them to go to the extent that they do. They see themselves as women. And they are popular. They are perfectionists. Whatever they do, they do to perfection. They can even do hair better than us . . . They have that sense that 'I need to do my best. I need to do it to perfection'. As if they love what they are doing, whatever the community thinks. 'Inside I feel like a woman. I can do what they do and do it even better.'

These anecdotes from trainees, clients, salon owners and hair-stylists reflect a widespread perception that gays are naturally skilled at hairstyling and are hence likely to be successful. Proprietors are more likely to hire gay stylists and clients are more likely to frequent their salons. Nobuhle, the owner of the N.M.B. Hair Saloon, recognised the potential of this positive public perception and established her enterprise with a well-known gay figure as an integral part of her business strategy.

Dumisani and Nobuhle entered into a business partnership. On the one hand, it was a very unequal partnership. Nobuhle brought the start-up capital and owned the business, while Dumisani was in the position of an employee. On the other hand, it was also not a simple relationship between employer and employee. Nobuhle met Dumisani through his work – he had been her hairstylist; she, his client. It was in this realm of intimacy and familiarity that the idea of the salon first came into being. Nobuhle, like many other people in the aspirant middle classes, sought to open her own business as a way of bolstering her income as a salaried employee. She discussed these aspirations with her stylist and gradually the idea of the N.M.B. Saloon took shape. For Nobuhle, Dumisani would be a good business partner, not only because of his skill as a stylist but, most importantly, because of wider public perceptions of this skill. So Dumisani occupied an important symbolic position in her enterprise, which Nobuhle sought to encourage and promote with varying degrees of success. Dumisani was without doubt the person in charge of running the salon on a day-to-day basis. He was, in his own words, 'like a manager', but this did not translate into a good salary; far from it. Dumisani's start-up salary was equivalent to that earned by Dadi, the immigrant from the Congo who did braiding work and it was not significantly more than the salary of his apprentice, Xolani. Yet Dumisani had a special relationship with the owner that involved a lot of hidden perks, not reflected in the formal monthly accounts.

His status and prestige rested on the symbolic role that he played at the N.M.B. Saloon. This consisted of his ability to draw clients and thus bring a certain competitive edge to the salon. Nobuhle was not naive about the industry and neither was she complacent about Dumisani's hairstyling abilities. For example, she had planned to send him to Johannesburg during the quiet winter months to attend one of the courses run by the companies that produce the leading black hairstyling products, Black Like Me and Dark and Lovely. She asked me to find out more about them – the fees they would charge and the schedule of the courses. She understood that Dumisani needed to keep up with the latest fashions and she recognised the need to invest in him and, through him, in her business. As an experienced gay stylist, Dumisani occupied a more central place in her business than other employees. Even if his skills could do with a bit of brushing up and he might benefit from a course in Johannesburg, it would be difficult to fill the symbolic space that he occupied at the salon. This gave him status and a degree of power and influence above his designated position of 'like a manager'. Dumisani's position at the salon reflected his ambiguous position as simultaneously special and vulnerable. A low salary combined with a high level of trust and a variety of unofficial perks kept him in high status, but also in a dependent relationship with his patron, Nobuhle.

Nobuhle explained to me her rationale for planning to stage a beauty pageant, several months after Miss Gay Ten Years of Democracy, in which 'gays and girls would compete against each other'. She told me: 'Gays say they are better. I want to organise a pageant in the Wesselton Hall to see who is the most stylish girl.' Her idea was to strengthen the association between her salon and gays by sponsoring a beauty pageant, while at the same time advertising her business and attracting more clients. Even though Bhuti was sceptical and told me that he thought that Nobuhle was exploiting the form of the gay beauty pageant for her own business purposes, she nevertheless persuaded him to organise the event and it did take place. But as it turned out, there were only five competitors and hardly any audience. However, the motivation for the event was born of astute business awareness about the economic potential of publicly promoting her salon's association with 'gay style'.

Inadvertently, Nobuhle had stepped on a gay preserve. For several years beauty pageants had served as regional community events and as public awareness-raising exercises, rather than as vehicles for advertising a particular business. Yet, even before the failed pageant and, in spite of it, she felt that her choice of Dumisani as the core person in her business enterprise was 'perfect'. She said that 'clients come out praising me'. Gays, she told me, are 'full of design'. According to Nobuhle, they are also 'trustworthy, honest and they talk so nice'. She also said that gay stylists outperformed women stylists. Dumisani had his own ideas as to why 'gay people have more clients than straights'. He said that they were able to produce a wide range of

different kinds of styles. And they are cleverer and more talented. And they design their own styles. If they [the clients] go to a gay stylist, the stylist won't go to a book to look for a style. They just say to the stylist, 'Make me look beauty'. They know that gays are talented.

Nobuhle's clumsy efforts to organise a beauty pageant that would have gays and girls competing on the same stage in order to show 'who is the most stylish girl' was an attempt to harness the symbolic allure of a stylist like Dumisani in order to enhance and promote her fledgling enterprise. Like all advertising, it sought to play on aspirations and positive associations in order to draw more clients. According to Nathi, who was one of Dumisani's close friends and a stylist at Professional Hair Salon, 'Money is getting inside from the gays'. And Nathi would know because every day he walked from the salon, in feminine apparel, through the streets of Ermelo to the bank, several blocks away, to deposit the daily takings.

Popularity and personality
Hairstyling can be a laborious business. As seen above, a good set of extensions, for example, can take up to several hours.

According to Nobuhle, it is important that stylists have good communication skills. Several gay stylists pointed out to me that women clients need to feel comfortable enough to talk about their problems, including intimate family issues or their relationships with men.[6] And women clients can gossip with gay stylists in a way that they would not necessarily be able to do with another woman or a heterosexual male stylist.

An interest in men is something that most women clients share with their stylists, which allows for the exchange of certain confidences. As Ayanda explained about his clients, 'They talk about men, about men in general. They talk about the problems they encounter about men, like heartbreaks.' A common perception is that gays are able to empathise and advise. Yet they are also at a comfortable distance from the social world inhabited by their clients. According to Ayanda, 'Clients think that gays are better. They have a sense of confidence that gays are not jealous. They would keep them happy every time.'

Mondli, who used to run his own salon in Wesselton, was bemused by the fact that he was forever the confidant to his female clients, who shared many of their relationship and family problems with him. In particular, he was asked for advice on marriage: 'Whereas,' he reflected, 'I myself am not married.' It is true that in the Cynobrey Hair Gallery, for example, there is a seemingly endless banter about men – finding them, keeping them, leaving them, sharing them and converting them to gay life.

Bongi heard about Siyanda by word of mouth. A friend told her about 'this lady who has just arrived and is doing hair nicely'. So she entrusted her treatment-damaged hair into Siyanda's care. She soon became a regular customer, with an appointment every two weeks for remedial treatment and every six for 'relax and style'. At first she could not tell whether her hair had improved, but she continued to keep her regular appointments at Cynobrey Hair Gallery because she was drawn to Siyanda, whom she described as 'very friendly'. However, over time she also told me that her hair condition improved dramatically and that Siyanda forbade her from any further braiding and plaiting, which, according to him, had been the source of her hair problems. Another regular client, Yolanda, while acknowledging Siyanda's particular skills, also cited his friendly disposition as the main reason for her loyalty to Cynobrey Hair Gallery: 'He is a right guy. He is nice to me, always smiling and joking. He doesn't mind if he knows you or doesn't know you. He just chats. He is always very, very friendly . . . Very talkative, Siyanda.'

In a conversation between former hairstylist Bongani and Bhuti on the popularity of gay stylists in general and Siyanda, in particular, Bongani suggested, 'It is that friendliness'. Bhuti thought that a capacity for gossip and a sense of humour was essential 'and speaking that dirty thing in public. If you are stressed you forget your own problems and laugh'.

Gay stylists thus have a reputation for being personable. Lindiwe, who is the daughter of the owner of the Professional Hair Salon in Ermelo where Nathi is employed, remarked, 'Clients love them; they love them the most. They are talkative, friendly and full of jokes.' Nathi, like Dumisani, is treated 'like family' and is held in high regard. He stays in the 'gay palace', owned by the same family who own and run the Professional Hair Salon. As Lindiwe explained, customers were drawn to her mother's shop by the presence of a gay stylist. She also reflected on Nathi's particular allure: 'I think that Nathi is accepted by everyone because of who she is. She is something else compared to the others. She is friendly to everybody. She is a hard worker.'

'Friendly', 'talkative' and 'being something else compared to the others' all allude to a particular form of self-presentation that is characteristic amongst individual gay stylists. It is an elusive quality, but it is as if in the world of the salon, gays can express themselves in overtly effeminate ways without fear of criticism or censure. In addition, it is a sphere in which their creative talents and skills are respected and admired. In the salon, they are in charge. 'Hairstyling is the profession if you really want to express yourself,' was how veteran stylist Martin Machapa from Johannesburg expressed it. And the hair salon is a place where, often using very little by way of material resources, a world of glamour, style and fashion is evoked. This, in turn, translates into an ever-increasing list of available and possible styles for clients.

The popularity of gay stylists, which is hard to measure quantitatively but impossible to ignore, is based on a number of factors. The most important of these is the liminal gender position that the gays occupy. As the 'profession that accommodates the dragging queens', most gay stylists (there are exceptions) tend to be strikingly and overtly feminine in their daily dress, mannerisms and behaviour. This is similar to the self-evaluation of hairdressers in Annick Prieur's study in Mexico City: 'None of them believe their flagrant homosexuality is a financial liability here – quite the contrary; some claim that everybody knows homosexual men make the best hairdressers, and that it would be a handicap if their dressing as women became too convincing'. (1998: 69–70)

In the ambit of my fieldwork, overt femininity was part of what made gay stylists appealing to women clients – the reassuring sense that their hair is being entrusted to someone who knows, through first-hand experience, about women's hair. For example, one of the clients who entered the Cynobrey Hair Gallery asked to have the same style as Ayanda, who had recently had hair extensions done in Ermelo. Even the hairstyles worn by the stylists can be trendsetting models for their female clients. This illustrates another important aspect of their popularity – the fact that clients can look to Ayanda for a fashionable, feminine hairstyle shows his ability to produce and perform femininity in a flawless and seamless way. It is the success of his performance as a woman that makes him attractive as a stylist. Women appear to be more likely to entrust hairstyling (which is emerging as one of the key markers of feminine appearance) to gays who are themselves experts at making and performing gender. After all, women, like *ladies*, also engage in the daily performances that constitute femininity.

Rivalries and bewitchment

However, popularity can come at a price and in a highly competitive informal industry, such as the hairstyling business, jealousy and resentment, whether real or perceived, are invariably lurking in the background. Success and the dangers associated with success are common themes evident in a number of stories told to me about jealous rivals employing witchcraft against their competitors.

In 2001 Siphelele found lucrative and fulfilling work as a stylist in the Triangle Hair Saloon in Mamelodi township on the outskirts of Pretoria. He had moved there after a series of unsuccessful ventures and short-lived jobs in some of the most obscure towns in Mpumalanga, including Amsterdam and Mayflower. The proprietor of Triangle, Dawn, was pleased with his work and, Siphelele told me, since his arrival business had improved. Siphelele then took seriously ill and consulted a sangoma, who put him on a rigorous and painful treatment regimen. I spoke to Siphelele in the concourse of Park Station, Johannesburg. He had lost a lot of weight and his skin had the pallor of ill health. He had small sores, almost like a rash or a bout of acne, on his skin. He explained how he had become ill as a result of being bewitched by people who worked in the shopping complex that also housed the Triangle Hair Saloon: 'The minute I arrived, the saloon started to be busy. People were jealous of the owner of the saloon. They wanted to destroy her through me. I went to see an old guy. He is the one who saved me. He gave me some *muti*.'[7] Siphelele submitted to a lengthy and expensive treatment regime, which he explained to me 'helps, because I believe in it'.

Bongani, who worked in eMzinoni township on the outskirts of Bethal, also claimed to have been bewitched. Well known and highly respected for his braiding work, Bongani found that his hands were less and less dexterous, until eventually he was unable to continue braiding hair in the manner that he was used to and on which his reputation rested. He told me that he was bewitched during a braiding competition, where his model had *muti* in her hair. Again the culprit, according to Bongani, was a competitor using devious means to close his hairstyling business. In a conversation with Bongani, he told me the story from his perspective:

> I once had a saloon. I was previously owning a saloon. I had a lot of support but I had problems and I had to close down the saloon. I was getting sick. There was this competition with other beauticians. It was strong competition because I was getting more customers. So others used *muti*. They were using *muti* when they came for plaiting, so the hands got sick. I did not have an idea who it was because of the number of customers. It affected my hands. They became too sore to work. It happened during a plaiting competition. I am doing plaiting. They knew that I am the one doing plaiting, so someone went to me knowing that there is *muti* in their hair.

In these stories, the perception of jealous rivalry rests on a presumption of inordinate skill, of having a competitive edge, which allows the gay hairstylist to assume the role of celebrity in a highly competitive informal sector. In both these cases of bewitchment, fingers are pointed at jealous female rivals, reinforcing the idea of a competitive relationship between gays and women in the hairstyling profession. These stories of witchcraft are paradoxically about success as well as failure. Gay hairstylists, the narratives suggest, are bewitched because of jealousy and resentment spawned by their success, which, in turn, leads to their downfall. Thus, on the one hand, they serve to reinforce the idea that gays are equipped with special skills, a perception endorsed by proprietors of hair salons, cherished by clients and reinforced by stylists. On the other hand, these narratives suggest vulnerability.

Hair, women and danger

There is a story I was told so often during the course of my fieldwork by hairstylists, customers and salon owners alike, that it has become something of a trope to explain the popularity of gay stylists, especially amongst women clients. The story revolves around women, menstrual cycles and potential hair damage: If a woman stylist were to handle hair when menstruating, she would run the risk of damaging her client's hair. Indeed, the client's hair may even start to fall out. Clients need to be especially careful and discerning because it is quite possible that, for economic or more malevolent reasons, a woman stylist may not inform her client that she is menstruating or may not refrain from styling hair. In this narrative, female stylists cannot always be trusted. By using the services of a gay stylist, this particular danger is averted.[8]

A male trainee at the Black Like Me hair academy in Johannesburg felt he might have had the edge over women stylists in his salon in Rustenberg for this very reason. Although he was a little vague on details, he told me about the potential damage that could be inflicted on a client's hair by a stylist who continued to work regardless of her menstrual cycle. The owner of a string of salons in the sprawling township of Sebokeng spoke about clients' fear of hair loss as one of the reasons for his preference for employing gay stylists, aside from their superior skills and sense of fashion. Bhuti confirmed this idea:

> Gay hairstylists are most popular because there is this thing, this belief that you won't lose your hair if you go to a gay stylist. If you have your hair done by a woman who is menstruating, you are in danger of losing your hair. Also, personally, it is easier to pour out your problems to a gay. So that is another reason why women prefer a gay stylist.

Bongani, who worked as a stylist in Bethal before witchcraft rendered his hands ineffectual for the intricate work required, explained it in these terms: 'Other women stylists won't say when they are having a period. The hair will be damaged and will fall out. That is why gay stylists are popular.'

There is some danger, these stories, anecdotes and warnings suggest, in entrusting intimate work, such as hairstyling, to a female stranger. She may be motivated by jealousy and deliberately ruin your hair. Alternatively she may be careless or in need of the work and hence continue to ply her trade even when menstruating. Whatever the motivation, these stories about the inherent danger of an untrustworthy woman doing clients' hair at an inappropriate time in her monthly cycle provide some insight into the social and symbolic space that gays occupy in the hairstyling industry. In the cluster of anecdotes about the dangers of women, menstruation and hair, the figure of the gay stylist emerges as effeminate, but safe. In other words the gay stylist brings together the best of both worlds.

In so doing, gay stylists are able to become celebrities and sometimes adopt celebrity names. However, they become famous, not as women, but as gays. It is the liminality of their gender that allows gays to aspire towards the feminine, to perform a hyper-femininity, to compete with women and yet remain non-female. Women's hair (like gossip) can be entrusted to gays, as they are able to empathise with women and bring a feminine touch to hairstyling, while simultaneously remaining at one remove from the ambit of the female world.

Styling the self

The salons serve as a locus for interaction between gays and the wider community via the stylists' contribution to the creation and perpetuation of a particular gay style. The year 1994 was a period of transition in which South Africa's first democratic government was elected. In terms of gay folklore in Wesselton, it also signalled an expansion of existing possibilities for the public expression of gay identities. SisFiki was already a visible presence in Wesselton in his drab housecoat and slippers. But in 1994 three pupils at Cebisa Secondary School in Wesselton decided to come out and they did so in style. Dumisani was seventeen years old at the time, a contemporary of Siyanda and Ayanda. They arrived at school wearing make-up and their own versions of the girls' red and black uniform. Dumisani recalled that Ayanda wore a particularly short skirt, while he and Siyanda opted to wear trousers and high-heel shoes. Sibusiso, a *gent*, who at that time was in a lower grade at the same school, remembered them as the first gays that he was aware of. He recalled that the three friends joined the high-school girls as drum majorettes. Dumisani recollected, 'I felt comfortable at school. There was no criticism. We were wearing make-up while we were going to school. There were no comments. Even the teachers were saying "Keep it up, guys!"' All three went on to become hairstylists and, in this highly visible role, they have had considerable influence in public presentations of gay identities.

Histories of homosexuality in South Africa (see Chapters 1 and 7) show that cross-dressing associated with same-sex practices is not new and is one of the ways in which social sanction has been achieved in certain contexts (Chetty 1995; Louw 2001). This has been well documented on the mines, for example, since the early twentieth century (Epprecht 2004). What was new about the coming-out episode described above was that it took place in a school, was closely associated with the language and gestures of gay liberation (especially in relation to coming out) and the three gays were not sanctioned for their actions and behaviour. Gays and lesbians were already protected under South Africa's Constitution, which meant that, for the first time, official sanction was given to a visible gay presence in the public domain. And because homosexuality was conflated with effeminacy (gays are *ladies*) Siyanda, Dumisani and Ayanda dressed themselves up and made themselves up to express their gayness in a public institution – a high school that fell under the auspices of a government department. This resonates with hairstylist Nathi's experience in the provincial hospital ten years later, where the non-discrimination clause of the Constitution was interpreted to mean that Nathi had a right to be accommodated in the women's ward of the hospital (see Chapter 5).

This combination of style, legal protection and public visibility was to be the hallmark of emergent forms of gay identity in the public sphere and the folklore that developed around this particular incident expresses just that. Stylists such as Siyanda, Ayanda, Dumisani and Nathi enjoyed flaunting their success. Or rather, given that in material terms this success was only relative; it was the idea of success that was flaunted in ostentatious ways – particularly through dress and accoutrements such as jewellery and trendy cell phones. Dumisani, Ayanda and Nathi were all mugged during the course of the same year. All had clothes, money or cell phones stolen. Were these homophobic attacks? The muggings appeared to be robberies rather than 'hate crimes'. It seems likely that the muggers perceived gays to be relatively affluent, helped along by a flamboyant display of the material trappings of success. Gays were seen as easy pickings. They were regarded as being relatively well off and at the same time as easy, vulnerable targets. Nathi concurred: 'It was not because I am gay. They saw me and they know that gays are having money.' Individual gays may or may not have money, but considerable investment goes into perpetuating the idea that gays have money and style. Henry, who had moved from Johannesburg to Standerton, commented on his first impressions of gay life in Ermelo, 'Gays have money. Like Nathi for example – stylists can always give money.' It is in this realm of appearances that gays excel. They follow the maxim that to be a celebrity one must behave like one. Gay hairstylists are often at the forefront of this form of flamboyant self-presentation. It is the idea of success that Siyanda conveys through extravagant drag, excessive accessories and startling high-heels, and it is his manner – confident, sassy and slightly aloof – that makes a statement about his social position. The fact that his rented room is sparsely furnished and that his salon is in a humble single garage with no running water is somehow rendered incidental and immaterial to the manifestation of success through dress and gesture.

However, hyper-feminine style is not invariably a ticket to success, as Siyanda discovered when his 28th birthday party, which took place at the town hall of Ermelo, turned into a dismal flop. Bhuti organised *stokvel* birthday parties for gays in the region, to which Siyanda was not invited.[9] So Siyanda excluded Bhuti, underestimating the extent of Bhuti's network and the sphere of his influence. While on the surface this conflict and the reasons for it were trivial, it represented a subtle contestation about styles of self-presentation and ways of being that went to the heart of questions of identity in the region.

Bhuti's *stokvel* birthday parties, for example, provided opportunities for extravagant dressing up, as did the various beauty pageants, but these were self-contained performances that took place beyond the realm of the everyday, whereas Siyanda's form of self-styling, regarded as 'too much' by some gays, was a sustained, ongoing performance. I will explore these conflicts in more detail in the next chapter.

Whatever the distinctions made amongst gays and the conflicts that arose from these, many gay activities were associated with style and performance. The *stokvel* parties and beauty pageants were obvious examples, but a distinctive style was also evident at other occasions. At Dumisani's funeral, for example, the gays who were not in drag were easily recognisable by the distinctive style of the clothes they wore, the way that they walked and presented themselves and the activities they engaged in. This composite gay style meant that gays were seen to be fashionable and gay lifestyles were often conflated with fashion. Thirty-five-year-old Samuel from Driefontein who was married to a woman and had sexual relations with gays had a discussion with me about gays and fashion:

Samuel: Others think that it is a fashion to be in this life.
Graeme: Why is that?
Samuel: It is because of the area that we living at. As you
           know we are living at rural areas. They are not clear
           as to what is going on about this.

Graeme: What do they mean when they say it is 'a fashion'?
Samuel: I can say it is a modern way, a modern way of living.
Graeme: What is modern about it?
Samuel: It is like you see when someone is talking like a lady.
            It is a style. In fact, it is a new style, a new style that
            is a fashion.

Miss Gay Queenstown 2000 said of his hometown, 'We don't
have a problem here in Queenstown, only the uneducated people
don't understand.' Another informant explained his mother's
incomprehension in similar terms, 'My mom is not educated,
so she didn't know anything about this thing.' He went on to
say that he had tried to explain to her that being gay was an
innate orientation: ' "Mom, that thing is inside me. It was something I was born with." But she thinks that it is a fashion.'
Sipho commented that when it becomes obvious and common
knowledge that someone is gay, 'it is shocking for people,
especially in the rural areas. They still don't believe that it is a
real thing. They think that it is a fashion'.

A set of dichotomies is invoked: rural, cultural, traditional
and uneducated compete with urban, fashion, a modern way,
sophistication and style. Gays occupy a fashionable, modern
sphere that is symbolically located outside culture and tradition.
However, exclusion from cultural norms and values also means
that gays are associated with style and fashion; as such, they
embody the aesthetics of modernity.

The idea of homosexuality as fashionable is not a new one.
In the late 1980s, a prominent spokesperson for the exiled African
National Congress (ANC) dismissed rights-based claims of
lesbians and gays in a post-apartheid dispensation by describing
homosexuality as a phenomenon that 'seems to be fashionable
in the West'.[10] This comment, which links 'fashionable' and 'gay'
with 'the West', is a revealing one. Similar sentiments were
expressed at public hearings on same-sex marriage organised by
the National House of Traditional Leaders (NHTL), which took
place in Mpumalanga, KwaZulu-Natal and five other South

African provinces over a two-week period in February 2005. At these hearings, homosexuality was consistently denounced as both un-African and un-Christian (see Chapter 7). Fashion, when juxtaposed with tradition, culture and belief, emerges as ephemeral, frivolous and insubstantial. Fashion captures the idea that being gay is a transient identity of choice and, furthermore, that it is a product of a particular time and place. Fashion is about change, not tradition (Entwistle 2000; Van Dijk 2003; Wilson 1985). As Clive (who was unsure whether he was a *lady* or a *gent* in Chapter 2) put it:

> Most of the young boys these days they take this thing as a fashion. They want to experience it. They see these things in the media, on TV and radio. They see men can be in love with men and women with women. Though they are not gay, they want to have the experience. That is why it is most developed now.

A detailed analysis of youth fashion trends is beyond the ambit of this book, but a cursory glance at the ANC Youth League website is instructive. In the lifestyle section, South African designers are invited to submit their designs for the Vukani! Fashion Awards on the theme of Evolution '76. After a brief description of the 1976 uprising, 'which triggered a long and often violent confrontation between black protesters and the white South African government', potential participants are urged to 'reflect the political events of 1976 in fashion'. Innovative trend-spotting agency Instant Grass has this to say about these politically formative years:

> It was youth day in South Africa recently, marking the anniversary of the Soweto uprising in 1976 – a spec-tacularly sordid affair even by apartheid era standards. Anyway, fast-forward 30 years and things in Soweto have changed somewhat . . . South Africa, like a number of other African countries, has a fast-growing black middle

class that has fused Western culture, with township and traditional influences to create one of the most original and potentially powerful international youth culture movements.[11]

Euromonitor International advertises its report *Cosmetics and Toiletries in South Africa* as 'a comprehensive guide to the size and shape of the market at a national level' and is on sale at $2 350. The opening heading of the executive summary reads: 'Emerging black middle class boosts sales of cosmetics and toiletries.' This is obviously a claim designed to whet entrepreneurial appetites and boost interest in the report, but it is backed up by the experiences of Herman Mashaba, who founded cosmetics company Black Like Me in 1985. Twelve years later he sold 75 per cent of the business to Colgate-Palmolive and bought it back again in 1999. His company had a record 47 per cent growth in 2001 and the following year the company went international when it launched in the United Kingdom. Journalism student Sherri Day wrote: 'Still, for now, hair stylists said the business of doing hair is at an all-time high. Consumers can't agree on why this is so. Some said experimenting with their hair is about getting back to their cultural roots, while others admit they are following fashion.'[12]

In post-apartheid South Africa, there has been an exponential growth in the South African black hair product industry. There has been a similar proliferation of styles. Certainly the lengthening list of styles on offer at hair salons and the burgeoning market for black hair products is evident even at the most humble rural salon. In an article entitled 'Year of the Black Hair Revolution', Judith Watt mentioned 'the S Curl, the German, the pomade, braids, cornrows, extensions, bobs', remarking that 'all indications are that black South Africans are leading the way in terms of real design creativity within the area of hairstyling'. The Optimum Hair Saloon in Wesselton offered an extensive range of styles, including 'Frizi wave, Simba wave, Pop corn wave, Pineapple wave, Mushroom Bob, Python singles,

Mushroom and Macaroni, Shongololo Style, Banana and Macaroni', while at Ladin'Co. clients could choose from a list of seventeen styles including Z-curl, Chillies and G-String. The story of changing fashion norms can perhaps best be told through anecdotal evidence about the perm hairstyle. Clive, who grew up in the rural district of Driefontein, near Piet Retief, was used to wearing 'dress things, like ladies' things' since his sexual debut with older farm workers at age twelve (see Chapter 2). It was only while attending high school in KwaThema that he was introduced to gay life and where he first recognised himself as gay. The idea that same-sex practices could constitute an individual and collective sexual identity was initially very disturbing to him: 'I was shocked actually, so shocked to see that there is a group of such people. Where do they hide themselves?' One of the earliest markers of his newfound affiliation with the likes of his friend Mpumi and others who frequented the gay shebeens, was his perm hairstyle: 'In those days we used to perm our hair.' Clive said that it was the distinctive perm hairstyle that made Mpumi publicly recognisable as gay.

The perm as a marker of gay identity is echoed in the following extract from a letter written by a gay man living in KwaZulu-Natal and sent to the Johannesburg office of the National Coalition for Gay and Lesbian Equality in January 1996:

In the early eighties, permed hair was new to African people, it became a common belief in KwaMashu and other black townships that it was homosexual and un-African for a man to perm his hair. Many young people with permed hair were bashed.

One particular incident, always cross my mind, whenever I hear or read of Rev Meshoe's bigoted statements.[13] It was year 1982, I was a pupil at one of the high schools in KwaMashu, a boy of about seventeen years was on his way to pick his girlfriend to the tennis court, he was attacked with bricks and sticks and left unconscious. The reason for the attack was suspected homosexuality on his part, deduced from the size and lustre of his curls. With his lustrous perm, Rev Meshoe would not have been spared.

What was once seen as gay is now commonplace and unremarkable. In this sense gays can be seen as trendsetters, anticipating new styles. After all, the perm, once seen as a marker of gay identity, has became a fashionable style amongst young men in general, including, apparently, for Reverend Meshoe himself. An older informant, 49-year-old Brendan, recalled how the perm was a marker of homosexuality when he lived in Standerton in the mid-1980s:

> During our own times while we were still young it was the perm . . . When we were young gays in Standerton it was the gay style, because the straight guys used to insult you, if you were having a perm on during those days, saying, 'Jissus, you are too much of a sissy'.[14]

Yet in the space of twenty years, this was one of the signs of dramatic change that Brendan noted. He agreed that not only were straight men sporting perms, but that 'they are even worse because they are wearing earrings, which of course we don't even wear'.

When a trainee at the Black Like Me hairstyling academy remarked that hairstyling 'fashions came down from upper Africa', she was alluding to an important point, the symbolic economy of hair and hairstyling. In a South African context, the politics of black hairstyles is relevant to my argument about the niche occupied by gays within the black hairstyling industry. Broadly speaking, the proliferation of hairstyles is one of the signifiers of a new black aesthetic that has characterised South Africa's transition to democracy. Interestingly, while gays are sometimes dismissed as un-African, in the context of the hair salon they are also entrusted with producing a specifically African femininity.[15]

Gay lifestyles are seen as a 'fashion' in themselves.[16] This perception is fed by the performance of a particular gay style that is seen as a new development, coinciding with South Africa's transition to democracy. There is a further ambiguity in the social position occupied by gays: few people from the smaller towns in my fieldwork would want to be seen as un-African or un-Christian but, increasingly, few would want to be seen as unfashionable, either. The acceptance or rejection of gay lifestyles has becomes a marker of sophistication, of a cosmopolitan worldliness, of being fashionable.

The competitive edge that gay hairstylists have is more than a shared taste in styles, an ability to empathise or a friendly disposition. Feminine self-styling is an intrinsic part of what it means to be gay. Styling plays a vital role in the public performance of a gay identity that in the context of *ladies* and *gents* is feminine, by definition. For some gays and this is particularly striking amongst hairstylists, a gay identity is also closely linked to dress. For hairstylist Mondli, his willingness to wear dresses even to important public occasions such as funerals was indicative of his being out as a gay. Gays were self-conscious about the need to dress up and style the self in order to perform femininity.

Judith Butler's (1991) emphasis on performance as constitutive of gender is useful in understanding gay hair stylists' self-conscious expression of a particular brand of femininity. Both hairstylists and their female clients perform femininity through various – in Michel Foucault's words – 'techniques of the self', through mannerisms and deportment and by using various props at their disposal, such as dress codes and hairstyling. For women, however, their gender is seen as 'natural', whereas gays occupy a liminal space. Gender is hard to achieve and, as Ayanda complained in relation to his driving licence, his feminine gender identity is not something that is ever fully recognised. Gays are acutely aware of the repeated performances that are required to successfully present themselves as convincingly feminine. They are thus especially well placed to do hairstyling as seasoned experts in creating, producing and performing feminine styles. Gays are intimately familiar with what their women clients require of them – to help produce femininity through hairstyling. Or as one of Siyanda's devoted clients put it, 'I like his style; he is so stylish.'

Notes

1. See Besnier (2003 and 2004) for comparative examples of English fluency as a marker of social status in Tonga.
2. Mamelodi is a township on the outskirts of Pretoria.
3. I first met Siyanda when I undertook preliminary research for the film *Dark and Lovely, Soft and Free*. I was told that everybody knows Siyanda, you just have to ask in Wesselton. This seemed to be true; I had no trouble at all in locating him at his busy salon.
4. Nkosinathi made this trip to Johannesburg at least every two months, although if he ran out of stock, he would buy some of his supplies locally, in Piet Retief.
5. Nkosinathi's salon hours were flexible, depending on prior appointments. The salon was open six days a week, closed on Sundays. He normally opened at 8.30 a.m., but on busy weekends he was prepared to make his first appointment as early as 6.00 a.m. and was also willing to work until late at night. This flexibility is something that clients also appreciated about other gay-run salons, such as the Cynobrey Hair Gallery. One of Siyanda's clients remarked, 'Like now it is after five. I am from work. Siyanda has to take time off but, because I am here, he sacrifices to do my hair.'
6. See Gimlin (1996) for a discussion on 'emotion work' amongst hairstylists in a Long Island beauty salon.
7. *Muti* is traditional medicine. In this instance, it was of herbal origin.
8. Female hairstyling is a task that has historically been entrusted to close female relatives or the most trusted women friends. It is a common cultural practice in many African societies that mitigates against the dangers of ritual misuse of body products, including nails and hair – see, for example, Sieber and Herreman (2000) and Van Dijk (2003).

9. In its classic sense a *stokvel* is a savings scheme based on the fixed weekly, fortnightly or monthly contributions from members. In this way a common pool is created and money is drawn either in rotation or when a particular need or occasion arises. In this case the whole arrangement was a lot more haphazard, but nevertheless gays who participated were expected to contribute financially to the birthday parties which took place on a regular basis and as often as once a month.

10. In 1987, ANC spokesperson Ruth Mompati explained that the ANC did not have a policy on flower sellers and did not intend to have one for gays either. She claimed that homosexuality was something that only affected the affluent middle classes: 'I cannot even begin to understand why people want lesbian and gay rights. The gays have no problems. They have nice houses and plenty to eat. I don't see them suffering. No-one is persecuting them' (*Capital Gay*, 18 September 1987).

11. Instant Grass provides market research through a network of 'specially recruited, highly connected, trend aware informers, or "grasses", in key urban areas'. They describe the endeavors of international youth brands to market their products to the emerging middle classes as 'the second scramble for Africa' (see http://www.instantgrass.com/).

12. See http://journalism.berkeley.edu/projects/southafrica/features/hair.html.

13. Reverend Meshoe is the leader of the African Christian Democratic Party (ACDP), which claims amongst its policies, 'family values' and is not supportive of gay rights.

14. 'Jissus' is a corruption of an Afrikaans expression of amazement.

15. See also Van Dijk (2003) for a discussion on Ghanian women's perceived skill in producing African styles.

16. In this respect there are strong parallels with transgendered beauty pageants described by Mark Johnson (1997) in Tausug and Niko Besnier (2002) in Tonga. In the former the interplay between 'own' and 'other' worlds and in the latter the negotiation of 'locality' and 'non-locality' are strongly reminiscent of the ambiguous associations with homosexuality and fashion in South Africa.

CHAPTER 5

How to be a 'Real Gay'
Workshops on Identity

In 2004 Bhuti organised a series of workshops under the broad theme 'how to be a real gay'. Initially this struck me as a rather absurd idea and an impossible project on which to embark. I also thought it was very funny. 'I am going to Ermelo to attend a workshop on how to be a real gay. I will keep you informed,' I would tell my friends. 'When I have completed my research at the very least I will know how to be a real gay,' I would joke. I was not alone in my amusement and sense of fun. The organisers and participants created a jovial and light atmosphere at the workshops, characterised by a camp, easygoing banter, quick responses, in-house jokes and asides at other people's expense.

However, it was also a serious exercise with important outcomes and consequences. How one becomes a 'real gay' is indeed a serious question and has been the subject of numerous historical and ethnographic studies (see, for example, Chauncey 1994; Moodie 1989; Prieur 1998; Kulick 1998). It is a truism that distinctive gay identities emerge in different cultural contexts and historical periods. This has been demonstrated repeatedly across space and time, generating a substantial body of work in support of the thesis that sexual identity is a social construct. In situations where identities based on sexuality do emerge – and as Michel Foucault (1978) has demonstrated this is a relatively recent phenomenon – there are norms and values, protocols and styles that are subject to cultural and temporal variation. The global gay hypothesis anticipates a gradual homogenisation of sexual identities along the lines of a hegemonic (Western) model of gay and lesbian identities (Altman 2001). Emerging forms of gay and lesbian identity outside the Western paradigm have been cited as indicators of transnational flows and the dynamic interplay between global and local forms of gender and sexual identity formation (Altman 2001; Besnier 2002; Johnson 1997). The workshops on 'how to be a real gay' were a self-conscious and deliberate attempt to shape or to give precedence to a particular model of gay self-identification and categorisation (see Brubaker and Cooper 2000). The workshops took place at a moment of transition where competing notions of gay identity vied for hegemony and were likely to reveal 'new forms of understanding and regulating the sexual self' (Altman 2001: 100) as well as the cultural and historical context that shaped these new understandings and practices in particular ways. These two aspects of the workshops, namely, what they reveal about subjective (and contested) understandings of the sexual self and what they reveal about the broader historical and cultural context in which these new understandings emerge, provide a useful framework for thinking about the concept of 'real gays'.

The political project seemed doomed from the start: how could anyone, I thought, try to impose a standard norm on the myriad practices, performances, desires and identities that constituted gay life in the area of my fieldwork? At the heart of the workshops were two competing yet intersecting ideas about gender, sexuality and identity that circulated in Ermelo. On the one hand, a particular set of gender ideals was promoted and reinforced by my informants (what it meant to be a *lady* or a *gent*) and, on the other hand, sexual orientation and gay rights that suggested a modern gay identity, based on object choice, were the primary discourse of the workshops.

As shown in Chapter 2, gender – in terms of *ladies* and *gents* – plays a central role in self-identification amongst gays in Ermelo. The performance of femininity also goes hand in hand with the possibility (even likelihood) of social integration for gays. The workshops offered some alternatives, creating a forum for dialogue between the language and terminology of human rights and a modern gay identity and the participants' strongly held views on gender and sexual identity. As it turned out, it was a dialogue in which the locally self-evident wisdom of *ladies* and *gents* ultimately triumphed over the lexicon of lesbian and gay identity politics.

The workshops showed that 'being gay' was a contested terrain. If there was a real way to be gay there must then be other, presumably less real or even fake ways of being gay. The workshops were likely to reveal some of this conceptual territory, including the fault lines around which gay identities were currently organised. As such, they promised to provide considerable insight into the lives of gays in towns such as Ermelo and, by extrapolation, some of the conditions under which particular forms of gay identity are produced in contemporary South Africa. This was a context in which what I will call traditional understandings of sexuality and gender, coexisted with a modern gay identity, which underpinned the provision for freedom of sexual orientation in the Constitution.

There were three workshops and I attended the first two. The first had a general focus and included topics such as 'hate crimes', 'coming out' and 'you and HIV'. The second workshop, the only one to be held outside of Ermelo, took place in Bethal. This was mostly concerned with homosexuality and Christianity and was followed by the launch of a gay church community. The third workshop focused on legal aspects and was partially facilitated by the Johannesburg-based gay and lesbian advocacy group, the Lesbian and Gay Equality Project (LGEP). In this chapter, I focus on the first workshop, although I will also refer to the subsequent ones. The definition of terms, under the agenda item 'outlining the sexual concept', was pervasive in the first two workshops and I pay particular attention to these termino-logical debates.

How to be a 'real gay' in Ermelo

The following description, based on my field notes, describes the first workshop.

Although it is a Saturday evening, hymns and prayers can be heard emanating from behind the lace curtains (adorned with a light pink floral motif) in a small face-brick room. The lace curtains hang loosely over a window that looks onto the back of a row of shops in a recently established area of Wesselton township, situated on the outskirts of Ermelo, Mpumalanga. The buildings are all rudimentary and functional, the finishes elementary and cheap. Inside this room, which is Bhuti's bedroom, the walls are unevenly plastered and covered with a dull undercoat of paint. Electricity is channelled to a central light bulb through thick white plastic tubing resting on the wooden roof beams in the ceiling-less room. It is raining and, earlier in the day, the opening prayer included thanks for the rain: 'The farmers are happy and we are happy', although the latter statement was qualified with 'those of us who are out of the closet are happy'. It is doubtful whether the farmers would in fact be happy with the persistent rain on this weekend in March 2004 as it is autumn and a time for harvesting, not planting.

There is a proliferation of housing, both formal and informal, in this new section of the township as Wesselton, like many other towns throughout South Africa, struggles to accommodate the rapid influx of people from farms and villages to towns and cities. The infrastructure, however, has lagged behind the rapid spread of housing. With the rain, the dirt roads quickly turn to mud while cars attempt to weave their way around the deep craters formed along the more regular routes. Here and there gullies are filled with stones and dry grass so that minibus taxis, the only means of public transport in these parts, can pass. In the twilight, shadowy figures still make a dash for the shop, taking shelter under the tin veranda before entering. Inside chips are cooking in a large vat of recycled oil. These are popular as a take-away meal accompanied by atchar sold in small opaque plastic containers with bright red lids. Collapsed cardboard boxes keep some of the mud and rain off the untreated cement floor.

The shop sells all the basics – including soap, tinned fish, Vaseline, tea, sugar, biscuits and large plastic bags filled with orange crisps, popular with shebeen proprietors. A metal grille separates the customers from Missus and Baas,[1] the storeowners. It is here that the tenants of the four backroom flats pay their rent. At R300 per month, this is a bit more than the going rate elsewhere in the township, but here security is good. Baas makes a point of driving by late at night or in the early hours of the morning to check up on things, the grounds are fenced and someone always stays in the old caravan, a rickety structure resting on bricks, near the gate. Security was one of the main considerations that led Bhuti here less than a month ago, having being plagued by a series of break-ins and burglaries at his previous place. So when Missus complains to Bhuti that the gays are becoming a security risk because their boyfriends are forever jumping over the gate late at night or in the early hours of the morning, he is both hurt and annoyed and reaches for his closest linguistic weapon: 'Homophobia,' he claims. Yet Missus continues to let rooms out to gays, to the extent that these rooms have become known as 'the gay palace'.

Bhuti stands in front of a sheet of newsprint clipped with pegs to the pelmet, wearing a jersey against the cold and a hat for style. He is explaining the meaning of terms that appear on the newsprint: 'homosexuality; heterosexuality; transvestite; transsexual; hemophrodite; bisexual; gay; lesbian; butch; femme; dragging queen'. Eight participants are listening, commenting and questioning. Later the group is divided into two and in these smaller groups, they discuss coming out to family, friends and in the workplace, as well as other topics relevant to their lives, such as domestic violence. So, for example, participants discuss coming out in their groups and then one person from the group reports back to the gathering as a whole. Codes of behaviour and styles of self-presentation, etiquette and dress codes feature prominently in these discussions on coming out. Tsepo, as one of the group leaders, reports back that in his group they felt that 'gays should not make themselves a joke'; they should not arrive for a job interview 'wearing twenty earrings on each side, a lady's two-piece suit and long nails'. And gays at school should behave like normal students; lesbians should not insist on wearing trousers and gays should not insist on wearing skirts. Bhuti jokes that for some it was easy to come out to family and friends 'because your families always called you *intombazane*'.[2]

Contrary to the sentiment of the opening prayer, the organisers, like the farmers, are not entirely happy with the rain. This is because the small number of participants is a big disappointment to them and the cold, wet weather is blamed for the low turnout. Instead of holding the meeting in a nearby community hall, as initially planned, it is simply held at Bhuti's home, in his two rented rooms. The participants shift around Bhuti's bedroom during the course of the afternoon, sometimes standing, or reclining on his large double bed, or sitting on the precarious green plastic stools that he keeps in his rooms.

Tsepo and Bhuti have been trying to organise a workshop for some time now. The aim of the workshop is to teach gays and lesbians in Ermelo and surrounding towns, such as Bethal, Piet Retief and Standerton, about gay life because, according to Tsepo, it 'seems as if they are very confused'. In Bhuti's view, the gays in Ermelo are accepted, but as women and not as gays. He explains that 'the gays of Ermelo don't know how to be real gays' and so he came up with the idea of running a workshop on how to be a 'real gay'. For Tsepo, the workshop promised to be useful in providing answers to difficult questions, 'so that we have answers if people ask or attack us'.

Before delving into the details of the workshop, I will introduce some of the participants. In jolly-talk, Bhuti is affectionately known as 'aunty' amongst the gays, denoting both his status and relative seniority. When discussing the plans for a forthcoming gay beauty pageant in Wesselton, Tsepo jokes that Bhuti should get an award as 'Aunty of the Millennium' or 'Aunty for Life'. Bhuti is a veteran activist in this region. He was born in the township of Sakhile in Standerton, although he spent part of his youth in Soweto where he was looked after by an aunt. He stayed in Soweto in order to be close to Baragwanath Hospital, where he received ongoing treatment for a bout of polio that he had contracted as a child. From 1976 until 1989 he wore specially designed footwear, or 'disabled boots' as he calls them. He still has a slight but unmistakable limp. In 1995 while living in Sakhile, he started the organisation GLOSA (Gays and Lesbians of Sakhile), which operated as a prayer group and support network as well as a social space. At the time he was doing temporary work in a restaurant kitchen and for the Independent Electoral Commission during local government elections. He also did a stint of volunteer work at the National Coalition for Gay and Lesbian Equality, based in Johannesburg and became actively involved in the Hope and Unity Metropolitan Community Church (HUMCC). He got an administrative job at the Department of Heath and Welfare in Standerton in 1997 and moved to Ermelo in 2000 where he works as a receptionist for the same government department.

In Sakhile Bhuti was regarded as something of a mother in gay life, rather than an aunt. Initially he too had a 'mother', a role model and confidant who helped him to find his feet as a gay living in Standerton. Bhuti sports a light beard and a slightly more prominent moustache, which is unusual for a gay, an aunty and a mother. The ambiguity of his appearance alluded to the complexity of his position as a well-networked gay with a secure job and a *lady*. From his home in Sakhile and his job in the Department of Health, he organised regular GLOSA activities as well as more ambitious events such as Miss Gay Personality and a workshop that aimed to educate members of the broader community about gays and lesbians. This workshop, held in October 2000, was attended mainly by colleagues, friends and supporters, but it was an innovation in Standerton and a journalist from the *Standerton Advertiser* was there to cover it: 'Ag shame, everybody deserves to be in the *Advertiser!*' she told me. Since then Bhuti has established himself at the centre of a loose network of gays and lesbians in small-town Mpumalanga which he refers to as GLOM – Gays and Lesbians of Mpumalanga. It is an organisation that has no formal structure. It exists only as a network and an acronym.

Bhuti maintains contact with the HUMCC, the gay Pentecostal church community in Johannesburg, and is also able to convince organisations such as the LGEP, for example, to attend and participate in local events, such as a workshop on the legal status of gays and lesbians in contemporary South Africa. He was the regional organiser of a mini gay and lesbian film festival held in Ermelo,[3] which is poised to become an annual event. His activism, organising abilities and contact with city-based organisations meant that 'Aunty' had cultivated a certain authority in the region and he is now at the centre of gay social life.

More specifically, Bhuti's home is the centre of gay social life in the area. His irregular *stokvel* birthday parties are well-attended events, drawing people from Johannesburg, Durban, as well as smaller towns within the vicinity of Ermelo, such as Piet Retief, Bethal and Standerton. Thus, while the number of people participating in the workshop is small, the group is influential. Indeed the group represents the nascent elite of 'workshopped gays' or, in Bhuti's terms, 'real gays'.

Tsepo is young, energetic and ambitious. His parents are poor, falling into arrears on the modest rental for a house in Wesselton, yet he is always well dressed, his slim figure invariably clad in tight jeans and a designer-label T-shirt. He is a hard worker, who is not easily cowed by circumstance. It was Tsepo who would explode with indignation during the workshop when Bhuti explained how he had found a church community that accepted gays. Bhuti said that he had left one local Pentecostal congregation, Christ is the Answer, to join another, Praise Messiah Praise Centre when the pastor at the former spoke out against homosexuality. His current pastor was prone to visions, including a vivid revelation about the house he would build for God.[4] In fact, Bhuti reported, it was the founding vision of the Praise Messiah Praise Centre that had inspired the pastor to welcome 'thugs, prostitutes, gays and divorcees', to which Tsepo responded vehemently, 'I don't see gay life as a crime. I don't remember doing crime. I don't remember selling my body, but I am associated with these people!'

It is a slightly awkward event for Tsepo because his ex-boyfriend, Sibusiso, is also at the workshop. Sibusiso is contrite. It was here, at one of Bhuti's parties a few months back and starting in this room, that he and Tsepo had started the fight, which had escalated into a row, then a scuffle (see Chapter 2). When Tsepo returned to the party, distressed and with his shirt torn, he vowed that that was the end of the road, as far as he and Sibusiso went, and so it was. But in spite of Tsepo's firm resolve, Sibusiso had not given up yet and was determined to make amends.

For Sibusiso, the workshop provided an ideal platform for doing just that. For him, the theme of 'domestic violence' is both pointed and potentially redeeming. Although his stated aim was to 'learn about gays and lesbians', perhaps in doing so he would understand what had transpired between himself and Tsepo on that fateful night. He told me later that he regretted his actions to the 'depth of my heart' and insisted, 'Honestly, honestly, I never beat anybody that I am in love with . . . either a gay or a woman. Tsepo was the first person.' Ironically, it was his sense of his role as Tsepo's protector that led to the argument. Sibusiso did not want Tsepo to return to his place unaccompanied at that time of night. And in this respect he did not see Tsepo as blameless: 'He should have listened to me or, if he was still enjoying the company, he could have said, "No, you can leave to that place and I will ask somebody here to take me over there".' In any relationship Sibusiso believed that both parties should make decisions, but in the event of a deadlock, 'I have to promote my powers that are vested to me as a man'. Sibusiso did not see himself as gay, although the workshop would help him consider just where he would place himself amongst the many options in identity's lexicon.

In a discussion with Sizani and Bongani about the various problems faced by gays and lesbians in eMzinoni township near Bethal, Bhuti suggested that a workshop would be a good beginning. He cautioned against Bongani's idealistic enthusiasm for turning the youngsters away from 'drinking and sleeping around', suggesting that they needed 'to have patience and endurance as gay people can be so difficult'. Bhuti proposed that in any workshop, clarity around terminology is always a good starting point: 'We need to start with the true meaning of "gay" and "lesbian". Some people don't know what the words mean.' Sizani and Bongani were readily convinced and became active participants in the Ermelo workshop and, subsequently, helped to organise one in their hometown of Bethal.

Formerly a hairstylist, Bongani left this profession when he discovered that he had been bewitched by a jealous rival (see Chapter 4). The bewitchment affected the mobility of his hands and so he became a shebeen queen instead – the proprietor of a tavern run from his shack, which is comfortably furnished, but prone to occasional flooding. The unpredictability of this circumstance means that all furnishings need to be elevated off the mud floor with stacked bricks. This gives a slightly surreal sense to the room in the juxtaposition between suburban comfort and shack settlement practicalities. The headboard of Bongani's double bed, like the chairs in the part of his large L-shaped room designated as 'sitting room', was still covered in the thick protective plastic in which it had emerged from its packaging at the shop where it was bought at considerable expense.

Bongani and Sizani are close friends and share a concern about the gays and lesbians of Bethal and in particular the youth who, in their opinion, need guidance and strong role models. From time to time they discuss going into business together, but at this stage their vague plans serve as an expression of friendship and solidarity, as a way of talking about the experiences that they hold in common and their willingness to try and make a go of things in Bethal.

Sizani has lost both her parents. She lives in the house that she inherited. She tries to make ends meet by taking in a tenant from time to time and also by selling cold drinks, alcohol and basic cooked meals in the form of pap and meat. She has several girlfriends. One lives in Pongola,[5] one in Ermelo and another, Florence, stays with her parents who live just around the corner from Sizani's house. Florence's mother and father had different reactions to this relationship; her father understands better than her mother does because he 'learned about that life' when he lived in Johannesburg. Sizani tells me that Florence is attracted to those women who 'have a beard and are strong'. Sizani is undoubtedly strong and although Florence's preference for a beard is clearly metaphorical, Sizani does not have a beard, but she does perform masculinity. Sizani says that at first there was some confusion about her sexuality. The men thought that she had a 'male inside', that she was a man trapped in a woman's body, or alternatively was a stabane (hermaphrodite) but now they have a better understanding. She told me that ultimately, she would like to take two wives. She has adopted her sister's daughter, now seventeen years old, who lives with her. The adoption, like many of its kind, is both informal and typical. It is quite common for family members to take children into their home when the biological parents cannot cope for whatever reason, financial or otherwise.

Sizani is the person to whom all the younger lesbians in Bethal go with their problems. At the time that Bhuti was promoting the idea of a workshop, one young woman, Zodwa, had just given birth to a baby boy. She is seventeen years old, a child herself and small in stature. She is now out of school and has no means of support. Her uncle's wife and older sister are there to help with the needs of the baby. She explains that she started dating women at the age of fourteen and then tried dating men in order to console her bewildered mother. She soon fell pregnant, but after the baby was born she went back to her schoolmate girlfriend, Busi. Her mother tried to intervene and had gone as far as storming into the local police station to lay a charge against Busi. Frustrated by the law, she had now given her daughter an ultimatum – if she wants Busi she must go to her, but then she should not come back to her mother's house because she never wanted to see Busi in her house again. The family had hoped that the young man would be just what their daughter needed to turn her from her lesbian ways, but for Zodwa, while she says that she loved him, 'there were things he did which I could not stand' and the family are left with their daughter, now a young mother, and her assertive, strong-willed girlfriend.

Young Manti attended the workshop, but that is to be expected; he and his close friend, S'thembele, attend almost everything at Bhuti's place. They virtually live there. At the time they both invariably slept in Bhuti's room, either sharing his generously proportioned double bed or, when space was an issue, sleeping on a foam mattress on the floor. Manti exudes an air of well-being and wears his slightly plump features with a playful, easygoing confidence, engaging in teasing banter with Bhuti about the relative attractiveness of their respective weight. Bhuti is slim and remonstrates with Manti for being slightly overweight, each arguing for what is most fashionable and sexually alluring to men. Manti has a talent for clothes design, making clothes mostly for himself. For both Manti and S'thembele, their youth and attractiveness help to sustain them. They help out here and there, in an easygoing, non-calibrated form of reciprocal exchange. A bit of help with the dishes perhaps, while Bhuti is at work, or collecting water from one of the communal taps that service these rooms, or some washing in return for a place to sleep, to wash, or for a meal.

Nathi is one of the gays that Bhuti was referring to when he said that gays in Ermelo were accepted as women and not as gays, precisely one of those gays that sparked, in Bhuti's mind, the need for such a workshop. In fact, Bhuti would dispute whether Nathi should be called gay and prefers to call him transgender, while Nathi sees himself as gay – a 'real gay', in fact. I emerged from my rooms one morning to find Nathi making his bed with the help of another young gay. The bed was about all that could fit into Nathi's room, although he had managed to squeeze a dresser in as well. With the sheets and duvet in place, the next step was the large cushions that were fluffed out and then placed, in an exact spot known only to Nathi. And finally, the teddy bear, which was placed as a centre piece between the cushions. When the whole thing was complete, Nathi stood back to admire his handiwork, made one final adjustment to a cushion and then left his room for another long day at the Professional Hair Salon. Saturday is a working day for Nathi. The salon usually stays open until the early afternoon, depending on how busy it is. Wednesday evenings and Sunday mornings are reserved for church, where Nathi can be seen dressed in a bottle-green and white uniform, the skirt, sash and blouse of Inhlanhla Yezikhova Ezimnqini (Ethiopian Holy Baptist Church in Zion), replete with a green headscarf. Nathi sings soprano. I hardly recognised him when I first saw him heading off for church one Wednesday evening.

Nathi's work precludes him from attending the workshop, but it is unlikely that he would do so anyway. Nathi is self-confident and he is certainly accepted and respected at work and at church. He was one of two gays to enter Miss Igwalagwala and won a hotplate as a prize for being selected as one of the top five finalists in Miss Ermelo.[6] In both competitions he was competing on an equal footing against women. He was disappointed not to win Miss Gay Ten Years of Democracy; he did not even secure one of the top three positions. He complained that the judges were not really looking for genuinely feminine qualities, but for someone with masculine features who carried himself like a woman. Nathi regarded himself as a real gay. He was born this way and had no time for 'fake gays': 'Me, I was born like this, Graeme, so I see the others they are changing, you see? They are no longer gays. They are fake. To be a real gay you are born like this and you don't have a feeling for ladies [women].' He spoke with contempt and disapproval of Sipho,[7] originally from Driefontein and now based in Johannesburg: 'He wants to fuck the gays and then he wants the others to fuck him? Uh-uh.' Nathi is not sure, but he thinks that this has something to do with 'white gays'. Sipho, Nathi says, is attracted to white gays and he has evidence: 'You remember at Andrew's engagement party? Sipho had a cell phone and he was phoning a white gay.'

For Nathi, life in Ermelo is good. He is well known. You cannot walk with Nathi for two minutes without stopping for him to greet, chat and flirt: 'About gays, they understand, because now they take us as girls.' He gets propositioned by men in his church, but he tends to decline any advances from fellow congregants, with one exception and in that case the man did not live in Ermelo. Two years ago he had an affair with Sibusiso, which lasted for about six months, but he left him after he decided that 'he is a play guy, that one'. Recently he dated a strikingly handsome man who was a semi-finalist for the Mr Africa competition, the finals of which were held in Middelburg in Mpumalanga. He is currently dating a policeman. For the most part, he is content with his straight boyfriends, although their girlfriends sometimes frustrate him. But he too has his roll-ons: 'A roll-on is when we are not alright. Like maybe when I am fighting with my husband.'

Manti and S'thembele have parents who live in Wesselton and they keep rooms at their parents' homes. But socially it is more comfortable at Bhuti's place, there is more happening here and, importantly, they can bring lovers here, which they can't easily do at home. S'thembele does some hair braiding when the opportunity arises, while Manti helps hairstylist Dumisani when he has a particularly busy day at the salon or when he is called upon to do hair for a special occasion, like a wedding. In these cases Manti helps out with washing and applying hair-relaxing chemicals, while Dumisani tends to the styling. Manti sometimes stays with another older, more established gay, Thulani, who lives in the back room of a house in a formerly white suburb near a truck stop. For Manti the truck stop is a source of disposable income when lonely truckers on the road to somewhere join him for a bout of sex, either in the truck, or at the Truck Inn or at Thulani's place. Sitting on the stairs leading to a suite of rented rooms one Sunday morning after a party, he presented himself to me in a camp drawl: 'Hello, I am Manti, exotic dancer and hooker.' He has a reputation for gossip, a habit that is colloquially known as GGC, the gay gossip column. In the past his gossip caused a rift between Dumisani and Bhuti; they did not speak to each other for weeks. Similarly Bhuti and Thulani stopped speaking to each other when Manti mentioned to Thulani that Bhuti thought that he was flaunting his material assets. The last time that Thulani and Bhuti had a serious and protracted fight – this time over a man – it took the intervention of the landlady, Missus, to resolve it. She did not want discord in her back yard and would act as mediator if necessary to resolve brewing disputes and conflicts.

Themba was at the workshop to learn more about 'lesbian and gay'. He had a hard time at home because his mother strongly disapproved of his lifestyle and discouraged his friends from visiting. He practises as a sangoma, but his client base is minimal and he struggles to make ends meet. While he is the only sangoma attending the workshop, there are several others working in the vicinity who, like Themba, have a penchant for other men, or gays, as the case may be.

Emmanuel is a sangoma who lives in Bethal, where he has a boyfriend who works on Kutala mine near Ogies, Mpumalanga. He is from a family of six children: four boys, a girl and 'myself', he tells me. He spends a lot of time in Ermelo, where he stays with an aunt. He is regarded as 'too much' by Bhuti and his friends because he invariably wears feminine clothes, usually a blouse and an ankle-length skirt. He is also teased by young men, in particular: 'When walking down the street, I meet with these boys. [They say:] "Oh this one comes with this style! You annoy us by making yourself a girl when you are a boy. You are scared of the ladies. You want us to propose you, but we won't".'

So they say. But some do propose, he tells me. The only time that he is not teased is when he is in his sangoma attire: 'Maybe they are scared that I will do something to them with my *muti* or something.' Another Ermelo-based sangoma with a reputation for effeminacy suggests that gender norms in the social sphere don't apply in the realm of divination and healing: 'There is neither woman nor man when it comes to work'. Themba says, 'When I became a sangoma, I was already gay'.[8]

In the workshops, coming out is promoted as an ideal, a declaration of identity that is seen as an essential rite of passage to becoming a 'real gay'. Bhuti expresses the philosophy behind coming out through an image of fruit: 'You are an apple, juicy, succulent and sweet. Don't expect everyone to love you. If you end up trying to please everyone you will end up being a second-rate banana.'

The participants learn that coming out is a personal decision that promises to be both 'enriching and beneficial'. It is a step to be taken when you 'arrive at a stage where you want to live your life as you are'. A workshop participant cites television talk-shows as a good opportunity for initiating discussions about sexuality in the immediate family and thereby facilitating the coming-out process. In particular, *The Felicia Show*,[9] hosted by talk-show host Felicia Mabuza-Suttle, is singled out as 'your stepping stone to tell them that you are gay'.

Workshop participants also stressed the importance of modifying behaviour by 'educating yourself' and learning moderation; for example, 'sometimes going to taverns, but not becoming a curtain at Roy's Place (a popular tavern in Wesselton where many gays go)'. Importantly, coming out and becoming 'real gays' entailed particular modes of self-presentation. For example, in the group report-back, overtly flamboyant styles of dress are announced as inappropriate at school or in the workplace, unless the workplace is a hair salon.

Terminology featured prominently in the workshops under the agenda item 'outlining the sexual concept'. Terms drawn from a global gay lexicon are identified and applied to a local context, often emerging in the process with an endemic meaning. In introducing both himself and the purpose of the workshop, Bhuti explains the importance of understanding the 'sexual concept' and thus provides insight into the locally accepted norms that conflate being gay with effeminacy:

> What are people thinking of gay and lesbian issues? We need to workshop ourselves, like coming out the closet. What type

of a gay he is? If I say I am a woman, the next person in the taxi will ask, 'How can a man be a woman? We need to know: is it your sexual orientation, or your whole body that is a woman?'

The workshop participants learn about gays and lesbians, butch and femme, hermaphrodites and bisexuals, homosexuals, transsexuals, heterosexuals and drag queens. They learn that the captain of the English football team, David Beckham, is a transvestite – according to Bhuti, Beckham is a man who likes to express his feminine side by wearing his wife's clothes. This fact, like many others conveyed in the workshop that day, is conscientiously jotted down by participants in their notebooks or on scraps of paper. The terms are all written in blue marker pen on the large sheet of newsprint hanging from the pelmet in Bhuti's bedroom. Participants go through the list term by term, discussing, questioning and naming examples. In some instances, as with David Beckham, these are drawn from a wide tableau of international figures. In other cases, they are drawn from national icons such as Brenda Fassie,[10] who features in a discussion about whether gays and lesbians are born or made.

In a context of rapid legislative change premised on the ideal of gender equality, an understanding of the law and possible avenues for complaint and redress are of compelling interest to the workshop participants. It is interesting that, for the *ladies*, new legislation concerning marital rape is seen to be of equal importance to the fact that: 'South Africa's Constitution protects gay people. You mustn't be scared to go to the police station. You mustn't stand that rubbish.' Workshop participants are told: 'If you don't want to sleep with your partner, you don't have to. You have the right to say "No", even if you are married. If you are forced, then it is rape.'

The details may be unclear, but the substance of an inclusive form of human rights is quite apparent. A sense of engagement with the democratic process is also apparent. The workshop takes place on the eve of South Africa's third democratic elections and Tsepo urges the workshop participants:

Voting is just around the corner. Let's go and vote. Now that we are free. We have parades and stuff because of the vote. Our rights are recognised. Know the stand of your party. I won't vote for the ACDP [African Christian Democratic Party].[11] Don't just look at the ballot paper and say to yourself: 'Oh, this is a Christian party'. No. Vote for the party that will accommodate you and your rights.

They also undertake to persuade other gays to vote. There is no doubt that the Constitution and the law, in its broadest sense, have created an environment in which projects of self-assertion, including these workshops, can take place.

As the workshop draws to an end, snatches from a hymn, 'You are Alpha and Omega' compete with the din of rain on the tin roof and the music from a jukebox in the shebeen where, if you are prepared to 'pop R2', you can play a tune. Inside Bhuti's rooms, sections of the wall have already became visibly damp from the persistent rainfall and the chairperson, in his closing remarks, thanks those who have taken the time out in bad weather and urges those present at the workshop not to 'let a day pass without doing something valuable'. Most people feel that the day has not passed without value. In fact Sizani told Bongani and me in the car on the way back to their hometown of Bethal that she had learned a whole new vocabulary. She told me that she had noticed other women and one in particular who, like her, was more like a man. Did they feel the same? Did they do the same, she'd wondered? Now she knew – they were both 'butch'. 'I didn't have a clue before,' she said.

Ways of being: Style versus activism

When Bhuti claimed that 'the gays of Ermelo don't know how to be real gays', he explained that they were accepted as women and not as gays and he was proposing an alternative model. When he spoke about gays being 'accepted as women', he had some readily available examples to draw on, individuals who constituted a type – a particular expression and performance of femininity – that in his view was out of sync with the times.

Nathi was one such figure and, as seen above, he had his own ideas about 'fake gays' and 'real gays' that were in sharp contrast with the aims and intentions of the workshops.[12] For Nathi, it was quite clear-cut: there were those, like himself, who were born gay. To be gay was to be effeminate; Nathi performed as a woman. The way he styled his hair, the clothes and accoutrements he wore, his way of walking, the intonations of his voice, his mannerisms, sexual practices and public performances were all shaped by a feminine ideal. His boyfriends were, in his view, straight men. He was shocked by the disruption of these seemingly obvious facts by someone like Sipho who seemed to contradict everything he knew. As mentioned, he struggled to find an explanation, settling eventually on the possible influence of white gays. However, Nathi was not the only one to fit Bhuti's description. Siyanda, now working from his salon in eMbalenhle, would be another individual who, in Bhuti's terms, was 'accepted as a woman', as would hairstylist, Mondli (see Chapter 3).

Bhuti's workshops represented a more overt political project. Even the form of his intervention, 'the workshop', was ubiquitous in the era of political struggle, as well as in the post-apartheid democratic dispensation. The ideal of the workshop is to provide a forum that is informative and participatory, instructive and quintessentially democratic. In this respect, Bhuti aimed to play the role of facilitator, rather than expert and invited maximum engagement from the participants, facilitated by small group discussions on several important topics. The opening prayer at the beginning of the workshop included the phrase 'those of us who are out of the closet are happy', a sentiment that points to a distinguishing feature of the workshop, namely that coming out is essential to personal fulfilment and political activism and it requires information, education and the articulation of a particular identity. When Tsepo explained that the workshops would also ensure 'that we have answers if people ask or attack us', he was alluding to the need for gays and lesbians to seek self-understanding as a prerequisite for educating others.

This distinction is fundamental to the difference between the two forms of self-expression that I have characterised here as 'style' and 'activism'. When, in that watershed year of South Africa's political transition, 1994, three young gays arrived at school wearing make-up and skirts, it was a particular way of announcing themselves through dress and the performance of a particular style. According to Bhuti, the 'real gays' that he envisaged emerging from the workshops would privilege activism over style, while for the stylists 'real gays' were gays like them.

Hairstylists such as Dumisani, Nathi, Siyanda, Ayanda and Mondli and sangomas such as Emmanuel had developed ways of performing an overt femininity and refined it to an art. They are far from closeted, but their identity does not require lengthy discussions, workshops or announcements. They have become publicly recognisable as gay through the particular styles of self-presentation. There is no need for them to come out, not only because their families have always called them *intombazane* as in Bhuti's joke, but because they carry a feminine demeanour in all aspects of their lives. What became clear from the workshop is that in Bhuti's terms 'real gays' need to tone down these overt forms of feminine expression in everyday life, embracing instead an identity based on sexual orientation, which is gradually disclosed through a process of coming out.

This division between adherents of style and those of activism was evident in who attended the workshop and who stayed away. Bhuti and his cohort of workshop participants constituted an activist core. Bhuti embodied a cosmopolitanism achieved through networking with city-based gay and lesbian organisations and through individual contacts and connections. He kept abreast of national gay and lesbian politics, while at the same time busying himself with local activism, such as the work that he undertook through GLOSA and, under the rubric of GLOM, 'Aunty for Life' organised beauty pageants, held regular social events and has increasingly become a recognised community activist and leadership figure in the region.

Nathi, on the other hand, would not see the point of participating in such a workshop. Why would he when he has found acceptance and respect as a gay on his own terms? Or as he put it: 'About gays, they understand, because now they take us as girls.' He is an integrated member of his church community and regarded as a strong asset in his workplace, where he enjoys the protective patronage of the salon owner and her family. He had no shortage of suitors. A coming-out workshop would indeed be superfluous for the likes of Nathi.

Earlier in this chapter, I described the sharp exchange that took place between Tsepo and Bhuti when Bhuti proudly explained how he had found an accepting church community that welcomes 'thugs, prostitutes, gays and divorcees'. Tsepo objected to being lumped together with the socially marginal and undesirable. If this was acceptance, he wanted none of it. The incident raises a question: if acceptance and integration was a goal (and the workshops strongly suggest that it is), what was the likely outcome of these two approaches that I have characterised as 'style' versus 'activism'?

The activist approach rested on coming out, on claiming and declaring a distinct identity as gay and in downplaying the role of dress and highly feminised performances of the self. On the other hand, those who express their identity through style don't need to come out as gay. They see themselves as gay and are accepted as girls even in environments that are regarded as bastions of Christian and traditional morality and culture, such as the African Independent Church congregations. And yet the distinction between these two approaches is subtle. The boundary between coming out as an act of disclosure and coming out by way of dress and feminine performance is not clear-cut. As one informant, a sangoma, put it: 'To wear dresses and be gay is one and the same.' Mondli also saw coming out as integrally connected to the way he dresses: 'You see now I have just come out of the closet completely. I no longer wear trousers. Even if I go to a funeral, I don't wear trousers. It is too difficult for me to go back to wearing trousers.' For him, activism is synonymous with beauty pageants, or 'shows', as he calls them, which he helped to organise in the tavern Dube Tonight in Wesselton in 1999 and 2000: 'We actually started making shows. Many of them are like contests, so that we can explain to people about being gay or lesbian. We explained how it happens.'

Claiming rights and educating the public is a familiar rationale for organisers of beauty pageants. Posters advertising Miss Gay Queenstown 2000, for example, carried the slogans: 'We want "to claim our rights" and to be "recognised with our relationship" in Queenstown', while the name of the Ermelo beauty pageant – Miss Gay Ten Years of Democracy – speaks for itself.

When Mondli wears a skirt to a funeral, rather than trousers, as an essential part of being 'out of the closet completely', it points to the making of a particular form of gay self-identification that combines elements of a modern, rights-based concept embodied in the Constitution and more traditional concepts about dress, femaleness and gay identity. Thus the distinctions between style and activism become blurred in practice – as when the display of style in beauty pageants is mobilised for an activist cause. They are at once competing and complementary discourses and practices. Importantly, style allows for social integration and acceptance within an existing sex/gender system. The gays are accepted as women, based on a perception of sameness, not difference. The activist discourse evident at the workshops, while it does not break with the gender binary, does suggest a playing down of feminine dress, mannerisms and style. It promotes an identity based on the assertion of difference and distinction (as gays), rather than familiarity and inclusiveness (as women).

The experiences of Bhuti and Nathi in their respective church communities highlight some of the choices available and the possible consequences of these two approaches to the public display and articulation of identity or coming out. For someone like Nathi, who is a fully fledged, skirt-wearing member of his church and the church choir, Bhuti's tenuous integration amongst the socially ostracised in a newly formed Pentecostal congregation would be less than attractive. Bhuti's acceptance in the congregation was largely dependent on the inclusive vision of the founding pastor that inspired him to seek out and embrace the socially marginal and ostracised members of his community – in this respect, gays had a certain salvation appeal, along with thugs and prostitutes. However, when the founding pastor was replaced by a preacher who condemned homosexuality, Bhuti left and settled for an informal service of hymns and prayers in his rooms when there were enough friends and associates to constitute a congregation. This situation led to the gays at the workshop resolving to start their own church along the lines of the HUMCC in Johannesburg. These plans were realised when the church was launched at a workshop in Bethal in 2004.

In contrast, while the word 'gay' is unlikely ever to be uttered in Nathi's church, he experiences a sense of acceptance as a fully integrated female member of the congregation; as does Mondli who at the time acted as church treasurer, a highly responsible and respected position. When I asked some of his fellow congregants if it had ever been a problem having a gay church member, they found the question puzzling and perplexing. I was told that he sings beautifully, attends church regularly and even the Archbishop loves him. The politics of style offers the possibility of integration for gays, as women, so they can be relatively unproblematically integrated within the existing gender order. Ironically, the activist approach runs the risk of fuelling the very homophobia that it anticipates and seeks to address. Yet neither approach fundamentally breaks with the sex/gender system.

'Real gays' in this context are gays who, according to Bhuti and his followers, are in tune with the times. 'Real' translates into an identity based on sexual orientation that is made possible through the political space opened up by the Constitution and the legal changes that have followed. It is a form of understanding the sexual self that is in certain respects different from one based on the performance of a distinctive gay style and, in other ways, remarkably similar. Nowhere are the similarities more evident than in common understandings of gender and sexuality.

Style, activism and the gender order

In relation to gender and sexuality, Bhuti and Nathi represent both complementary and contrary views. Bhuti asserts that gays are accepted as women and Nathi makes a similar observation, 'About gays, they understand because now they take us as girls'. Given that Bhuti had observed that gays were accepted as women and *not as gays*, I expected that the workshops would offer an alternative to this gendered ordering of relationships and identities. I assumed that 'gay' would be understood as a distinct category of sexual identity that was not conflated with women or effeminacy, but in this respect, 'style' and 'activism' seemed to converge. Instead of providing an alternative model, this unexpected similarity served to confirm the resilience of gender as a foundation for the construction of self-identity and categorisation amongst gays in the ambit of my fieldwork.

Bhuti is clearly inspired by a modern gay identity and a global gay culture – this is the implicit meaning of 'a real gay' in the workshops. In a context in which identity seemed both malleable and innovative, as suggested by the workshops, the rules of gender are, by contrast, apparently rigid and inflexible. Bhuti's concerns about gays being accepted as women (concerns that are echoed by the workshop participants) are more to do with self-presentation, with dress and demeanour, than with this gendered ordering of relationships. A gay remains a *lady*, whether an activist or not. The similarities between these two approaches rest on seemingly inviolable rules of gender that render gays by definition effeminate, as activists or stylists, wearing slacks or skirts.

Sizani expressed a similar issue in relation to her experiences as a lesbian. She said that many men in Bethal thought that she had a 'male inside her body', that she was a *stabane*. Now she has come out of the closet and they have a different understanding, namely that she is a lesbian. But being a lesbian for Sizani is not about 'women loving women'; her identity as a masculine partner remains intact and she draws her role models from images of polygamous patriarchy.[13] When Sizani identified with the term 'butch' in the workshop, it had the quality of a revelation. This is because it is a term that has the capacity to denote her sense of self as a lesbian and as a man. To a certain extent, the workshops achieve their modern (or in Bhuti's terms 'real') gay goal – new terms are introduced and, with them, new forms of self-identification. But the workshops also undermine this aspiration by reinforcing a gender model that is contrary to a modern gay identity in which the aspiration towards egalitarianism is an integral part. According to David Halperin, the possibility of transcending hierarchy is the essence of modern homosexuality: 'Homosexual relations cease to be compulsorily structured by a polarization of identities and roles (active/passive, insertive/receptive, masculine/feminine, or man/boy). Exclusive, lifelong, companionate, romantic, and mutual homosexual love becomes possible for both partners' (2002: 133–4).

The workshops set out to highlight the differences between those who rely on dress, mannerisms, demeanour and a particular set of skills in certain niche occupations (such as hairstyling) and those who follow the path of coming out, of announcing themselves as gay and engaging in forms of community activism, alert to instances of homophobia, seeking paths of legal redress and organising separately as gays. Yet when Siyanda, Dumisani and Ayanda went to school in the girls' uniform, this became etched in local folklore as a foundational moment for gays in Ermelo. They became role models for younger gays to emulate; style became a potent form of activism.

New terms, old meanings
The next workshop, held less than a month later in Bethal, focusing on gays and religion, was preceded by a similar elaboration of terms. Once again the participants, some of whom had attended the previous workshop, went over the terms, although this time and in contrast to Ermelo, the workshop was well attended and the proceedings took place almost entirely in Zulu, including the explanations of English terms and, as in

Ermelo, terms were illustrated by examples drawn from the audience. For 'dragging queen', one of the workshop participants was pointed out by the facilitator and dutifully stood up in his hand-crocheted, sleeveless dungarees with bell-bottom flares, expertly crafted using a dark brown wool, offset with borders of light cream breaking the brown monotony at the hips and upper thighs.[14] He used the brief opportunity both to demonstrate the term 'dragging queen' and to do a demure modelling session in his distinctive outfit. Once again the terms homosexual, heterosexual, gay, butch, femme, transvestite and transsexual echoed in the room as participants strove to meet their expectations, stated at the outset. A woman who had travelled from Johannesburg said she came to the workshop because she wanted to know if she was 'doing the right thing to be a lesbian. If you are a lesbian, how do you handle yourself in life?' She echoed a common expectation from local participants, which was to learn more about homosexuality or what it meant to be gay or lesbian.

Some terms did not fit easily into local understandings of gender and sexuality. This could be seen in the term 'butch'. In the workshop Sibusiso was singled out as a butch and after the workshop he confirmed that the term 'butch' was closest to his sense of self: 'I learned a lot that I did not know, even about my own position. I did not know before about butch.' Sibusiso was similar to *gents* in most respects – he also had girlfriends and two young children, but he liked to socialise with gays and attend gay events, such as this one, which was exceptional for a *gent*. According to the definition offered at the workshops, a 'butch' is a 'lesbian or gay but who looks masculine. Someone like Sibusiso is gay, but he is a man, not a femme'. Everyone present knew that Sibusiso was not exclusively attracted to gays and that he, like most *gents*, had relationships with women. Thus the term 'butch' denotes a masculine-defined social and sexual relationship with gays, distinct from *gents*, who would not regard themselves as gay, butch or otherwise. However, in an interview during the same period (see Chapter 2), it was apparent that while Sibusiso reiterated his attraction to gays, he did not regard himself as gay. While he could identify with 'butch', he could not identify with 'gay'. There is a gap between categorisation and self-identification. The workshop had limited success in applying concepts such as 'butch gay' in a context in which, as one informant explained, 'If I am a man, I must be a man'. Typically, it was the terms that acquired new meanings in this exchange between divergent views on the relationship between sex, gender and sexual orientation; the participants emerged relatively unchanged, but armed with a new vocabulary with which to describe their world, albeit on their own terms.

Terminology was the entry point to the workshop and provided an indispensable framing device for subsequent discussion and debate. Without these terms, there could have been no fruitful interaction and the workshops would have failed. The terms allowed for the naming of behaviour, mannerisms, preferences and desires and also provided the building blocks for self-identification.

To a large extent these new terms, drawn from a global lexicon, remain infused with locally familiar meaning. This is evident even in Bhuti's introductory remarks when he imagined the question posed by an anonymous stranger in a taxi: 'How can a man be a woman? We need to know: is it your sexual orientation, or your whole body that is a woman?' This conflation of sexual orientation with gendered subjectivity perhaps disappoints the project of universalising homogeneity implied by the phrase 'sexual orientation' and suggested by the aspiration towards being a 'real gay', but remains true to a locally shaped world of gender and the erotic imagination shared by *ladies* and *gents*.

Yet even these discrete worlds of gender differentiation – *ladies* and *gents*, active and passive, gay and straight – cannot be entirely contained in these neat dichotomies. As the terms attempt to define – and in so doing provide a fixed meaning to a range of desires and practices – so too is the elusive nature of these categories and the terms that represent them exposed. We can see how Sibusiso resisted the definition of himself as a 'butch gay', retaining the 'butch', but dropping the 'gay'. Similarly, local phrases are coined, such as the term 'somehow bended', used to describe straight men with a penchant for gays. This term 'somehow bended' suggests that there is indeed a kink in the armour of heterosexuality, something that is, at the very least, not quite as straight as it may appear. Thus terminology also serves to refine the received wisdom of existing categories, allowing for subtle distinctions between various gender-based forms of desire and sexual practice, which, in this context, are essential markers of selfhood.

The slipperiness of the terms and the need to constantly invent new phrases points to the difficulty of fixing identities, even in a context where, on the surface, the marked distinction between *ladies* and *gents* seems very clear-cut. Interestingly the terms *'ladies'* and *'gents'* (and other local expressions such as *'sisButi'* and 'Greek salad') do not feature on the list at all – too familiar and commonplace perhaps to warrant close attention. But this is also because the workshops draw on a pool of international 'expertise', in this instance terms with a global resonance that are in turn reinterpreted and made local.

Just as 'gay' means one thing in Ermelo and another in Amsterdam, so too are terms with an international register such as 'butch', 'transvestite', 'femme' and 'drag queen' infused with local inflections. And in everyday practice it is the colloquial terms (such as *ladies* and *gents* and men who are 'somehow bended') that reassert themselves, while the formal terms from the workshop are seldom used.

Another perspective on terminology, categorisation and self-identification

Some of the underlying reasons for the workshop were crisply articulated in a conversation that took place two years later in May 2006 between two activists from different generations, Bhuti and Brendan. Brendan is an older man who was actively involved in the fledgling black gay and lesbian movement of the late 1980s (see Chapter 7). An extract from this discussion shows how ideas about identity have changed over time. This is particularly apparent in relation to new categories of identity, such as 'transgendered'.

The conversation took place in a very small house, which was built in an informal settlement on the edge of Sakhile township, a historically black residential area on the outskirts of Standerton. Bhuti and I were there to meet 49-year-old Brendan. The owner of the house, a younger gay man, was also present, as was his boyfriend. While I was ostensibly the interviewer, once the conversation got going, the exchange was mostly between Bhuti and Brendan. I hone in here on a fragment from that conversation, which grew out of a broader discussion about different churches – those that accepted gays and those that rejected them. The Zionist church groups, for example, were widely known to be accepting of gays and this, Brendan said, was reflected in their uniform:

Brendan: The dressing of the Zionists suits both sexes.

Graeme: Yes, it is almost indistinguishable.

Brendan: Exactly! So the most important thing there, you can find a boy wearing a dress, which is exactly like that of a woman . . . They accept that person exactly as he is because of the dressing and no one can just get in and say whatever he wants because that is their uniform.

Bhuti: The only problem with Nathi and Ayanda, *really* they are wearing *women's* clothes.

Brendan: Really?

Bhuti: In church they are wearing the women's turban and they are wearing a head-wrap. And when you go to the Bible, what does it say? Let's be realistic.

Brendan: No, if we are realistic about that, a man is not supposed to wear a head-dress, only a woman.

Bhuti: Yes, it is just that only those people they are . . . what are they, Graeme? [I don't answer his question.]

	Transgendered people, they are not exactly gay. They are transgendered. Do you know what I mean? They feel they are women completely; they are not homosexual.
Brendan:	No, I understand that. That is a very frustrating life, I can say, the one of pretending to be completely a woman, whereas you know exactly that I am not a woman, because it makes you not to be comfortable with your relationship. Because when a person loves you as a gay, he knows exactly that I am in love with Bhuti and Bhuti is having all the organs that I am having, but the only thing that binds me with him is love. He knows exactly that the kind of sex that I am going to have is not exactly like the sex that is being orientated by a female and a male. But if you are pretending now to be completely – wearing corsets, wearing pantyhose, high-heels and all those things – no! I don't feel comfortable with that. I don't want to lie.
Bhuti:	But you have to compromise. I also have a problem with transgendered people, but I have to compromise because we are in a same struggle with them.
Brendan:	Okay, no I understand that. But now if we are in our gathering, I don't mind what you wear. But now, if you are exposed to the community . . . that is where you draw the attention of the community. Learn to respect other people's feelings so that people can be able to respect you.
Bhuti:	But with these two, I don't have a problem with them, because you cannot easily identify whether they are men or women, because even their structure, their physical structure, it's completely of a woman.
Brendan:	But these two actually, what are they?
Bhuti:	They are men. They are men. What I have a problem with is just a man with a beard wearing a dress and make-up.

This conversation formed part of an ongoing dialogue through which various players, myself included, were trying to understand (or negotiate), for somewhat different reasons, the shifting and contested nature of what it means to be gay in a small-town setting in contemporary South Africa. These processes of identification remained opaque and difficult to unravel, precisely because they were contested, overlapping and contradictory.

In my role as researcher, I was paying particularly close attention to the complex interplay between sex, gender and the construction of meanings around the term 'gay' (both in terms of self-identification and categorisation by others). As a gay activist, Bhuti was preoccupied with similar themes and, as such, was very concerned with terminology, through which he sought to define what it meant to be gay. In the conversation above, it was not only the dialogue, but the silences that were telling. I remember feeling uncomfortable with Bhuti's question to me about the hairstylists – 'What are they, Graeme?' – which I did not answer. I knew the answer that Bhuti wanted from me and that he came up with himself, namely 'transgendered', but I resisted giving it to him. Why did I resist and what was the source of my discomfort? Why could I not answer Bhuti's apparently straightforward question?

Bhuti was classifying Nathi and Ayanda as transgendered and therefore 'not exactly gay' and he was inviting me to participate in this process of naming and defining – of categorisation. It was clear that these distinctions did not trouble Brendan in the same way that they bothered Bhuti. Brendan was more concerned with what he perceived to be unnecessary and arbitrary divisions amongst gays. In fact, he told me that he found it 'quite disturbing' that gays would want to draw these distinctions and thereby further divide an already vulnerable group. He was much more concerned with the impact that cross-dressing could have on public perceptions of gays. Brendan said that he was concerned that gays who pretended to be women when they knew that they were not might provoke community disapproval and disrespect. But in his view, there were different ways to be gay and they remained gays,[15] while for Bhuti, there were borders, lines that defined what was gay, and these two hairstylists belonged to a different category altogether – they were transgendered – people that he was willing to 'compromise' with, recognising that they were all in the 'same struggle'. To complicate matters further, as mentioned previously, one of the stylists identified as 'transgendered' in the discussion above, Nathi, identified himself as gay. In fact, he saw himself as a 'real gay'. Gloria Wekker has argued persuasively that 'emic constructions and explanations of same-gender sexual behaviour need to be taken seriously. There is no reason to assume that the Western folk knowledge about sex, which has been elevated to academic knowledge (cf. Lutz 1985), should have any more validity than folk knowledge anywhere else' (1999: 134).

As silent witnesses to this discussion were a couple – a 'gay' and his 'straight' boyfriend. As the conversation veered to straight boyfriends, Brendan strongly agreed with the need to have clearly defined gender roles in male same-sex relationships. He said:

> At all times, if your relationship is going to continue for a long time, there must be a submissive part. In other words there must be someone who is going to be passive and another one active. So the one who is active will be regarded as a man and the one who is passive will be regarded as a female.

Nathi and Bhuti might agree on Brendan's fundamentals, although the terms they would use to describe this gendered ordering of relationships and their respective sense of themselves within it would differ. They might also concede that there is appropriate gender-based behaviour. After all, what Bhuti objected to most strongly was 'a man with a beard wearing a dress and make-up'. Beyond a common agreement that same-sex interactions were based on gender dichotomies, competing terminologies reflected the process whereby new forms of self-identification were being explored.

These categories and practices were some of the building blocks used to cobble together new forms of self-understanding from different, sometimes conflicting models. Imagining, creating, naming and performing what it meant to be gay remained a work in progress, necessarily inconclusive and open-ended. This is why the snippet of conversation reproduced above, this seemingly obscure fragment, which took place in a makeshift home in an informal settlement on the edge of a township adjacent to a small town – in the heart of the hinterland, as it were – can shed light on local, national and global intersections that make up the life worlds of gays living in Mpumalanga. An understanding of these life worlds in all their paradox and ambiguity can provide insight into the uneven and contested nature of social change in South Africa.

Identity as a resource
The material circumstances experienced by the gays of Ermelo and surrounding towns would put paid to the kind of remarks made by African National Congress (ANC) spokesperson Ruth Mompati in London in 1987: 'I cannot even begin to understand why people want lesbian and gay rights. The gays have no problems. They have nice houses and plenty to eat. I don't see them suffering.'[16]

When I rented a set of rooms next to Bhuti's place in what would become part of the 'gay palace', I became intimately aware of the circumstances in which most of my informants lived. One thing grew quickly apparent: nothing belonged to me alone; all resources were scarce and therefore shared. For me, this took some getting used to. From minor material possessions – where is my mug? Or, what are the contestants doing with my mirror in the Wesselton Hall during a beauty pageant? – this applied also to other resources such as space, where people would simply wander in and out for a quick chat, to borrow this or that, or for a place to sleep, to wash or to change. Things circulated, but miraculously always seemed to come back to me. They were always somewhere to be found in one or other part of the gay palace and its environs. The mirror was back in its place, the mug was next door, and when I really needed it, my rooms were my own.

When one morning both outside taps that service the gay palace once again did not produce a drop of water and the two toilets with the metal doors, which did not close, remained conspicuously unflushed and clogged with scraps of newspaper, I was told, 'Yes, there is no water'; an everyday fact and a common occurrence. No water – a simple fact of life. At some point it will flow again. Maybe later today, maybe this evening. Who knows? Usually, I can't even think about starting my day without at least being able to wash my face and clean my teeth. My instinct would be to phone someone, complain and insist on the water being turned on. Who to phone? Complain to whom? What result would it have? Who has airtime to make the call? I could see that resignation was a more appropriate response than agitation – and I could get in my car and buy mineral water from a garage.

It is thus a context in which there is also enormous competition and envy in relation to resources. Thulani is a source of jealousy because of his new car, television and designer clothing – and hence his ability to attract men. 'He can get any man he wants,' I am told, and from the constant string of handsome suitors that I am introduced to, this seems to be more or less true.

Under these circumstances, identity is deployed as a valuable resource. Like the washbasins, crockery, cutlery, my mirror, a television – items to be shared and used to maximum advantage – so too the presentation of self is able to generate social capital and can help to secure an economic niche. The economic advantages of the politics of style are most apparent in the hairstyling industry. Through the cultivation of a certain style, gay hairstylists are able to attract and maintain a substantial client base in a highly competitive profession. They are seen to be especially skilled and gays use this public perception to their economic advantage (see Chapter 4).

What about the economic advantage of Bhuti's strategy of being a 'real gay'? Do the politics of activism offer other economic incentives similar to those that are a by-product of style? Economic motives are never far in the background of organised events, although even modest financial goals are often not realised. This is evident in beauty pageants, for example, where the organisers tend to anticipate a healthy profit, although invariably end up running at a loss or, at best, breaking even. The workshop on coming out and domestic violence, and the subsequent workshop on religion took place without any external funding. Individual participants paid for their own transport and food and were accommodated by their hosts. Only the workshop on the law, run by the LGEP, had some external funding and resources allocated to it. Some social gatherings were funded through a form of *stokvel* whereby all participants contributed towards the costs. Other events, such as beauty pageants, relied on the takings at the door. Yet Bhuti was aware that there were other resources available, it was just a question of how to access them, and the funding world was operating, to an extent, in his favour.

South Africa's 1996 Constitution, which protects citizens from discrimination on the basis of sexual orientation, is particularly distinctive in a region where vitriolic homophobia is openly expressed by political leaders, both in neighbouring countries, such as Namibia and Zimbabwe, and elsewhere on the subcontinent, including Uganda and Kenya.[17] Political outbursts of this nature ensured that gay and lesbian rights were placed firmly on the human rights agendas of international donor agencies, which began supporting gay and lesbian organisations in South Africa from the late 1980s, and elsewhere in the region beginning in the 1990s.

In recent years the resources allocated to these organisations increased dramatically when gay and lesbian rights were identified as a strategic node for strengthening democracy and civil society in South Africa.[18] Several gay organisations in the country received substantial multi-year donor funding. One of the conditions of funding was a strong outreach component and a demonstrable effort to address historical imbalances and inequalities. An under-resourced black initiative in a rural town would have strong appeal as an outreach partner for one or more of these organisations. Bhuti was well aware of this. He managed to draw individuals from various organisations to attend functions and events, which enhanced his status and reputation in the region and put him in touch with organisations interested in doing outreach. His networking approach began to generate financial benefits too, beginning on a very modest scale. The organisation OUT in Pretoria made a small contribution to some of the costs involved in Miss Gay Ten Years of Democracy, while the LGEP bore the costs of holding a workshop in Ermelo. The most significant development was the decision of the Out in Africa Gay and Lesbian Film Festival to launch the 'video suitcase' in Ermelo with a mini gay and lesbian film festival in October 2005. Bhuti was paid a generous stipend as local organiser of the event and became the custodian of the video suitcase. In this role he was responsible for hiring out the video resources to gays and lesbians in the region. The 2006 festival took place in the town hall and the mini film festival has been held in Ermelo several times since then. Local activism was able to tap into resources allocated to gay and lesbian organisations in South Africa under the rubric of strengthening civil society and a culture of human rights. Being an activist, like being a stylist, thus has the potential to generate resources. When, towards the end of 2005, Bhuti started planning another series of workshops on the theme of 'love' and HIV/AIDS, he began by drawing up a funding proposal.

I was also a resource. When the taxi driver teased Ayanda that he was a friend of white people and he responded, 'Yes, I have class!' he was making a joke of it. At other times, I was paraded about, going on pointless excursions for spurious reasons in order for gays to be seen driving around in my car or in my company. As a white middle-class person, my presence with sangomas or hairstylists could also be used to enhance prestige.

I am also well connected to gay and lesbian organisations and I
am well aware of funding possibilities. These too were harnessed
as resources – for example the Out in Africa mini film festival
came to Ermelo as an indirect result of my research there.
Increasingly, gays are working in local government departments. Bhuti, Henry and Thulani are all employed in this sector,
where they enjoy the protection afforded to them by the
Constitution and are relatively well paid in secure employment.

SisButis and citizens

What all the workshops had in common was a preoccupation
with establishing social codes and conventions, the ground rules
of behaviour for 'real gays'. This is a project which, as Pierre
Bourdieu (1984) has demonstrated, serves to create and reinforce
social distinction, in this case between 'workshopped' gays and
gays 'who don't want to be workshopped' because they are 'only
interested in boyfriends and drink' or because they have developed
other effective ways of social integration. This distinction
between 'real gays' and others promised to be important amongst
gays in underlining difference and marking hierarchies of
enlightenment, but it also marked a significant shift in the
possibilities for interaction with the broader community. Workshopped gays were expressing and embracing a new concept of
citizenship made possible by political and social change. These
new possibilities for interaction provided the context in which
the workshops could take place. This is evident in the importance
placed on naming and defining in local and global terms – 'What
type of a gay is he?' – in the emerging guidelines for gays
interacting harmoniously with others and in efforts to render
the law meaningful and useful for local disputes.

Political and legal changes in South Africa have allowed new
forms of citizenship to emerge. A workshop on legal issues and
three specific legal cases provide a useful prism through which
to look at the way that constitutional equality and the subsequent
legal changes have affected the day-to-day lives of my informants.
Some commentators have suggested that legislative change in
South Africa and specifically the equality clause in the Con-

stitution remains the preserve of the affluent (Fester 2006; Cock 2005; Jara and Lapinsky 1998; Barsel 2006). Others have suggested that legislation which has attempted to usher in an era of gender equality on the foundations of a deeply patriarchal system is not only unlikely to succeed in rectifying existing gender imbalances, but may in fact exacerbate gender-based violence, as men react violently against the perceived threat to formerly undisputed masculine preserves – control over women in the domestic realm and relative dominance in economic and social spheres (Niehaus 2005; Wood and Jewkes 2001). Other research has focused on men's attempts to repudiate violence in the context of a rapidly changing gender order (Walker 2005; Sideris 2005).

In terms of South African legislation, marital rape was only recognised in the Prevention of Family Violence Act, passed in 1993. In the same year the possibility of male rape was legally recognised.[19] This means that domestic violence and sexual harassment within a male same-sex relationship now has the potential for legal remedy and gays can use the law to protect themselves. Knowledge of the law, however scant and provisional, was seen as sufficiently important to devote an entire workshop to the current legal position of gays and lesbians in South Africa. The law also featured in many discussions and it is not surprising that it was uppermost in the minds of many participants.[20] Historically. homosexuality has been the focus of intense state surveillance and prohibition (Cameron 1994). Without the 1996 Constitution and the sweeping legal changes that have taken place in its wake, the workshop discussions about different ways of being gay would not have been possible. The workshops are thus indicative of a new sense of belonging, of citizenship, which comes from a dual emancipation – the abolition of laws that were oppressive in terms of race and, equally importantly for the workshop participants, sexual orientation. Yet the detail of the law, while seen as important in the abstract, is often rendered incomprehensible in translation or ineffectual in practice.

The workshop on the legal position of gays and lesbians held in October 2004 illustrated this ambiguous experience of the law. The LGEP, a gay and lesbian organisation devoted to advocacy and legal reform, paid for workshop expenses, including transport, accommodation and catering. They also dispatched experts in jurisprudence relating to lesbian and gay equality to Ermelo. For the LGEP, this rural constituency formed part of their outreach work. It was a relatively well-resourced organisation and, unlike at the other two workshops, there was no shortage of funds for basic essentials and no shortage of documentation, which was ferried in by the cars that travelled from Johannesburg to Ermelo. The workshop took place in a community hall in Wesselton. Yet the workshop was, by all accounts, a disappointment.

According to participants from Ermelo, this was because the language was alienating and boring, driving many participants to sit outside and chat, catching up on news and gossip while their legal status was being explained in the hall. It is not only the complexity of legal language that is a hurdle to mutual understanding between urban and rural, but also that local cases, complex, confusing and messy as they often are, seem to fall beyond the ambit of what an entity such as the LGEP is willing, or indeed able, to do.

In the workshop on domestic violence and sexual harassment, anyone who experienced sexual harassment was encouraged to go to the police and if their grievances were not satisfactorily attended to, they were encouraged to report their experiences to Bhuti, who undertook to contact the LGEP. Bhuti made a point of contacting the organisation whenever legal cases arose. He told me that he did so when Nathi was stabbed and robbed of his cell phone; he said that he did so when Dumisani was sexually assaulted and when Themba was accused of having sex with an underage youth.

The LGEP had little to do with the resolution of Nathi's case. Nathi fell in love with the policeman who took a statement from him while he was still in hospital. Well connected within the local constabulary, Nathi was satisfied when arrests were made in connection with his assault. The assailants were ultimately sentenced to lengthy jail terms (see Chapter 2). The second case involved Dumisani and is described in some detail in Chapter 3. Briefly, he was accosted and sexually assaulted by two young men. The matter was reported to the police and the youths arrested. Various attempts were made to reach an out-of-court settlement, but these failed. Again, the case was regularly postponed and eventually dropped altogether. In both these instances, legal representatives from the LGEP were approached and apparently undertook to intervene but, according to Bhuti, did not do so.

The third case involved the sangoma Themba and is described in more detail in the next chapter. Themba was accused of having sex with an underage youth. According to Bhuti, the legal representative from the LGEP reprimanded Themba for having sex with a fifteen-year-old youth, telling him that he had obviously not paid enough attention when he attended the legal workshop. If he had, he would know that the age of consent was sixteen and there was nothing that the LGEP could do for him. He was clearly in breach of the law as it had been explained at the workshop.[21]

When family negotiations broke down, charges were laid at the police station and Themba was arrested, but ultimately the family dropped the charges against him. Whatever the merits or otherwise of the case, the accumulation of ineffectual intervention, even in cases that seem relatively clear-cut, reinforced the idea of an ineffectual legal system and downplayed the possibilities for redress or protection, even when organisations such as the LGEP were invited to be involved.[22]

Thus the articulation and explanation of the detail of the law might be met with incomprehension and boredom, as was the case with the legal workshop, or the day-to-day experience of the law may be frustrating and inconclusive, as with the rape, robbery and assault cases. Or the interaction with organisations that are seen to protect gay and lesbian interests according to the provisions of the law may be seen as ineffectual, as with the engagements with the LGEP. Nevertheless, the Constitution and the subsequent changes in the law allow for new possibilities for individual self-expression, as well as a collective project for gays, underpinned by a sense of citizenship and equality before the law. It was in this context that the statement made by a hairstylist from the town of Balfour was made: 'I know gays have rights and gay rights are human rights. I know that gays are protected constitutionally.'

However, domestic violence and sexual harassment are not only legal matters – as the workshop devoted to these topics demonstrated – but as forms of violence that represent extremes of interaction in both intimate and social settings, they also provided the opportunity to find other, more harmonious ways of engaging between *ladies* and *gents* and between *ladies* and the broader community. The workshops thus provided some useful strategies for social interaction. It is equally true that without the equality provisions in the Constitution and the legal protection offered to gays and lesbians, these strategies for harmonious interaction would not be viable. Here the provisions on gender equality were seen to be just as important as those relating to sexual orientation. The kinds of problems that *ladies* experienced were similar to those faced by women, notably domestic violence, sexual harassment and rape. The empowerment of women – the legal provisions that have been put in place and a political commitment to gender equity – were also seen to be tools that could empower gays, as *ladies*.

The stated intention of the workshops, to encourage the emergence of a 'real gay' identity, akin to modern ideals of egalitarian same-sex relationships, was a project that failed because the sex\gender system remains intact. Thus in the workshops, the terms are imbued with new local meanings. They are translated in a local context and rendered intelligible to the workshop participants. So it is not the participants who are transformed into modern sexual subjects, it is the terms themselves that are imbued with new meanings.

Thus the basic premise remains intact: homosexual relationships necessarily involve, not two persons of the same sex and same gender, but two partners of the same sex but crucially and emphatically of different genders. Yet this dichotomy is increasingly unsustainable and was to a certain extent, if not undermined, then subject to critical scrutiny, within the context of the workshops. This is apparent in the informal terms used outside the workshops, such as 'somewhat bended', to refer to a heterosexual man with a penchant for gays or 'Greek salad' to refer to those who are unsure of where they fit within the gender order.

Another compelling aspect of the 'real gay' workshops is to be found in the political project that informs them. It is striking to me that the forms of behaviour and ways of self-presentation being discouraged at the workshops, namely flamboyant forms of self-expression, also allow for a remarkable degree of integration. As mentioned, this includes integration within conservative church communities, notably branches of the Zionist church and the Apostolic Faith Mission. Within these church communities gays may, for example, enter spaces and perform tasks that are the exclusive domain of women and are, in fact, taboo for men.

The workshops raised interesting questions about identity categories. Drawing on a recognised system of classification, Bhuti categorised Nathi as 'transgendered', while Nathi and others like him who dress and perform in overtly feminine ways regard themselves as gay. They see themselves in fact as the 'real gays' and, as Nathi explained to me, the gender confusion being introduced (and here the workshops are the thin edge of the wedge) is proof of the fact that some of these gays are fake and not real at all. In this model, a 'real gay' is born a gay and expresses an innate gay identity by dressing and conducting himself as a woman. The debates and discussions about these identity categories show them to be unstable, fluid and difficult to pin down. What makes a gay transgendered and vice versa? Who has the authority to name, to categorise? In a metropolitan context, the hegemonic view would be to call the overtly feminine gays transgendered, but in this context they see themselves as unquestionably gay. Similarly the term 'bisexual' fails to be meaningful in a context in which men do not have sexual relations with other men; they have sex with women or effeminate gays known as *ladies*. The metropolitan tendency to categorise on the basis of sexual and gender difference is strangely discordant here, where gender is the primary organising principle of sexual identity.

All these new possibilities – the seemingly endless potential for self-reinvention – remain constrained by or shaped by fixed and persistent notions of sex, gender and sexual identity. It is this very conflation of gender and sexuality that has allowed for the possibilities of social integration. It remains to be seen what the consequences of the 'real gay' workshops will be. Coming out is a way of identifying yourself, declaring yourself as different and distinct, and may pose problems for integration, as some of the experiences of my informants, in church communities, for example, suggest. This brings me to the conclusion that the very project of gay emancipation that asserts an identity based on difference and sexual object choice rather than gender may very well produce homophobia, by radically disrupting the sex/gender system, which currently offers gays and their boyfriends the possibility of integration.

The workshops were reformist, not radical. They did not challenge the basic underlying premise of sex and gender and so still allowed for the possibility of social inclusion. Even in the context of a same-sex relationship, heterosexual desire remained essentially unchallenged. After all, if gender is the basis for a sexual identity, heterosexual desire is always present in the relationship between two male persons of different genders – a man and a woman or, to use local parlance, a *lady* and a *gent* are invariably still involved.

Notes

1. The black proprietor's name is Basie (which literally translated means 'young boss'). The use of the names Missus and Baas (Madam and Boss) are also used ironically and denote deferential terms that were a familiar part of the vocabulary of racial inequality, here applied in terms of class to the owners and landlords, by the customers and tenants.
2. *Intombazane* means 'girl' in Zulu.
3. Out in Africa South African Gay and Lesbian Film Festival, 28–29 October 2005.
4. The pastor had shown me a detailed ink-on-paper drawing of the house, which he had drawn himself based on a dream and which he kept on hand. At the time it was tacked to the wall of his makeshift office. It looked remarkably like many of the suburban homes in the largely white, middle-class suburbs of Ermelo, replete with security fencing and an electronic sliding gate.
5. Pongola is a town in northern KwaZulu-Natal, near the Swaziland border.
6. *Igwalagwala* is the name of a regional radio station as well as the colourful lourie bird.
7. Sipho was attending the workshop as my research assistant, specifically as a photographer and translator. However, given that he was from the area and saw himself as part of the community, he was also an active participant in the workshop.
8. Themba interviewed by Busi Kheswa, Ermelo, 24 August 2002.
9. *The Felicia Show* ('where extraordinary people say extraordinary things') was launched in 1992 as *Top Level* with the stated aim 'to get South Africa talking'. It was the first audience-participation television talk-show of its kind in South Africa. Gay and lesbian topics have featured regularly on the popular programme.
10. Dubbed the 'Madonna of the townships' by *Time*, Brenda Fassie was a gay icon who died in May 2004, aged 39. Special tributes were paid to her in the Miss Gay Ten Years of Democracy beauty pageant held in Wesselton in August 2004.
11. The small but vocal ACDP was vehemently opposed to the inclusion of sexual orientation in the Bill of Rights and was the only political party to oppose the Constitution when it was ratified by Parliament in 1996.
12. For a comparison perspective on 'real' and 'fake' lesbians in Thailand, see Sinnott (2004).

13. However, Sizani admits that, if she followed her polygamous inclinations, she would be the only member of her family, to the best of her knowledge, who has more than one wife.

14. This outfit was made for him by an adoring aunt, although the wearer ultimately found it 'too much'. Concerned that he may be seen as a prostitute, he sold it to a more flamboyant 'dragging queen' for R30 and went back to his more sedate dress code.

15. The discrepancy between emic and etic uses of the terms 'transgender' and 'gay' is explored by David Valentine. He suggests that the generic use of the term 'gay' 'indexes any gendered or sexual difference that marks you off from heteronormativity' (2002: 235). Similarly, in my fieldwork, 'gay' was used as an emic term that covered a wide range of etic sexual categories, including transgendered and intersex. Whether these could usefully be seen as a distinct marker from heteronormativity is in question though, given that same-sex relationships were so deeply embedded in performances of heteronormativity.

16. *Capital Gay*, 18 September 1987.

17. The public discourse on homosexuality in Kenya has shifted in a more positive direction since the adoption of the new Kenyan constitution in 2010.

18. The broad rationale for this approach is that the state's ability to protect vulnerable groups (and to uphold fundamental principles of human rights, even when these are contrary to popular opinion) is a measure of the success of the democratic project in post-apartheid South Africa. The sexual orientation clause in the Bill of Rights is one such litmus test for the efficacy of constitutional democracy in South Africa. For these reasons, strengthening gay and lesbian civil society is seen as a strategic intervention.

19. For a fuller account of the history of rape in South Africa, see Posel (2005a).

20. Even a relatively obscure legal provision concerning cross-dressing and disguise was raised in a workshop. Bhuti sounded a note of caution on cross-dressing when he warned that one could be arrested for wearing drag in terms of an obscure legal provision against the wearing of disguises (see Cameron 1994: 90).

21. It is important to note that these are perceptions of the role of the LGEP as experienced by workshop participants and activists. I have made no attempt to verify these accounts, as I am primarily interested in how the law and an urban based-organisation, such as LGEP, is subjectively experienced and perceived.

22. The other complicating factor in these cases was the tendency to mediate and resolve disputes between families, rather than through formal legal channels. This was not unique to cases involving gays. For example, it is not unusual for heterosexual rape cases to be dealt with between families, thus bypassing the law altogether. In the statutory rape case involving Themba and the youth, the two families were deeply involved in attempting to resolve the dispute. The main aim was an out-of-court settlement. The threat of arrest and possible conviction was used as part of a broader negotiation strategy.

CHAPTER 6

'Gay' Sangomas

'Traditional' or 'Millennium' and Un-African?

In the previous chapter I showed how the workshops served as a platform for debate about what it meant to be a 'real gay' and how the real/fake debate was highly contested terrain that revealed not only different conceptions of sex, gender and sexual identity in Ermelo, but also pointed to broader shifts in self-identification and categorisation that were taking place as a consequence of social and legal changes at a macro-level. The workshops indicated that the effects of the Constitution could be felt in small towns and remote areas. The true/false dialectic came up again in another field of my research, in relation to gay sangomas. While hairstyling was a popular occupation for gays, a number of them were sangomas. I knew eight gay sangomas practising in Ermelo, Bethal and Standerton, although they were not the only ones working in the region. Sangomas clearly played an important symbolic role – several of them were reputed to be gay, yet they were seen to be unquestionably African – and, as such, they carried a symbolic value for gays striving to claim an authentically African gay identity. However, precisely because of their symbolic currency, they were also subject to close scrutiny by other gays.

In this chapter I explore the ideas behind a current distinction made by my informants between 'old' (traditional/genuine) sangomas and 'millennium' sangomas and show how traditional healers serve as African cultural icons. In particular, ideas about the authenticity of gay sangomas relate directly to discursive contestations about whether homosexuality can be regarded as African or un-African. How does the debate about 'old' versus 'millennium' sangomas relate to pervasive ideas about being African? Why is it that gays have such a strong vested interest in showing that their sexuality is compatible with African cultural norms? And, a parallel and related theme, why the efforts that gays invest in showing how Christianity and homosexuality are reconcilable.

Genuine versus millennium sangomas

This distinction between genuine and millennium sangomas came up for the first time in my research during a conversation that seemed to lead in a number of different directions. The full context might be important to site the everyday implications of this distinction; notably, the debate on gay and un-African that has played such a prominent role in South Africa for many decades.

On 1 May 2006, I met and interviewed Brendan in a small house in Sakhile township in Standerton (see Chapter 5). I had first heard about Brendan from Bhuti, more than a year before the interview. His name had come up during a discussion that took place in Bhuti's rooms on the topic of Zulu gay lingo.

In the background, as we were discussing the vocabulary of the gay language, a group of *ladies* was congregated on Bhuti's bed. At the centre of their attention was a young gay from Pongola who was wearing a doek on his head as a sign of respect for Happy, the man for whom he was waiting in agonised anticipation. So intense were his feelings for this man that the *ladies* were taking care of his lovesickness and offering him a calming cup of tea. Bhuti, who was by that stage slightly irritated by the emotive scenes, reluctantly intervened and called Happy on his cell phone. He asked him to please come because the youngster was missing him so much.

While this was going on, Bhuti and I continued our discussion on Zulu gay lingo. Bhuti believed that Brendan was one of the inventors of this lingo: 'It was a language that was used in the old apartheid time amongst black people who did not accept gay people.' He had given me a sheet of paper, a typed list of 86 key words drawn from this language, which had been compiled by Thulani. He also said that younger gays had learned their vocabulary from older gays and that the language was now used 'to gossip in front of other people who don't understand'. Bhuti told me that Brendan was a founding member of the Gay and Lesbian Organisation of the Witwatersrand (GLOW) in 1988, together with Linda Ncgobo and Simon Nkoli, amongst others.[1] Apparently Brendan, who was originally from Durban, had lived in Standerton while studying towards his teacher's diploma, before moving to Johannesburg. He had subsequently fallen on hard times and returned to Standerton in November 2004. Bhuti knew someone who knew someone who knew where he was staying and we resolved to try and meet with Brendan.

Meanwhile Happy had arrived and shortly thereafter left Bhuti's ròoms, together with the young gay from Pongola, now sans the doek. Bhuti told me that things were not going well between them because Happy found his young paramour too old fashioned, 'too cultural'. He did 'many cultural things that are done by straight ladies', such as, 'if you are a gay femme you must wait for a man to declare love to you'. And there was the business of the doek which, while intended as a sign of respect, had only added to Happy's irritation with his ultra-traditional *lady*. From what Bhuti told me and from what I witnessed that evening, the removal of the doek foreshadowed the heartache that lay ahead.

During 2005, whenever Bhuti visited Standerton (which he did frequently because his parents' home was there and he had a number of friends there) he tried to contact Brendan, but for one reason or another his leads had come to nought, until that meeting on 1 May 2006, which was Worker's Day, a public holiday, when we finally met Brendan. The house where he was staying was in an informal settlement, one of many that had mushroomed around Sakhile over the last decade. The house was made of precast concrete walling called Vibracrete that is ubiquitous in South African suburban gardens. Vibracrete consists of concrete slabs and poles that can be easily assembled. The walls of that house offered little protection against the cold. The wind that blew that day easily found a way through the gaps between the concrete slabs, and it was only May. I imagined what it would be like in mid-winter. The roof was made out of old strips of rusted corrugated iron and there was no ceiling. Inside, it was sparsely furnished and impeccably neat. There was a double bed on one side of the room and a small round table with four chairs on the other. In one corner there was a kettle and a hotplate, some crockery and cutlery and a plastic tub for washing up. There was no running water in the house but there was electricity, activated by the prepaid electrical meter that serviced the house. The house belonged to Dan, a gay who was much younger than Brendan and who had taken him in. Also present was a young man, Dan's boyfriend, who did not say a word throughout the interview. His only engagement was to smile with diffident bemusement during a discussion about the suitability of straight men as boyfriends.

Brendan was heavier and taller than the rest of us who sat at the round Formica table. His large stature, coupled with a loud, clear voice, gave him a commanding presence in the room. His hair was greying and receding and wrinkles showed around his eyes and mouth, features that made him appear older than his 49 years. Brendan was thoughtful and articulate and brought a wealth of experience to the discussion. Both Bhuti and Brendan were passionate activists and they enjoyed exchanging ideas and opinions, and so, instead of me interviewing Brendan, what followed was an exchange between Bhuti and Brendan, sparked by the questions that I posed. Their style of interaction was both deeply serious and engaged and at the same time filled with laughter, gossip and bemused incredulity at the perceived antics of some of their peers. Brendan was the oldest gay I had met in my fieldwork in Mpumalanga. My conversation with him provided the opportunity to explore changes that had taken place since he had first lived in Standerton from 1984 to 1986, twenty years previously. One of the topics that I broached was that of gay sangomas and my question (which pre-empted the focus of the discussion) was phrased in terms of changes that may have taken place over time. Ideas of old and new were picked up in relation to sangomas and I found myself in familiar terrain, a discussion about what constituted 'real' and 'pretend'. Below is an extract from the discussion:

Graeme: Another interesting thing . . . is that a lot of gays also seem to practise as sangomas . . . I wonder if that is something that is old, or something that is new, gays being sangomas?

Brendan: To the old people it is something that was there because what we Africans believe is that if a person is a sangoma, it is a person who has got the spirit of the ancestors. So now . . . it depends which ancestor is on you, which spirit of that ancestor is in you. If maybe it is your female ancestor, then possibly you are going to act like a female because you have got that spirit of that ancestor. So now most of the gays [sangomas] they are becoming homosexuals because most of them they are being controlled by a female spirit. So that is the reason that makes the gays mostly to be sangomas. But not the latest sangomas . . .

Graeme: Not the . . .

Brendan: The latest sangomas. The latest sangomas, they are just playing in order just to look for men. That is all.

[Laughter]

Graeme: Do you think so?

Brendan: No, I am not thinking; I am telling you.

Bhuti: But there are those . . . I can support you.

Brendan: All right, quote one.

Bhuti: Let us agree to disagree.
Brendan: Okay.
Bhuti: Nhlanhla. Do you know Nhlanhla?
Brendan: Who is that Nhlanhla?
Bhuti: He is a gay sangoma and he is working . . . miracles.
Brendan: When has he starting to be a sangoma?
Bhuti: 1996.
Brendan: Ja, I can agree with that. I am just talking about these
            2000 . . . the millennium, the millennium sangomas.
Bhuti: I am just talking about Themba. I fail to understand
            where is his . . .
Brendan: Spirit?
Bhuti: No, his duties as a sangoma is concerned. You know
            I didn't see someone that he has healed. I didn't hear
            him saying that 'I was working there as a sangoma'
            . . . I can agree with you because he is a millennium
            sangoma.

[What followed was a brief discussion about Mafika from
Standerton, another millennium sangoma.]

Brendan: Graeme, one thing is for sure, there is a difference
            between an old sangoma and the millennium
            sangomas . . . They are pretending because they want
            to get there in order to get men. If they are tired of
            those men, they just take off all their sangoma stuff
            and they just throw it there and they just go back to
            their original personality.
Graeme: So they don't even go to training or anything?
Brendan: No!
Graeme: They just wear the clothes, in order to attract men?
Brendan: Exactly. [Laughter] *Haai*, you know sangomas, hey?
Bhuti: You know Manelesi, he is having this notion seeing
            a gay guy and maybe he is attracted to this guy . . .
            He has got these tactics of going to that guy and
            saying I have been sent by your . . .

Brendan: Ancestors, ja.
Bhuti: . . . to make initiation so that you can be a sangoma.
            Like Dingane, he was once a victim to Manelesi, then
            after you enter the initiation then there will be . . .
Brendan: Sexual intercourse and all that . . .
Bhuti: . . . sexual intercourse
Brendan: Ja . . .
Bhuti: . . . and the frustration of the relationship
Brendan: The relationship, ja . . .
Bhuti: . . . the initiation and after that you will be . . .

[Bhuti explained that Dingane was not called by his ancestors.
He was seduced by his trainer, Manelesi. Dingane was persuaded
to undergo training and then, when the relationship soured, he
abandoned it.]

Bhuti: To my belief, if you are going to be a sangoma, you
            must dream, you must have a dream. The dream must
            channel you to that head trainer who will be training
            you and who will be putting you through the process
            of becoming a sangoma.
Brendan: You don't just wake up becoming a sangoma. It
            comes through time. Others may disappear from
            home and they are taken to a river or a dam and
            they stay there for about two months.
Bhuti: No, not two months, a lot of time.
Brendan: Yes, maybe six months or a whole year, staying inside
            the river. But those sangomas who are millennium,
            I can wake up the following day, going to that house
            if I want a boy from that house and say, 'I dreamed
            of your granny, saying this and this and this so you
            must come and join the initiation'. And then from
            there the boy comes in here and I just put him into
            the bed and thereafter I am finished. [Laughter] No,
            it is true. I am just saying something that we are very
            familiar with.

The idea of millennium sangomas echoed other debates that I had come across about what was real and what was not. Amongst gays there were many discussions in which these ideas of real and fake swirled around like an undercurrent. Questions of authenticity seemed to have a particular salience amongst gays and notions of 'real' and 'fashionable' also informed public discourse about gays.

Bhuti's workshops on 'how to be a real gay' (see Chapter 5), for example, presupposed that his activist sensibility held the key to a new, authentic way of being *gay* that stood in sharp contrast to the model of being *accepted as women*, which the workshops sought to challenge. The workshops thus equated 'real' with a process of education, enlightenment and modernity. Paradoxically these are precisely the characteristics that may render gays 'fashionable' by some of their detractors, those who see gays as a contemporary phenomenon and gay lifestyles as 'a fashion'. And there were those who, like Nathi, did not attend the workshops and who saw in their highly effeminate selves the true image of 'real gays'.

The idea that there are 'real' gays and those for whom being gay is 'just a fashion' also foregrounds questions of authenticity, of what constitutes genuine experience. In this case, the 'real gays' are seen as a natural, biological variant (they are born that way), while 'fashionable gays' have been drawn to a particular lifestyle as one may be to a trend in clothing or hairstyles. The fashionable gays are seen as part of a broader process of social transformation, at once liberating and deeply threatening. As such, they are symptomatic of broader social changes and the associated aspirations and anxieties. Fashionable gays suggest that even basic elements of personality, such as gender identity and sexuality, are infinitely permeable. Real gays allow for a reassuring certainty in the vagaries of nature.

The category of 'real' can be seen as a way of policing the boundaries of identity – for example, when used amongst gays to define the limits of gay and straight sexuality. Appropriate forms of behaviour are defined through a form of social commentary, often expressed in rumour and gossip. For instance, according to the gossip, Themba, noted in the conversation between Bhuti and Brendan above as a millennium sangoma, had a girlfriend when he relocated temporarily to the town of Witbank. And hairstylist Nkosinathi was also rumoured to have abandoned his gay life and become straight when he stopped attending gay functions and socialising with other gays. When Themba and Nkosinathi strayed too far from the parameters of the group, they risked losing membership of that group by stepping outside the boundaries of being gay. In this context the idea of 'real' paradoxically highlights the instability of the very categories used to define sexual identity.

In the discourse of the Hope and Unity Metropolitan Community Church (HUMCC), a similar dichotomy exists between 'real' and 'fake' gays. I raise this instance here because it is one of the gay community formations that have had an important impact on gays and lesbians in Mpumalanga. Bhuti, for example, has been an ardent supporter of the church. The HUMCC's pastor, Nokuthula Dhladla, had close family ties in the town of Volksrust. A branch of the church was launched at the workshop on Christianity and homosexuality held in Bethal in 2004. Pastor Nokuthula was asked to lead the workshop and officiate at the launch. The HUMCC even dispatched one of its leading choir members, Martin Machapa, to the Miss Gay Ten Years of Democracy beauty pageant. The church had an important symbolic role. The HUMCC was widely known amongst gays in all corners of the country, including Mpumalanga, where most gays knew about it, even if they had never attended one of its services. The existence of the church served as a powerful counterpoint to the accusation that homosexuality was intrinsically un-Christian.

The theology of the HUMCC held that God made some people straight and some people gay and that it is the spiritual duty of individuals to be true to their inner selves. This theology suggests that individuals have an innate sexual nature that is God-given. If heterosexuals are drawn to homosexuality for whatever reason, such as bad heterosexual experiences, abuse, or trans-actional sex (to name some examples mentioned in the church), they were as transgressive as gays who tried, due to social pressure, moral discomfort or religious rhetoric to live a hetero-sexual life. In this model, like the biological model, sexuality is predestined. Not surprisingly, bisexuality did not fit comfortably within this schema, being too ambiguous to fit into the neat identity categories promulgated by the church.

The church also participated in the project of promoting a modern gay identity, which emphasised identity categories, such as 'gay' and 'lesbian', rather than the more gender-based variants amongst *ladies* and *gents*. According to the teachings of the church, God made certain individuals gay, while others were drawn into the life for dubious or unnatural reasons. In the context of the HUMCC, 'God-given' is the theological equivalent of 'natural'.[2] Thus the theology of the HUMCC posits that the demonstrable presence of the Holy Spirit in the church community signals divine endorsement of the church project. In other words, if the church is able to show that the Holy Spirit is at work through its members, it shows conclusively that God, the ultimate authority, approves of gay Christians.

The discussion between Bhuti and Brendan about old versus millennium sangomas is also concerned with what constitutes the 'real'. From the discussion, it emerged that in Brendan and Bhuti's view millennium sangomas do not receive a genuine calling. They do not dream, nor are they led to their trainers through the intercession of their ancestors. Their training is neither adequate nor complete; it is not long enough, for a start. Then there is the problem with practising their profession – millennium sangomas do not run thriving businesses. In fact, in some cases, they do not appear to practise at all. The issue of appearance was also raised. Millennium sangomas wear the garments of their trade, but this was presented in the discussion as duplicitous, where dress is used as a costume or a disguise. Thus millennium sangomas misuse their position of ritual authority and power, or worse, the trappings of that position, in order to acquire status and, in the case of effeminate sangomas, to secure sexual favours from men. Or, in the case of masculine sangomas, they may abuse their position as trainers and take sexual advantage of their gay *twasa* (initiate). All these observations made by Bhuti and Brendan were concerned with the various ways in which appearance could be manipulated for personal gain.

Genuine or old sangomas were seen in a different light. For one thing, they experienced the calling as a direct revelation from the ancestors. They could do little else but follow the path that the ancestors had chosen for them. Indeed, when possessed by the spirit of an ancestor, personal volition is subsumed by the wishes of the ancestor – in Brendan's words: 'Most of them they are being controlled by a female spirit'. For Brendan, this was the most significant sign of authenticity. In this scenario a sangoma's sexuality is determined, not by individual desire, but by the needs of ancestors.[3] Hence a male sangoma possessed by the spirit of a female ancestor is fulfilling the wishes of this ancestor by taking on a male partner. In this way, a same-sex orientation is socially sanctioned and imbued with ritual power. The ancestors guide initiates to a trainer and their training is long and arduous. This pays off because at the end of their training they are in a position to embark on successful careers as healers and diviners. The fact that they are described as 'old' (in this context 'old' is a synonym for 'genuine') also points to the idea that they are closer to tradition and culture. They are thus more authentic and closer to the traditions of their forebears than the new, millennium sangomas could ever be.

Interestingly, at the tail end of the discussion, Brendan and Bhuti disagreed about the training requirements of sangomas. Neither of them was clear about how long an initiate should train for and there was also a lack of clarity about the nature of the calling and how the training took place. They both had ideas about this and about what happened in the old days – ideas about what constituted real African traditions and customs and hence what was authentic. But the world of tradition is also elusive and subject to dispute. It is more *the idea* of what is traditional, old or customary that was being used in the discussion and that holds an important symbolic weight. What constitutes 'the real' was thus a highly contested terrain. Were gays real or were they just a fashion? Were gays born that way or did they just decide to be like that? Did God predestin some to be gay or were gay Christians an oxymoron? Could gays become straight? Which *gents* were really straight and which were 'somewhat bended'? Were gay marriages real or were they more like theatrical performances lacking in legal status and social sanction? And, as the exchange between Brendan and Bhuti shows, who was a real sangoma? Why is it that the question of real and not-real, or fake, seemed to dominate discourses around gay identity, both for the public at large and amongst gays? In the rest of this chapter, I expand on this discussion between real and fake, or old and millennium sangomas, through two portraits: one is of Nhlanhla from Platrand, cited in the discussion as a genuine sangoma; the other is of Themba from Ermelo, who featured as a millennium sangoma.

Portrait of a genuine sangoma

> It was 1996. I was repeating Matric. It was not my aim to repeat it, it is just that I got very sick . . . They told me that I have a calling from the ancestors. To me it sounded like it is not that. It is just an evil spirit . . . Then after I went home to the farm where I grew up, they took me to see another traditional healer. They told me the same thing about the calling . . . I dreamt about being a sangoma. I was together with the old people inside a room. Everybody in the house was wearing red clothes. And there I was dancing, dancing just as if I had been a real sangoma.

Nhlanhla lived on a farm in the district of Platrand. I first met him in 2000, when Bhuti accompanied me to his rural homestead. We took the road from Standerton towards Volksrust and stopped en route to ask directions at an old trading store, run by a middle-aged white woman, a farmer's wife. Our presence seemed to make her uncomfortable. She spoke only to me and pointedly not to Bhuti. The store was an old brick building with a deep veranda. It had the appearance of being too large for the modest stock it held, as if it were once a more important and busier trading centre. The building was encircled by a copse of blue gums and shadowed by a set of maize silos that could be seen from miles around in this gently undulating landscape. This small settlement – the shop, the silos and a couple of houses – marked the turn-off to Platrand. We drove a short distance along the tar, which soon gave way to the rough corrugations of dirt road. We then travelled for some time until we reached a fork in the road. Again, there was a trading store, owned by an Indian family. This one sold second-hand coal stoves, of the kind that were common in townships such as Sakhile or Wesselton. We followed the signpost to Kaffirskraal.[4] About half an hour after leaving the tar road, we came to a set of homesteads that Bhuti thought he recognised. I parked the car at the side of the road and we began walking through the veld. As we walked, the sturdy soil underfoot gave way to mud and then marshland – nothing impassable, but enough to cake our shoes with mud. Bhuti lifted his trouser legs by grabbing the material near his pockets with both hands and yanking them out of mud's way. Then he continued, tiptoeing gingerly through the marshland. I teased him. He teased me back. He called me 'country girl', I called him 'city girl' and those were the names we were stuck with, albeit with some variation, throughout my fieldwork. As it turned out, it was the wrong homestead.

Nhlanhla lived very nearby, on the other side of the road, on a farm called 'Goedgenoeg'.[5] The compound was accessed through a metal gate, which had a small wheel attached to the base, so that the gate swung open with ease onto a farm road, with grass growing between the two rudimentary tracks. At that meeting, which was to be the first of many over the next six years, Nhlanhla cut a slight figure. He had a striking face, with high cheekbones and a shy smile. His voice was very soft and he spoke in a thoughtful, considered way. As we sat and spoke, he held himself in such a way that made him seem smaller than he actually was: he held his hands between his knees and his shoulders were slumped forward. When he walked, however, he held himself erect, at full stature and with a graceful poise. He was evidently delighted to see Bhuti. I knew that they had a close connection and that he and Bhuti had a 'mother-daughter' relationship, as Nhlanhla put it:

> I called Bhuti my mother. I showed Bhuti my album. I gave him a photo, he gave me his photo. Once we had got close and if I did something wrong, he wouldn't just keep quiet, he would tell me. He taught me about gay life . . . He warned me here and there until I found a way.

Platrand is farming territory. There are vast tracts of cultivated land en route to Nhlanhla's home. Nhlanhla's father worked on Goedgenoeg as a farm labourer, as did his elder brother. He had two younger brothers who, at the time of our first meeting, were still at school. Two of his siblings had died in infancy. His mother worked as a domestic worker on the same farm. Nhlanhla's mother once asked him when she could expect his boyfriend to pay *ilobola* for him. Some years later, Nhlanhla's brother insisted that his boyfriend should behave like any prospective brother-in-law. He told Nhlanhla, 'That man of yours, he must respect us. He must go in a right way.' His father, Nhlanhla told me, 'is not so talkative. You know people who see things but don't say anything about it? If everything is okay with me, if I am happy, then he is happy too.' It was only his elder brother who did not understand and who made a point of criticising gays in front of Nhlanhla. For instance, whenever there was a radio talk-show on the topic, he would say, 'Come and hear what people say about gay people.' His wife, Nhlanhla's sister-in-law, disagreed, saying, 'This is not a bad thing, but gays must respect themselves'. According to Nhlanhla, his mother broached the topic in other ways, aside from her joking remarks about *ilobola*: 'There is nothing that I can say about you. You are my child. I love you. I don't want anyone to say anything bad about you.'

Nhlanhla's family homestead on the farm consisted of a cluster of wattle and daub rooms. The external walls had been decorated with colourful designs, while the interior walls were coated with dyes, blue in one room, pink in another, green in another. The uneven mud floors were covered with linoleum. The furniture was an eclectic mix of cast-offs. I wondered which homes they had been in before. In particular, I noticed a kitchen dresser that was in the lounge, displaying some very ordinary cutlery. It was the sort of dresser that I knew to be all the rage in Johannesburg, at least for those subscribing to a 1970s retro style. The house had been added on to and gave a sense of having expanded with the family – the arrival of the couple's own children, the stages of their growing up and the various relatives that had stayed with them over the years. There was a barbed-wire fence around the homestead. A goat was grazing, tethered to a piece of rope attached to a pole driven into the ground. There were geese and chickens clucking about.

Six years later, in May 2006, Nhlanhla had just returned to Standerton to stay with his aunt. We had lost touch for almost a year. During that time, his cell phone number was either unavailable, or answered by his mother who did not seem to know where Nhlanhla was, or when he would be coming back. Then, just as I was about to leave South Africa for a protracted period of time, he called me on my cell phone. I met him the following day, in Standerton. As I waited at the designated spot in the parking lot of Kentucky Fried Chicken, I caught a glimpse of him in my rear-view mirror. He was wearing jeans and a T-shirt and, while instantly recognisable, his familiar appearance was shaped by a much smaller frame. He had lost a lot of weight. His face was dominated by a broad, engaging smile, while his cheekbones looked even more prominent in his sunken face.

His skin had the pallor of ill health. His hair remained partially beaded and twisted into dreadlocks of even length and he still wore the bracelets made from animal skin. He had been very ill and incapacitated for seven months. During that time he had been subject to a rigorous treatment regime and a life-and-death struggle with the evil spirits that had bewitched him. Nhlanhla thought that he might have been bewitched when he helped one of his patients drive away evil spirits: 'When the witch heard that it is me who helped somebody, it started to bewitch me.' Guided by the spirit of his paternal grandmother, he had travelled to Hluhluwe in KwaZulu-Natal for help, from where he had just returned.

According to Nhlanhla, 'I was born being a gay'. The influential ancestors in his life were all women. 'The ancestors, the men, I don't see them. I see the women most of the time.' His grandmother was the woman who, in his words, 'makes me alive again' and she had done so on more than one occasion:

> I've got my old grandmother who controls me most of the time. And then there is my other grandmother, my father's mother, who is always there if I am in the trouble, like now when I am sick . . . when I woke up the other day and my body was well, I couldn't believe it. I said to myself: 'Okay, everything is fine now. My grandmother has made me alive again.'

Unlike some sangomas, Nhlanhla was not singularly dedicated to traditional medicine. He believed that allopathic medicine had a role to play and sometimes referred his patients to medical practitioners. At the onset of his illness, he went to a local clinic and was given some tablets that had no apparent effect. It was at that point that he decided that the only effective form of treatment would be provided by other sangomas. Shortly thereafter, his grandmother appeared to him in a dream and guided him to Hluhluwe, where he found the help that he needed:

It is where I get help. I don't mean that the doctors have nothing to do. It is only that evil and the doctor can't go together. If you have a natural disease you can go to a doctor. As a traditional healer I can say that it is more important if you have a patient that is very sick you must take him to the doctor . . . It is important to go to the doctor and see what is happening.

Nhlanhla distinguished between 'natural' diseases and 'evil spirits' and prescribed treatment to his patients accordingly. He was strongly disapproving of sangomas who did not refer patients to medical practitioners when this was necessary: 'Some don't want to share their knowledge. Sometimes it is rotten knowledge.' In seeking to understand his own illness, he had initially considered various alternatives:

It started just like a normal sickness, you know. I started dreaming about bad things . . . I didn't know what type of sickness that I had. I am losing weight. I don't have any appetite. I told myself 'Maybe I have got HIV positive' . . . When times went on I saw, 'No, this is a witch. There is something wrong with me.' And my patients no longer came. It was just quiet. Nobody came to ask me for help. I start to see that everything now, everything now, is dark . . . So that is when I started to go to other traditional healers. They told me, 'You've got an evil spirit. Some others they have bewitched you. They have got a jealousy with your work.'

The seriousness with which he took his calling and the desperation brought on by his protracted and debilitating illness is evident in his decision to go to initiation school where, as a 30-year-old man, he would be circumcised. This was very late in the day for a man to go through the rites of adulthood and Nhlanhla did not relish the idea, but he had been instructed to do so by his ancestors, who had appeared to him in a dream. The dream, interpreted by his aunt, was apparently unmistakable. Nhlanhla heard a song in his dream, an initiation song: 'That was the message of my dream: this child must go and finish his culture. That is why the ancestors put everything in darkness. So he must go and finish and then after that everything will be all right.'

Nhlanhla knew that his feminine demeanour was very evident. He had told me how men proposed to him at church, for example. He recalled how at high school older boys would declare their love for him and how it had made him feel afraid. Or how, in Hluhluwe, other young men had questioned him, saying, 'We take you as a gay'. And there was the more painful memory of a group of older boys at school who had tried to force him to smoke marijuana, in order to make his voice deeper, more manly. He also remembered how, in the days before he became a sangoma, he had been called names like *sisButi*, *stabane* and *inkonkonyi*.[6] After he completed his training, people became more circumspect and they were more afraid of him. Nhlanhla knew that as someone who patently did not conform to the norms of his gender – as someone who was clearly and unmistakably effeminate – initiation school into the rites of manhood would be a test of forbearance and endurance, perhaps more so for him than the other young men:

> Even when I go to the mountain [initiation school], I will respect the law. The days will go by. Time will pass. I will come home. If you are a real gay, your only thing is feelings. You can go anywhere, you can do anything, but without your feelings, you are nothing. Yes, you are like a dead person. So this is my life. These are my feelings. They are going to do anything they want to do to me. Then I will come home and continue with my life.

Nhlanhla treasured his relationship with Bhuti who, he told me, was also well liked by members of his family. This was

clear from the way in which he was received by Nhlanhla's
mother and aunt at the time of our initial visit. Nhlanhla had
other gay friends, including a young trainee sangoma from
Standerton, but he steered clear of gay social events. He never
came to functions organised by Bhuti, for example. He explained
to me that he was expected to wear 'quality clothes' and that,
'you know what, especially with gay people, if we are together
someone will say bad things about someone else. Most of the
time they like to put others in a bad way . . . that is why I don't
like to be with them. A few of them, it's enough.'

Nhlanhla was active in one of the independent Zionist church
groups called Emahlokohlokweni, where he was a member of
the youth committee, sang in the church choir and participated
in the Umasambisane Women's Club, standing in for his aunt,
when she was unavailable. In church, he worshipped with the
women members and sang soprano in the choir, and at the Club
he catered and sang and danced with the other women members.
Although, in his own words, 'everything that I do, I do as a
woman', he wore the male uniform to church, the white trousers,
green jacket and belt characteristic of many independent church
groups. Once, he had a boyfriend in the church, but he found
that the man was exceptionally jealous and did not like him to
travel for church activities, such as choir competitions, so he
ended the relationship and declined the three proposals that he
had received from other church members. For Nhlanhla, it was
especially important that he would, when the time came, receive
a proper burial from the church community: 'I hope that one
day, when God remembers me, that my church is going to put
me in a hole, in a cemetery.' He had chosen this church, because
it accommodated a mix of Christian and traditional beliefs, unlike
charismatic churches, where he found that, as a sangoma, he
was unwelcome: 'I like salvation [charismatic church], but in
that church I didn't last because I was in this situation of being
initiated by the ancestral spirits.' Once, he told me, he had asked
the reverend's wife, 'Do the people accept me?' She replied, 'Most

of us, we love you . . . we want everybody to feel free in the church.'

Aside from his healing practice and his involvement in the church, Nhlanhla's abiding passion was netball.[7] It was a sport that he took up in 1994, the year of South Africa's first democratic elections, when everything seemed alive with new possibilities. In the same year Dumisani, Siyanda and Ayanda arrived at school in drag and make-up, Nhlanhla took to the netball court wearing the standard netball kit – a shirt, bib and skirt, cut above the knee. He continued with the sport after leaving school. At one stage there were four gays and three girls in his team. When he returned to Platrand, a young woman asked him to join their team. He accepted and soon became the coach of the Young Lions, a team composed of young women living on farms in the district.

Nhlanhla's sense of himself as a healer was central to the life choices that he made, the decisions that determined the course of his life. It was the most salient fact in choosing which church to attend; it profoundly influenced his intimate relationships, sexual practices and the company that he kept. He was committed to professional development, investing his earnings in further training to enhance his knowledge and hone his skills. It was this quality – the fact that being a traditional healer was the lodestar of his life – that made Nhlanhla, in the eyes of other gays, a genuine sangoma. The dream that signalled Nhlanhla's calling, the dream in which he was dancing 'just as if I had been a real sangoma' was, for Nhlanhla, the moment in which his life's course was set for him. The next day he had packed a small bag and headed off to meet his trainer, returning home several months later as a healer. In the context of real and millennium sangomas, Nhlanhla's dream and his vision of himself dancing had additional salience.

Portrait of a millennium sangoma

Themba lived in Thusi Village, a suburb of Wesselton, in a small room in his mother's back yard. He was a slight figure, effete in mannerism and dress. When he was not wearing traditional sangoma clothing, which was most of the time, he would wear jeans and a slightly feminine top. On his wrists, he invariably wore the red and white plastic beads or strips of animal skin that characterised his craft. He had an erect posture and strong arms, which gave him an air of confidence. He had an open, expressive face and could make people laugh by his expressions of feigned sincerity and camp banter. On the left side of his face, beneath his eye, a pronounced blemish, dark and round, gave the impression of a highly accentuated cheekbone. He kept his hair short with a hint of styling, partial cornrows, for example. The story of his calling and his initiation into the world of the ancestors was similar to many stories of young men and women who feel compelled to become traditional healers. Certainly it was not dissimilar to the experiences of Nhlanhla. Yet, Nhlanhla was taken seriously as a sangoma, whereas Themba was not. Themba, in Brendan's terms, was a millennium sangoma.

Themba's mother wanted nothing to do with his gay friends. When we went to visit, Bhuti would try to determine whether his mother was home by interpreting various signs – an open window, a drawn curtain, washing on the line and so on. He was afraid that she would come out and berate us before we managed to rouse Themba from his room at the back of the house. Themba's parents saw his friends as a bad influence. He told me, 'They called me to question me about my lifestyle and told me my friend Tsepo was not a good friend. He was influencing me negatively. I stopped seeing Tsepo and never went to his home. They realised that there was no difference.'

Themba was born into a Christian home in which traditional beliefs and practices were largely eschewed. So it was not easy for his family to accept that Themba had been called by the ancestors, signalled by the onset of inexplicable illness and erratic behaviour, which began when he was sixteen years old: 'At home we did not believe in such things as traditional healers, ancestors. We were Christians.' He got ill, had dreams and started mis-behaving at school. Here too, his behaviour was interpreted as being anti-Christian, demonic in fact: 'At school there were many Christians and they said I was demon-possessed. When they prayed for me, my ancestral spirits would be powerfully activated. My ancestors would tell them they are not demons.' Ultimately he began his training when he was seventeen, during his final year at school, on the very day that he was supposed to be sitting his accountancy exam: 'They say I just jumped the school gate and ran away.' He graduated as a sangoma just over ten months later, in July 2000.

Unlike Nhlanhla, whose dominant ancestors were all female, Themba's dominant ancestors were male, associated with masculine prowess in war. Themba mentioned two male ancestors – the dominant one being Mahlasela, meaning 'the one who attacks'. Like Nhlanhla, Themba did not articulate a direct link between the gender of his dominant ancestors and his sexuality: 'Some people ask me, "Does homosexuality go hand in hand with the ancestors?" I tell them that when I became a sangoma, I was already gay.' However, the gender of his ancestor did affect the way that he dressed: 'When I have a female ancestor as a visitor, sometimes I change from trousers to a traditional cloth and cover my head.' It did not affect desire: 'When I want a man it is just my lust.'

As a *twasa* undergoing training, Themba was accepted, although his trainer found it hard to understand that he was gay. He was treated 'like a girl' – other women washed in front of him and he slept together with other girls. This was something that Themba was familiar with. He recalled how, during childhood play, he would prefer to play with other girls, a preference that led his family to call him *'bafazini'* (someone who likes to be in the company of women): 'I never played boys' games . . . even when we played house-house, I used to play a girl . . . I used to play sister or mother. We would marry and wear white gowns.'

Like his family, who called him *bafazini* but did not realise that he was gay, Themba was aware of his effeminacy, but it took him some time before, as an adolescent, he recognised himself in the term 'gay'. This was in part because of the *stabane* myth that held that gays were, in fact, hermaphrodite.[8] Themba said there was a time when he thought that gay people should be 'beaten up'. That was before he saw his friend Tsepo hanging out with a group of gays and before he learned that Tsepo himself might be gay. But the moment of self-recognition for Themba was when he saw a young gay naked for the first time: 'We visited Nathi, a gay boy, and we found him taking a bath. We looked at his body and we realised that he was a real boy, like us.'

From childhood games, Themba went on to become a 'grown-up girl', invested in the allure of clothing: 'When I am well dressed, I am very confident that I am attractive. When a man approaches, he sees a lady in me.' He kept a detailed written record of the men who had approached him and whose advances he had accepted. When asked in an interview about his boyfriends, he said candidly, 'I don't know where to start. I have the whole bus.' In total 70 names appeared on his list when he showed it to me during the first quarter of 2005.[9]

Themba was aware of the need to behave in a way considered appropriate to his calling. He said, 'It won't look right if people can see me dancing in clubs. When I am far away, like in Durban, I take out my beads because people there don't know me.' Thus he would remove his bracelets and the beads from his hair, so that he would not be instantly recognisable as a sangoma when frequenting gay clubs. He also told me, 'I have stopped my other ways. I am now focused on being a sangoma.' Yet these 'other ways' that Themba alluded to, had not actually stopped. When I first met him in August 2002, he was a familiar figure in the small gay community of Wesselton. He enjoyed the company of other gays and he loved to party.

As mentioned in the previous chapter, Themba also became embroiled in a legal case involving a fifteen-year-old youth that he had sex with (the age of consent in South Africa is sixteen). Themba did not deny the allegations; indeed, the youth's name appeared alongside the names of 70 other people whom he had listed on his sexual inventory. The letter 'S' – in a column devoted to the elementary facts about the sexual act – indicated 'thigh sex' in which the young man was the active partner. The young man's family informed Themba's mother and laid charges at the police station and Themba was arrested. Ultimately it was a fellow sangoma who intervened, persuading the family to drop charges against Themba.

This incident did not result in a conviction, but it did little to enhance Themba's social standing. While friends rallied around to help, he also became the subject of gossip and speculation and was subject to public humiliation by the family of the youth in question. Not only was he arrested and briefly detained by the police but his mother, who was already less than comfortable with her son's sexuality, was also subject to visits from the young man's family. As part of an original agreement with the aggrieved family, Themba undertook to pay for the youth to have a medical examination. This was because the young man had developed a rash and the family were concerned that he may have contracted a sexually transmitted illness. Themba had to borrow the R100 from me to do what he promised. Then the extended family became involved and soon uncles were demanding exorbitant payment for damages.[10] But Themba had no money of his own, which reinforced the idea that he had few clients, despite his claim to the contrary. Bhuti had always maintained that he had never seen Themba actually healing, or even talking about his work. The implication was that Themba kept up the pretence of success when in fact he had hardly any clients at all. His inability to produce even R100 and his ongoing dependence on his parents supported the view that he was not a busy healer.

During the course (and as a result) of my fieldwork, Themba and Nhlanhla met each other at Nhlanhla's home on Goedgenoeg farm. When they saw each other, they both fell to their knees and greeted each other, while clapping their cupped hands. Later, there was a joking exchange between the two. It was clear that Themba's easy camp banter, although not lost on Nhlanhla, was not Nhlanhla's preferred style. On the subject of boyfriends, Nhlanhla, with his characteristic reluctance to discuss his private life, deflected the enquiry. He said demurely and with affected modesty that he was a virgin. Themba retorted, 'If you are a virgin, then I am ten years old.' Themba said that it was lucky that Nhlanhla did not have to walk far to fetch water as it would be dangerous for him with all the men around. Nhlanhla made the exaggerated claim that there were no men around Platrand and that, no, he did not have a boyfriend. Themba joked about using a 'love potion' to attract a man and Nhlanhla responded with a sincerity that jarred with the camp banter of the exchanges. He said that there was no such thing as a love potion and that the only thing that you could do was to 'just show your love to that person'. This brief exchange suggested some of the differences between the two gay sangomas that, on the surface at least, gave clues as to why one might be seen as old/genuine, while the other was perceived as millennium.

Several features seemed to influence these perceptions of authenticity. Nhlanhla lived in a rural setting, while Themba lived in a township. Themba liked to party, while Nhlanhla avoided gay gatherings. Nhlanhla was circumspect about his private life, while Themba kept an annotated record of his sexual encounters. Where Nhlanhla was sincere, Themba was camp. On the one hand, these differences in personal style showed clearly how Nhlanhla and Themba might be judged differently. I too wondered about Themba's role as a sangoma and was more familiar with him socialising with other gays than with his work. I could see why Nhlanhla emerged as a powerful icon for other gays because of his singular devotion to his role as a sangoma.

On the other hand, was there really that much difference between Nhlanhla and Themba? Both Bhuti and Brendan emphasised the calling as a good indicator of authenticity. Themba followed his calling and overcame considerable obstacles in order to do so. He came from a Christian family and was accused at school of demonic behaviour. He literally had to jump over the school gate in order to follow his path. Bhuti pointed to

Nhlanhla's relative material success and the dearth of Themba's
clients as an indicator of difference. Yet Nhlanhla, like Themba,
lived with his family, on whom he was partially dependent. He
did not have a thriving business, an unlikely scenario in the
poverty-stricken rural area in which he lived and worked. His
greatest wish was to be able to assist his parents, but he found
that 'in this job of traditional healer, people have so many
jealousies that you can't work the way you wish to work . . .
As from now, I don't have any money, I have got just a little
bit.' Brendan's idea about agency as the marker of a real gay
sangoma – 'most of them they are being controlled by a female
spirit' – also does not stand up to scrutiny. Both Nhlanhla and
Themba saw themselves as gay first and then as sangomas and
neither saw a link between their ancestors and their sexuality. I
came to the conclusion that the answer was not to be found in
differences of personality, style and relative degrees of success.
Rather, it was in the realm of perceptions, impressions and
appearances about what it means to be African. To what extent
do Nhlanhla and Themba, as gay sangomas, manage to wear the
mantle of 'African'?

The idea that homosexuality is un-African is very pervasive,
expressed by leaders of neighbouring countries as well as by
ordinary South Africans, who see gay lifestyles as something
new, a fashion imported from the West. In order to illustrate
this point on a local level, in the next section I draw on a public
hearing on same-sex marriage that was held in Mpumalanga, in
which strong ideas about homosexuality were expressed. This
hearing and six others like it, held in different provinces over a
two-week period, provided a glimpse on a micro-level of
widespread discomfort with the ideals enshrined in the South
African Constitution, particularly those relating to gender and
sexuality. What is perhaps remarkable is that these kinds of views
are seldom heard in the South African public sphere. They are,
for one thing, against government policy and contrary to the
spirit of the Constitution.

Gays are un-Christian and un-African: Discourses of exclusion

On Valentine's Day of 2005, a charismatic Christian pastor and a disgruntled local chief enacted a brief same-sex marriage on the stage of the Nhlazatshe community hall, situated in a rural district near the village of Badplaas, Mpumalanga. The largely middle-aged and elderly group of men and women who had gathered in the hall exclaimed in dismay as Pastor Manana and Chief Nkosi walked hand in hand along the stage. The chief seemed uncomfortable with this display and the brief enactment was drawn to an abrupt close.

The pastor seemed to be having difficulty in explaining what exactly was meant by same-sex marriage. And so, through this dramatic vignette, he tried to spell out the implications of a recent high court ruling on the definition of marriage. The small crowd appeared to be both baffled and outraged at the prospect of legally sanctioned same-sex unions taking place in South Africa. Pastor Manana, in his role as Master of Ceremonies (MC), then turned to the audience and invited them to share their views on the impending Constitutional Court deliberations, which could open the doors to same-sex marriage: 'What we want to know is: am I allowed to marry Chief Nkosi or is a woman allowed to marry a woman? Is Swazi culture agreeing?'

In the circumstances, it was a largely rhetorical question that was nevertheless answered by a resounding 'no' from the audience. Badplaas is close to the border with Swaziland and many of the concerns that were raised at the gathering were about 'Swazi culture'. Similarly 'Zulu culture' was the focus of the next public hearing on the same topic that was held in KwaZulu-Natal. While the cultural focus may have been specific, it was clear from the proportion of luminaries gathered there that the meeting was intended to represent 'culture' and 'tradition' from all corners of South Africa. Traditional leaders from several provinces were present, including from the Eastern Cape, KwaZulu-Natal and the Free State. Chief Mabandla from the Eastern Cape, who spoke through a translator, addressed the audience by explaining that the meeting sought to bring together 'chiefs from all provinces'. He brought the discussion from the culturally specific to the general, situating himself as one of the chiefs in South Africa who was concerned about tradition and culture. He extended this further, beyond ethnicity to race, by suggesting 'we blacks in South Africa do not have a law that a woman must marry a woman and a man must marry a man'. Two central and interrelated tropes dominated the public discussion. One was that homosexuality is un-African and the other was that homosexuality is un-Christian. These views were just a faint echo of an all too familiar and pervasive discourse that has come to characterise public pronouncements on homosexuality in several eastern and southern African states. An official statement from the ruling party in Namibia – the South West African People's Organisation (SWAPO) – urged fellow Namibians to 'totally uproot homosexuality as a practice' and to 'revitalise our inherent culture and its moral values which we have inherited for many centuries from our forefathers. We should not risk our people being identified with foreign immoral values' (Gevisser 1999: 962). In recent years, public officials in countries including Botswana, Kenya, Swaziland, Tanzania and Zimbabwe have joined a growing chorus of voices heralded by Zimbabwean president Robert Mugabe's widely publicised declaration:

> [Homosexuality] degrades human dignity. It is unnatural
> and there is no question, ever, of allowing these people
> to behave worse than dogs and pigs. If dogs and pigs do
> not do it, why must human beings? We have our own
> culture and we must rededicate ourselves to our
> traditional values that make us human beings (Gevisser
> 1999: 962).

At the Badplaas public hearing, the first speaker, a woman, mentioned three main themes that would recur throughout the proceedings. These were culture and tradition, Christianity, and the nature of democracy in South Africa. First, she addressed the meeting by pointing out that 'we all know culture and we know that this thing [same-sex marriage] is not allowed'.[11] Second, she said that the proposed changes in legislation went against the teachings of the Bible. And third, she said that 'we did not know that democracy would bring this'. What followed was an outpouring of strongly held views on Christianity, tradition and homosexuality. Government policies were lambasted and cast in a morally dubious, even evil light, bound to bring calamity on the country. A man suggested that the government's laws on gender equality had produced stubborn women, who talk of 'rights and do not respect their men'. One speaker delivered a tirade against child-support grants claiming that this had led to a wave of teenage pregnancies. Another thanked democracy for 'bringing all the witches to light' and illustrated her point with reference to the termination of pregnancy legislation, which enabled young women to 'do abortion and die'. One man summed up the mood of the meeting in these terms:

> We voted but we did not know that we were destroying our land. I do not think our leaders pray. By just saying 'amen' that idea [same-sex marriage] would die . . . Women no longer respect men because of people in government. Children disrespect teachers because of these people . . . The devil is using the government to kill people. We must pray because the Parliament is going to kill people.

The MC made it clear that the National House of Traditional Leaders (NHTL), organisers of the event, were there to gather the views of ordinary people and not to impose their own ideas: 'The nation must be free to talk,' he said. The very existence of the NHTL pointed to an attempt to accommodate 'traditional' within the framework of a constitutional democracy. Nowhere was this fit more uncomfortable than in the realm of gender and sexuality, as these public hearings demonstrated. Over and over again, speakers juxtaposed elected leaders of government, who were associated with corruption, with the natural authority of chiefs, presented as guardians of the moral order. Gender and generational reversals were at the heart of the articulation of a collapsing moral order and apocalyptic visions of divine destruction inspired, in this instance, by Sodom and Gomorrah. The government and its laws had set children against parents, learners against teachers, women against men, good against evil, Christian and traditional values against secular laws. The final measure that was 'trying our patience' was the proposal that men would be allowed to marry men and women to marry women.

The MC's efforts to contain and focus the discussion by keeping broader issues of gender equality out of the debate were futile. Even he, despite his exhortations, began to speak about prohibitions on divorce in Swazi customary law. Thus, by being constantly linked to more general questions on gender, same-sex marriage emerged, not so much as an isolated aberration, but as the logical outcome of the government's systematic tampering with the natural and customary and moral laws governing gender. In a sense same-sex marriage was the logical outcome of gender equality, where men and women no longer knew their natural, God-given place. Women were being stubborn and disrespectful to men and this was somehow linked to the availability of abortion and child-support grants and now, 'this thing'.

The debate that took place in Mpumalanga also touched on issues fundamental to the nature of the democratic order in South Africa. It is clear that same-sex equality does not enjoy majority support in South Africa. When the National Coalition for Gay and Lesbian Equality received the results of its nation-wide survey on attitudes towards homosexuality in 1995, these were embargoed for fear of giving ammunition to the small but vociferous opposition to the inclusion of sexual orientation in the Constitution, led primarily by the African Christian Democratic Party (ACDP). It is significant that the ACDP sent representatives to the Badplaas workshop to garner support for their cause. It was ironic that 'un-African' and 'un-Christian' were seamlessly yoked together in the workshops as if they were synonymous. Traditional Swazi values were supported with reference to the biblical book of Leviticus, for example.

The participants at the hearings were quite correct in the assertion that 'this thing' was unpopular and did not represent the wishes of the majority of the population. In their view, a small group of elected officials was imposing legislation that ran counter to majority opinion. In this scenario, it is traditional, unelected chiefs who listen to the views of the people and are hence portrayed as the true voice of participatory democracy, a sentiment that one of the chiefs capitalised on when he said, 'I do not disagree, as a leader I agree with the people. As you lead people you have got to hear what they have to say.' The argument that the protection of minority rights is a litmus test for the success of the new democratic order would not have had much credibility at this gathering. Indeed, when, at the following workshop in KwaZulu-Natal, a lesbian activist from Durban drew a parallel between racism and homophobia, the crowd roared their disapproval of the analogy. In the words of the MC, 'If I was a gatekeeper in heaven I'd deal with the Swazis severely, because they know culture and the laws.' The implication was that Swazis, and anyone else concerned with moral values, could not stand by while the government imposed unpopular laws, and everyone present at the meeting was encouraged to sign a petition.

The NHTL hearings took place in a context in which the secular debate on homosexuality was almost settled and the legal framework for equality on the grounds of sexual orientation largely in place. A trawl through the gay and lesbian archives will reveal a set of historical sources on homosexuality from the nineteenth and twentieth centuries that are contained in police files, for example, or court records, or the documents produced by commissions of enquiry, or psychiatric reports. In these records, homosexuality was predominantly cast as criminal, pathological or immoral. With sweeping legislative changes, one would now be hard-pressed to find information on homosexuality from these sources. Sexual orientation no longer falls within the ambit of police investigations, commissions of enquiry or psychiatric consideration. Court cases tend to be testing the state's commitment to the principles of equality enshrined in the Constitution, rather than convicting individuals on the basis of the myriad laws under the Immorality Act. The debate about homosexuality has shifted from the secular realm and, by and large, confined itself to the moral sphere, where it is couched in terms of authenticity and morality, such as un-African and un-Christian. It is in this context that the gay sangoma holds a powerful symbolic position as a 'real African' and thus is an important figure in counternarratives that suggest a uniquely African form of same-sex practice and identity.

Counternarratives

One of the strong messages that emerged from the public hearings was that gays were un-Christian. The small group of gays and lesbians who attempted to launch a branch of the HUMCC in eMzinoni township near Bethal in April 2004 were attempting to overcome the alienation that some gays felt in their home churches. Through the workshop, the sermon, the prayers and hymns, gays and lesbians included themselves in Christian ritual and discourse that often sought to exclude them. Although its membership was small, the HUMCC held such an important symbolic place in the consciousness of many of my informants because it was testimony to their aspiration to reconcile their sexuality with their religious beliefs. The presence of a small gay church community in Johannesburg carried a symbolic weight disproportionate to the size of the congregation. Thus in launching a branch of the church in Mpumalanga, gays were responding to a perceived local need but also, on a broader level, registering a protest to the kind of argument made at the public hearing in Badplaas – that being gay was intrinsically un-Christian. It formed part of a counternarrative of inclusion.

The other message from the public hearing was that being gay was un-African, contrary to culture and tradition. If the HUMCC stood for the possibility of being gay and Christian, the figure of the sangoma was an important part of a counter-narrative that suggested it was possible to be both gay and African. Like 'God' or 'nature', the authority of the ancestors is seen as beyond dispute. The symbolic power of the sangoma is derived from the authority of the ancestors.[12]

From the discussion between Brendan and Bhuti, it is clear that Themba was not considered to be a real sangoma. One of the reasons for this was, perhaps ironically, his lack of distance from the local gay community. To be a healer, a mediator between the world of the ancestors and the world of the living, means occupying a special place in the social order, a liminal position. The ancestors are the moral guardians of society, the 'authoritative underpinning' (Hammond-Tooke 1981: 56) of the domestic and social order and the guardians of collective social mores and values. According to Jean Comaroff: 'If the ancestor cult subsumed the individual in the collectivity, it also subsumed the domestic group into the totality. Ancestors had the power of unmediated intervention in the lives of their descendants, acting in "moral" defence of the established order' (1985: 83).

It follows that someone with access to the world of the ancestors occupies a special social position with specific responsibilities. A sangoma's behaviour is likely to be interpreted and judged by others in the light of professional duties and responsibilities.

The blessing of the ancestors, as the 'authoritative underpinning' of domestic and social life demonstrates that it is possible to be gay and African. The sangoma figure allows gays to reinsert themselves into culture and tradition by co-opting a quintessentially African spiritual figure to their cause.[13] This goes together with numerous tales, some of them fantastic, others based on historical truth, about homosexual practices, same-sex marriages and cultural traditions that show homosexuality as being historically and culturally African.

Several informants had historical references at their fingertips whenever the discussion about the place of homosexuality in South African history came up. One was that Shaka was gay and another that his aunt was a lesbian.[14] Another view was that homosexuality was always part of the social fabric, but that it was not spoken about and generally hidden from public view. Another reference was to the Modjadji or Rain Queen and her many wives. These stories and anecdotes sought to locate gays in historical and cultural worlds. They are concerned with proving an African authenticity, hardly surprising considering the kinds of ideas that were presented at the public hearings on same-sex marriage. Thus, for contemporary gays, historical precedent took on a particular significance: it was a way of reasserting an identity as both gay and African. Yet these titbits of African historical experience were always vague and subject to dispute and contestation. As such, they were a less reliable measure than the figure of the gay sangoma – a living embodiment of and intercessor with the world of the ancestors.

However, African culture is not neutral or unproblematic when linked to a gay identity, as shown by the case of the lovesick gay who was regarded by his boyfriend as being 'too cultural'. The idea of being part of African culture and tradition was symbolically important, but in certain circumstances it was also important for gays not to be 'too cultural'. Several gay sangomas, including Nhlanhla, have remarked on the power of dress – they are less likely to be harassed, for example, when wearing their sangoma's attire since people are likely to be more scared of them. In this case, outward appearance serves to convey status and power. However, according to Brendan's reasoning, gays could potentially abuse this by dressing as sangomas in order to attract men, while not actually being sangomas.

Themba described how he was able to attract men when he was well dressed and they were able to see 'a lady in me'. But he also felt that his dress may be too convincing and that he needed to explain to his prospective lover that he was, in fact, a gay. In the workshops Bhuti organised on 'how to be a real gay', one of the strong sentiments that emerged from group discussion was that gays should not be 'too much'. In other words, they should not drag all the time. The sangoma Emmanuel was pointed out as one of those who is 'too much' because of his habit of always wearing cloth skirts of the traditional kind that Themba wore when he was possessed by a female spirit.

Nhlanhla also had specific views about the protocol of dress for gays. He felt strongly that while gays should be free to wear what they please, they should not wear feminine underwear:

> You can wear girls' jeans, no problem, but not the inside clothes. Oh! You can wear a top, maybe a lady's T-shirt, you've got no problem – or a shirt or anything. Yes, you can wear it, no problem. But not wear the panties. You give the other people a bad picture, especially people who don't understand very well about gay people. You must put the people in the right way: he is a gay but he wears very nice. You must respect yourself if you want people to respect you.

The distinction here is subtle, but important. What Nhlanhla indicates is that it is okay to perform as a woman and to dress as a woman, in outer appearance to style oneself as a woman. But at the level of your undergarments, your self-knowledge as a gay and therefore male should be retained. Wearing women's underwear went beyond the boundaries of what Nhlanhla saw as gay and also beyond the parameters of social acceptability. It is the reverse of the anxieties expressed by Brendan about sangomas' clothing – where external appearance had the potential to deceive.

In a context where gays are seen to be fashionable, un-African and un-Christian, performance and modes of self-styling are very important. We have seen how gays are able to use the idea of fashion in hyper-feminine performances of the self to their economic, erotic and social advantage. Fashion invites inclusion, even celebration of a highly stylised self. Being regarded as un-

African and un-Christian is more difficult terrain because gays are discursively excluded from religion and culture. Here too, modes of self-styling are equally important, but for different reasons: being visibly and demonstrably Christian and having cultural icons, such as sangomas, to demonstrate being African. However, this necessary emphasis on style and performance also produces anxieties about where the performance ends and the reality begins. To use the analogy of dress, are the sangoma's outer garments nothing more than a disposable costume? And is the gay's underwear the layer at which the performance must end?

These concerns about African identity and the tensions that exist between being gay and being African help to explain the animated discussion that took place between Brendan and Bhuti about genuine and millennium sangomas. It also explains why gay sangomas are subject to an unusual level of scrutiny and judgement. It is important that they are genuine and not millennium, faking it for their own dubious ends. It is important that there is more to their profession than the garments that they wear. The figure of the sangoma plays a powerful role as an intermediary between social and spiritual worlds. Powerful ancestors act through them. If sangomas can be gay, who can dispute the weight of generational authority? Themba says that the ancestors would not have called him to service if they disapproved of his being gay. When asked what the ancestors would do if they did not like it, Themba answered, 'They would not give me this work if they did not like it.'

In order to be seen as real, gay sangomas should avoid being too gay. Nhlanhla seemed to fit the bill; he was seen as closer to traditional African culture, beliefs and practices. This was an image helped along by the rural homestead in which he lived and his regular visits to remote areas to receive additional training or to seek healing from other sangomas. He was circumspect about socialising with other gays. Themba, on the other hand, spent too much time socialising with other gays. He was unable to sustain the allure and the elevated status of being a spiritual intermediary with the ancestral realm. The image of Themba removing his beads in order to enter a gay discotheque in Durban captures the tension that he felt between his secular life and his role as a healer. To be seen as real, to be genuinely African, the sangoma needs to be seen to be located in the old, not too closely aligned with the new, or they may, like Themba, be seen as millennium sangomas.

Although couched in similar terms to the real/fake debate evident in the workshops, old versus millennium is a temporal distinction that is more subtle. Old, in this instance, means to be steeped in traditional ways and to adhere to culture mores. It also entails being mindful of the place of homosexuality in a traditional context. Nhlanhla, for example, is manifestly different from heterosexual men in his mannerisms, the way he walks, his voice and the activities that he pursues. When he went 'to the mountains' for initiation, he was questioned about this by other young male initiates, but he was protected by an elder. His difference is not concealed and neither is it spoken about. Millennium, in this debate, refers to the performance of a particular kind of gay identity. In its extreme version, it is all performance and no substance, as seen in the allegations that millennium sangomas do not even go to training – they only wear the dress and accoutrements of traditional healers, such as beads.

Sangomas hold the symbolic weight of being African. In the debate about real and millennium sangomas, we see how gays become implicated in the logic of exclusion. Brendan preferred to think of sangomas inhabited by female spirits. Bhuti would like to see sangomas demonstrating their spiritual powers as out and proud gays who are unambiguously African. By endorsing some as 'genuine' and rejecting others as 'millennium' on the basis of a perceived affinity to African cultural norms and traditional practices, both are inadvertently endorsing a view of culture that was remarkably similar to one expressed by the participants in the public hearing. At the hearing, African culture (old) was contrasted with the Constitution (millennium). While for the Christian and traditional participants, a gay identity was intrinsically un-African, for gays such as Bhuti and Brendan, an African identity was more authentic if it was less gay. Thus for gay sangomas to demonstrate their authenticity, they need to show that they are African, in part by being less gay.

Notes

1. Simon Nkoli (1957–98), who died from AIDS-related causes, was a pre-eminent black gay activist who was one of 21 accused in the Delmas Treason Trial. He is regarded as an influential figure in placing the question of gay and lesbian equality on the agenda of the liberation movement. An activist from Soweto, Linda Ncgobo co-authored an article on gay life amongst Soweto youth (McLean and Ncgobo 1995). Ncgobo's funeral was the focal point of an influential article on the modernisation of gay identity in South Africa (Donham 2005).
2. The concept of 'sexual orientation' as part of a range of 'natural characteristics', including race and gender, was one that was successfully harnessed by activists and lobbyists campaigning for the inclusion of sexual orientation in South Africa's Constitution.
3. The question of agency amongst same-sex identified female traditional healers is explored in more detail in Morgan and Reid (2003). The research suggested that amongst older women, sexual desire was attributed to a dominant male ancestor, while younger women often came out as lesbians before they became sangomas.
4. This is one of the place names that have so far been passed over by the South African Geographical Names Council, responsible for advising the Minister of Arts and Culture on the trans-formation of place names, including the removal of offensive names. Anything with 'kaffir' (an offensive racial term) was amongst the first to go, although at the time of our journey, some had evidently slipped through the cracks.
5. Goedgenoeg, translated from Afrikaans, means 'good enough'.
6. These are all common terms frequently, but not invariably, used pejoratively. *SisButi* combines sister and brother; *stabane* translates as 'two organs' or hermaphrodite, while *inkonkonyi* is a Zulu name for the blue wildebeest. The etiology of *inkonkonyi* as a term for

homosexuality is unclear and none of my informants could offer a definitive explanation. SisFiki, told me that *inkonkonyi* referred to the flywhisk, often used by sangomas. It is tempting to speculate that there may be a connection to the sangoma, an association between traditional healing and gender liminality.

7. Netball was adapted from basketball and was originally known as 'women's basketball'. It is a popular women's team sport in South Africa.

8. The *stabane* myth was so pervasive that for someone like SisFiki, for example, it was one of the few terms that he used to describe himself. SisFiki, who was 42 years old in 2005, was seen by the younger gays as a kindred spirit. He had undergone training to become a sangoma during the 1970s. He claimed not to know the meaning of 'gay' at all and to be familiar with only two terms, namely *stabane* and *inkonkonyi*. While he would not be seen as a millennium sangoma, neither would he be taken seriously as a healer. He was often drunk and he did not take care of himself. He invariably wore an old blue dustcoat and slippers. SisFiki earned enough money to sustain a regular supply of cheap 'African beer' by doing household work in Wesselton. He was at the bottom rung of the social ladder, an object of fun and a figure of abjection. He lived in dire poverty.

9. According to this list, he had had 32 sexual partners in the previous year and 10 in 2003. He always assumed the submissive role in anal and intercrural sex.

10. According to Themba, the aggrieved family demanded unrealistic compensation because they believed that gays had access to money and resources. The compensation fee was at one stage set in terms of thousands of rand.

11. Homosexuality, sexual orientation, gay rights and same-sex marriage were never mentioned at the meeting and were only referred to obliquely. It was explained that the government was poised to allow men to marry men and women to marry women, but speaker after speaker only referred to the substance of the matter as 'this thing' (*lento*) or 'that idea'.

12. In his classic ethnography, Heinz Kuckertz provides a detailed description of the significance of ancestor religion in the context of an agnatic kinship system, showing how the authority of the homestead head is reflected and reinforced through the religious rituals associated with the ancestors: 'The reason for the conceptual

significance of agnatic kinship is the fact that the ancestors are at once the point of reference in defining authority within any given agnatic group, as well as (in the generalized form) the conceptual frame of any authority whatever' (1990: 267).

13. This point is not lost on activists. At the Constitutional Court hearings on same-sex marriage held in May 2005, several sangomas wearing traditional dress gathered outside the Constitutional Court carrying placards that read 'GALA and Sangomas Support Same-Sex Marriage'.

14. Shaka (c.1787–c.1828) was one of the great Zulu chieftans, well known for his military prowess.

CHAPTER 7

History and the Search for Identity
Can Gay be African?

But now, at this point in time, it is quite easy as ABC. Really, people are just comfortable and they are doing whatever. Because it was very difficult for us, doing it at that time . . . Oh, Standerton! It has drastically changed from the time when I was here (Brendan, 1 May 2006).

The young people are strong and free. The older generation were afraid. But they need structures to represent their interests, like in Johannesburg, Cape Town and Durban. Here they don't have structures to represent their problems. The things that they experience are only known by them. No one else knows the problems (Henry, 12 December 2003).

As these two quotes suggest, both informants – an older and younger man – agree that circumstances are much more favourable for gays in the present than they were in the past. Brendan, the older man, argued that it was much easier to be gay 'at this point in time' than it was 'at that time', while Henry, the younger man, distinguished between the experiences of 'young people' and 'the older generation'. Brendan emphasised broader social change: 'Oh, Standerton! It has drastically changed', while Henry alluded to the important role that activism played in securing gay rights, pointing to 'structures' as a vehicle for highlighting social problems and lobbying for change.

These quotes capture the historical moment in which my research took place. On the one hand, there was the Constitution and the changes that followed in its wake (including changes in the law, increased visibility in the media and changing social attitudes) and, on the other hand, there were the ordinary, everyday activities that served to create gay spaces in a town such as Standerton. These broader changes facilitated local activities: the idea of emulating the 'structures' of gay and lesbian organisations that exist in South Africa's major cities is a relatively recent possibility for gays in small-town Mpumalanga and is at the heart of a fundamental historical shift that has taken place in recent years.

Brendan's observation that the social environment has become more tolerant and accepting is an important one. It points to a slightly different strategy for gays to negotiate their social worlds, one that is subtly distinct from the one implied by Henry's 'structures'. In Brendan's terms, gays in small towns needed to find ways of inserting themselves into the social fabric as sexual outsiders. For Henry, the structures of a social movement were a prerequisite for accessing the rights promised by the Constitution and the subsequent legislation. As suggested in Chapter 5, these strategies were not mutually exclusive in the workshops; rather, they coexisted.

These kinds of discussions about how things were then compared to how they are now echoed a deeper preoccupation amongst my informants with the past, as a source of continuity and as a way of showing, through historical examples, that homosexuality is indeed African.[1] There was great interest amongst my informants in gay history but, as in most societies, there was a dearth of material in South Africa. As Stephen Murray has noted: 'For most societies, data on homosexual behaviour and societal reaction to it are so rare, recent, and incomplete that little can be said about patterns of change over time' (2000: 11).

In discussions about the history of homosexuality and how they perceived it, the most common response from my informants was that while homosexuality was always around, it was well hidden and never spoken of. As Brendan reflected: 'Actually, the gay life is not something that has just started. It started from long ago. Our forefathers, they did experience this although it was very, very hidden from them.'

As suggested by Brendan's words at the beginning of this chapter, in the twenty years since he last lived in Standerton, he noticed vast changes in the ways that gays were able to express their identities and live their lives. What changed between these two periods of time since Brendan first lived in Standerton from 1984 to 1986 and then again from 2004 to 2006? What would account for the 'difficulties' of the first period and the 'comfort' of the second? And what were the 'drastic changes' that had taken place? Brendan's comments resonated with some of my questions: to what extent were the hair salons, the workshops, the *ladies* and *gents* and the gay sangomas something new and specific to this particular time? Were these cultural formations a by-product of the broader political changes that had taken place in the preceding decade, which saw homosexuality elevated from a criminal status in the statute books to a protected category in the Constitution? And to what extent did they build on prior histories of same-sex practices? To echo the distinction that was made in the previous chapter about sangomas, were these identities, practices and institutions 'old' or 'millennium'?

One of the ways in which my informants articulated an interest in history was through ongoing discussions about *isingqumo*, a Zulu gay language. In subsequent sections I will follow the life story of Brendan, seen by my informants as the main carrier of this language. Different phases of his life illustrate the historicity of major themes in this book, notably the central role of gender in rural gays' self-identification, the effort to be African and modern at the same time and the impact of a novel, global model of being gay. These themes also stand out in my informants' search for their own history.

Inventing *isingqumo*

Bhuti told me that Brendan was one of the inventors of this language, *isingqumo*. This view of Brendan as one of the original inventors and scribes of a gay dialect was corroborated by other gays who were gathered in Thulani's room on a cold evening towards the end of June in 2004. I had in my hand the typed list of terms that I had originally picked up in Bhuti's rooms. This list had been compiled by Thulani, who was taking it upon himself to teach other gays more about the gay dialect which, according to my informants, had originated and continued to flourish in Durban. Thulani's room, the former servant's quarters at the back of a house situated in a formerly whites-only suburb of Ermelo, had space for a large double bed, a television, a fridge, a hot plate and very little else. The room was invariably occupied by a group of gays who stood around in the meagre spaces between furniture or sat on the small bench or the couple of stools that were available, but who mostly lounged on Thulani's bed. His bed had a large, ornate headboard that was made of chipboard, but with a dark varnish designed to make it look solid, durable and grand. This setting was to play an important role in the way we were to discuss the topic that I had already been trying to raise for some time: the broader background to this enigmatic gay slang. So some elaboration on the quite special aspects of this setting might be helpful here.

The bed was disproportionately large for the room. Thulani was someone who liked to present himself as outrageous: 'That is what I like: bitching and fucking around!' was one of his favourite comments.[2] So it seemed appropriate that the room could hardly contain his bed. Not that his bed was the only site of his sexual experiences, as many of the stories that he shared with me would testify, nor was the bed his exclusive preserve. Aside from his various lovers (and there were several), youngsters, such as Sihle, often stayed with him. A couple even shared this small space with him for a few consecutive months until they found a room of their own. Thulani was often away. On weekends, he frequently went to his family home in Piet Retief or travelled for work, in which case someone would usually stay in his room to keep an eye on things. Furthermore, given that his rooms were in walking distance of the well-frequented Truck Inn, where lonely truckers were willing to part with cash in exchange for sex, his bed was also used by others as a comfortable venue for 'trade'.[3] And it was this bed that was the site of Themba's passive, thigh-sex encounter (according to Themba's meticulous record of his sexual encounters) with the fifteen-year-old that had landed him in hot water and potentially in jail (see Chapter 6). So, as things often worked in accommodation-scarce Ermelo, the bed was a shared, rather than private space, replete with its own individual and collective history.

That evening the bed was covered with a dark bedspread in brown and black and the pillows were framed by images of wildlife – silhouettes of zebra, giraffe and lion, which fitted in with the affectations of an African-themed room – including wall-mounted wooden masks and small ornamental clay pots. Thulani's taste in interior décor was one of the more modest ways in which he distinguished himself from other gays who were less well off. His clothing and new car were other belongings that he paid particular attention to and which were the source of considerable envy, and hence a topic for gossip, amongst other gays. He could afford all this because of his secure and comparatively well-paying job in a local government department. Perched above the headboard of the bed was a large box of government-issue condoms on which someone had written with a felt-tipped pen: 'If you fuck around, please use me'. The presence of the box of condoms and its inscription reflected the pragmatic and protective side of Thulani. More frequently he expressed a fatalistic bravado in the face of HIV/AIDS. This duality, the tendency to fluctuate between taking precautions and throwing caution to the wind, was evident in what my informants told me about safer-sex practices. Everyone knew about AIDS, some speculated about the origins of the epidemic, others had their own strategies for avoiding infection, but while the ideal was always to use condoms, this was not the case in practice and especially where alcohol and the heat of the moment were involved. There was, however, a growing awareness of the toll that the virus was taking two decades after the first cases were reported amongst white gay men in 1983 (Walker, Reid and Cornell 2004). As Nathi expressed it, 'There is a lot of HIV in this area. That is why I am afraid of loving people now, because there are a lot of guys who are dying now.'

That evening Thulani was making dinner. He and Bhuti were the main organisers of a beauty pageant – Miss Gay Ten Years of Democracy – scheduled to take place in Wesselton in August, which was in two months' time. The dinner was to provide the opportunity for Thulani and Bhuti to discuss some of the planning details. I accompanied Bhuti and Tsepo to Thulani's room. We drove in my car from the place where Bhuti lived (where I also had rooms), which was colloquially known as 'the gay palace'. By this stage I was familiar enough with the route not to get lost, as I had done many times in the past, in a suburb where the seemingly indistinguishable streets separated similar box-shaped houses and small gardens enclosed by precast concrete walls or chicken-wire fencing. This was one of the suburbs where less affluent whites would have settled twenty years previously, the employees in the lower levels of state enterprise and industry – artisans and semi-skilled workers, for example. It was towards the bottom rung on the scale of Ermelo's expansive and diverse suburbia, designated 'whites only' during the apartheid-era. Yet this suburb, which largely retained its racial and class profile, was now also a site of aspiration for a few members of the emerging black middle class who chose to move out of the townships, such as the man who owned the house, from whom Thulani rented his room. As Tsepo, Bhuti and I drove towards Thulani's room we passed street signs with familiar names from a previous era. National Party government ministers and many prime ministers, including Malan, Vorster and Verwoerd, were amongst the luminaries of Afrikaner nationalism after whom streets in the neighbourhood had been named. And yet there we were, venturing down these streets, a white man temporarily staying in a formerly black township and two black men going to visit an openly gay man who worked in a government department and who rented the servant's quarters from the black proprietor of a home in this formerly whites-only suburb. Much had stayed the same, but much had also changed.

Once I had settled with Bhuti and Tsepo in Thulani's room, there were a total of seven males gathered in the small space. Participants in one of Bhuti's workshops would no doubt interrogate the category 'male' and, using the all-pervasive terminology of gender, would find five gay femmes and two *gents*, or a gay butch and a *gent*, depending on the criteria applied. Ignoring the terminology of the workshops and turning to the common everyday shorthand, it might be said that there were five *ladies* and two *gents* present, although some, including me, may have disagreed with this neat categorisation. Using the terms of *isingqumo*, as compiled and defined by Thulani, *iqenge* (a man or gay butch), *umchakisana* (a straight guy), or *isimet'hlana* (a gay femme) are some of the terms that might have been used to describe the men gathered in the room. Thando from Sakhile would have added the widely known terms *skesana* (femme) and *injonga* (butch) as well as *imvubu*, which, he told me, meant 'someone who is confused'. He told me that the meaning was derived from a stick used in Zulu warfare. An *imvubu* was a man who could surprise you. But you must expect surprises, he told me. SisFiki, aged 43 in 2004, who was considered by gays in Wesselton as an older kindred spirit in their midst, would have used the terms *inkonkonyi* or *stabane* to describe himself and his desire for men. The terms varied and the usage changed over time, although the categorisation into 'masculine' and 'feminine' remained consistent throughout.

Two of us perched on the bench in the narrow space between the bed and the wall, while the rest either sat or lay on Thulani's bed or stood in the two-metre space at the foot of the bed. Those who stood attended to the evening meal or made coffee or kept the cheap wine flowing from its box, or used the restricted space to clown around in. Thulani and Bhuti, for example, took turns pretending to be the Master of Ceremonies (MC) and introducing competitors at the forthcoming Miss Gay Ten Years of Democracy. In between they were filling me in on the meaning of the printed words on the page that were drawn from the Zulu gay language. There was some argument and disagreement between them and the five other gays present about the definition of several words, while a few were unknown, in which case no definitions were forthcoming. Kids, liquor, our gay vagina, a white man, an Indian person, a Coloured person, to kiss, sex, someone who is sexually available, food, eat, anus, money, discrimination, a penis, to come, a straight guy, a gay butch and a gay femme were some of the many English translations that were given, based on Thulani's list. Thulani said that the gays of Durban all knew this language well and spoke it fluently. In Durban, they told me, 'You will feel like you are on your own planet, if you don't speak it'.

Bhuti then took hold of an imaginary microphone in order to address a phantom audience. In this spontaneous skit, he was the MC addressing spectators at the forthcoming Miss Gay Ten Years of Democracy. In his introductory remarks, he drew the audience into his confidence by alluding to the changing nature of gender roles and social identities: 'Things are not what they were. These days you see ladies drinking like men and men dressing up like ladies.' He went on to say that there were surprises in store for the audience and that, despite initial impressions, the contestants were going to expose themselves as men. Thus, Bhuti playfully suggested, the gender order was turned on its head and nothing was what it appeared to be. This was typical of the theatricality of social occasions, where incidents drawn from everyday life were being constantly dramatised. Meanwhile Thulani showed off two snapshots of his 'best boyfriend', one of which was framed and placed at his bedside and Bhuti related how his boyfriend, Mandla, had said that he was going to compete in the beauty pageant, if one of the prizes was indeed going to be a television, as rumour had it at that time. Bhuti feigned strong disapproval. Everyone present found the idea of Mandla, a straight man, entering Miss Gay, let alone winning, to be preposterous and hence hilarious.

Once again, I found myself trying to find out something about the origins of this gay language and the meanings of some of the words in a slightly inappropriate context. There was a lot to distract our attention away from the vocabulary, but the conversation kept drifting back to the typed list that I had in my hand and the definitions that I was jotting down in the margins. It reminded me of the previous time that I had had this discussion, one evening in Bhuti's rooms, with a small drama unfolding between the lovesick gay from Pongola and his boyfriend, Happy. It was on that occasion that Bhuti first told me that Brendan was 60 or 70 years old and that he was the inventor of this language, a claim that seemed highly unlikely to me at the time, but Brendan was someone that I wanted to meet. And in Thulani's room I found myself in a situation where this topic had come up and I was again pursuing what I thought were the most relevant lines of inquiry: what was the origin of the language; what were the meanings of the words on the typed list; how widespread was its use? Yet again there was an elusive, disputed, hard-to-pinpoint quality to these discussions. It was as if my line of inquiry was entirely discordant with the occasion and, I began to see, with the larger meaning attached to the language, the excitement that its existence generated, the enthusiasm for learning the terms and the mirth produced by its use. My insistence on trying to establish 'the facts' started to make me feel like the most prim of fieldworkers, doggedly in pursuit of verifiable details that would not be forthcoming and hoping to find the truth in definitions and etymologies. My informants were in widespread disagreement about what some of the words meant and, I also believed, had an implausible explanation about their origin, with Brendan featuring in this narrative as the primary lexicographer. And yet clearly there were truths in the myth of origin that was being offered to me. One was that the language is widely considered to have developed in the Durban area. The other was that Brendan held an important place in the local gay world, as an older gay (although much younger than the purported '60 or 70' years) who was a participant in a gay history that contextualised and legitimated the world inhabited by younger gays. And the existence of a Zulu gay language fulfilled a similar role. It was a language that had served an indisputable function as a form of secret communication between gays, but seemed to have lost its urgency in this regard, certainly amongst my informants.[4] The language had become something of more peripheral interest, a curiosity that was primarily entertaining and amusing, but necessary only in certain circumstances.

Rather than focusing on vocabulary and etymology, what I became most interested in was first, how my informants talked about the language and what that said about a sense of history and a perception of social change, and second, how the evidence that existed about the language was both scant and contested, similar to other strands of homosexual histories in South Africa. The need for *isingqumo* and its use had shifted over time, reflecting the changing situation of gays themselves. Saying that Brendan was the inventor of this language was the same as telling me that he was 60 or 70 years old, when in fact he was only 49. Clearly, to my informants, the need to have a history, or older role models, sometimes got in the way of accuracy or was more important than the facts. This was hardly surprising for a group of people who have by and large been left out of the historical record,[5] or whose claim to a history is the subject of dispute.[6] While the origins of the Zulu gay language, the vocabulary and etymology, would without doubt be useful and fruitful avenues to pursue, what captivated me was how these stories spoke to a history, which was both real and invented, and how the existence of the language, as well as its changing role and function, points to the metamorphosis of the social position of gays.

As Gerrit Olivier has pointed out, gay lexicons serve the obvious purpose of concealment, but they also reveal and identify gays to each other: '[A gay language] allows members of that community to identify with one another and with the group through a mutually understood and exclusive code' (1995: 223). Yet this serves an ambivalent role by simultaneously enabling gays to communicate exclusively amongst themselves and, in so doing, isolating speakers from the rest of society.[7] As Brendan put it, 'So now that was the way of trying to protect us from being isolated that much. We had another way of isolating them from our own affairs.' Clearly, for the young gays gathered in Thulani's room, this language was fun to use and to banter with, although the need seldom arose, but it was also proof of a history. It was a language that gay folklore suggested was transmitted from one gay generation to the next.

The fact that there was dispute and disagreement about the meaning of words also revealed something about the nature of the lingo. Olivier (1995) points out that a 'gay vernacular' consisting of a limited vocabulary (or, in linguistic terms, 'lexical items') lent itself to rapid change and adaptation. Similarly, writing about black gay life on reef townships in the mid-1990s, Hugh McLean and Linda Ncgobo commented: 'As isingqumo is a rapidly evolving slang, much of it will either fall away or change in the next few years.' (1995: 184) So the language is, by definition, unstable: 'the "gay vernacular" is not a fixed thing. While some words may gradually become obsolete, new ones appear' (Olivier 1995: 222). All around me was a cacophony of gay language of various kinds – aside from the text on the page and the contradictory definitions flying about the room, there was a liberal dose of camp banter, often in the form of parody or impersonation that was the salt to any conversation amongst gays. And there was the GGC, the gay gossip column, and jolly-talk, the local slang, as well as the more formal exercises in terminology at the gay workshops. These various forms of articulation and styles of self-expression provided links to the past and insight into the present and, as such, they suggested both rupture and continuity.

There are also conflicting opinions about the origin of *isingqumo*. According to Marc Epprecht, the language only developed in the mid-1970s, in a context of increasingly militant trade union and political activity that opposed existing traditions of same-sex mine marriages (2004: 199). These same-sex relationships were seen to serve the interests of management by contributing to the docility of workers in the face of the deprivations of the migrant labour system. The language was thus developed, Epprecht suggests, as a coded way for miners to discuss same-sex marriages and liaisons within earshot of co-workers who disapproved of these practices. As such, it is embraced into his wider thesis that homophobic discourses were picked up by political resistance and, in particular, African nationalist movements relatively recently and that many of these homophobic sentiments can be traced to preoccupations with sexual propriety that were one of the defining characteristics of colonial and apartheid ideologies and practices. McLean and Ncgobo suggest that the lingo probably originated in Durban, given that most of the words are derived from Zulu. They speculate that '[t]his would seem to indicate that a gay sub-culture was more developed in Durban from earlier on' (1995: 184). While Ronald Louw (2001) refers to the 'homosexual argot', *isingqumo*, he does not explicitly speculate on its origins, but its presence supports his contention that the Durban district of Mkhumbane was a particularly important node for the development of particular types of 'homosexual relations'.[8]

Brendan, who in local gay folklore was presented as the 'inventor' of this language, said that *isingqumo* developed in the Durban area in the late 1940s – in fact he was even more precise, pinning it down to 1947 (ten years before he was born):

In Durban there is a place which is known as Mkhumbane where gay men and also gay women were getting married, an illegal marriage . . . but that is where you could find a man and another man staying together . . . That is where this language started . . . It was started by the gays who were having straight men who were married. Now trying to get these women not understanding what they were talking about. That was the language of keeping them away from interference with our own communication.

Brendan had learned the gay lingo in Durban where he had lived for most of his life. It was initially used, he told me, in order to allow gays to talk freely amongst themselves and in front of the wives of their lovers. This primary function of secrecy and discretion is a point corroborated by Louw (2001) who notes that the name of the gay argot – *isingqumo* – is derived from the Zulu word *ukungqumuza*, meaning 'to speak quietly so that others about do not hear of important matters'. However, even on this point, there is minor contention: McLean and Ncgobo claim that '*isinqumo* without the "g" means "decisions", and the *skesanas* say that the parole got its name because one must take a decision to use it' (1995: 182–3).

Brendan told me that the secrecy of the language as an exclusive lingo for gays had changed over the years and that most people now understood it. It was only amongst a small minority of the most ignorant that the language could still be used as an effective way of speaking in code:

Most of the women in Durban, they know this language from A to Z. The straight girls and the straight boys, they know it very well. You can't even utter a word in this language that they don't understand. Durban is so advanced in so far as gay life is concerned.

This points to a perception of the diminished need for the language to conceal and suggests that gays are becoming more integrated into the wider social order. What Brendan seems to be saying is that wider society has learned to speak the language of gays, so that the use of *isingqumo* as a language of concealment is only possible amongst the most ignorant and conservative pockets of society, a claim supported by Bhuti and Thulani.

One might expect a hidden language to simply disappear if its social use, as a language of disguise or concealment, falls away. Whether or not the gay lexicon is widely understood amongst the Zulu-speaking population in the wider Durban area is a claim that I could not test the veracity of, but nevertheless it struck me as a clue to the way in which some of my key informants saw the impact of social change on their lives, over time. These discussions about *isingqumo*, including its origin, dissemination and contemporary usage, provided a thumbnail sketch of the way in which my informants perceived and spoke about the past and their present situation.

There was disagreement, both amongst my informants and in the wider literature, about the origins of the lexicon as well as the extent of its usage, the meaning of the terms and the primary function of the language. What was clear was that the language had been used with varying degrees of intensity at different points in time, both as a strategy of concealment from wider society and as a gesture of commonality, in that it facilitated recognition and communication about same-sex desires and practices. It is also apparent that the role and function of the language changed over time, depending on the relative degree of integration or isolation of the speakers. The gay lingo is one of the historical threads that have passed through time to the present day, held by the likes of Brendan and Thulani. But, like the historical record, it is contested and disputed and means different things depending on who is using it. It also shows how gays network across space and time; after all, the language appears to have originated some fifty years ago and is still used extensively in Durban and amongst gays in Johannesburg as well as in Ermelo, Standerton and other towns in Mpumalanga. What happens in Mpumalanga is intricately connected to other centres. The disputes and uncertainty about the language echoed the lack of clarity about the histories of homosexuality in South Africa.

For the gays gathered in Thulani's room, the language was important precisely because it spoke to a history. It was a thread to an imagined past in Durban that served a legitimating function. Like the sangoma, who could be construed as a figure representing African culture and tradition, a Zulu gay language was a tangible link to a gay past. This was particularly important in a context in which the 'African-ness' of homosexuality is brought into question. According to Epprecht, in Zimbabwe, the word '*hungochani*' plays a similar role: 'They [gay rights activists in Zimbabwe] take the evident African-ness of the word to validate the integrity of black Africans who come out as homosexual' (2004: 4). Similarly, in South Africa, an Nguni-based dialect that had a plausible history was invaluable to the local gay community as an irrefutable link to past. This is why I was frustrated in my quest for details and etymologies – these were no longer important since the language had lost its urgency as a strategy of concealment. As Brendan observed, gays were much more visible, even in small towns and increasingly did not need the language of secrecy. But where the language was important was as a tangible link to the past, hence Thulani's concerted effort to write down some of the vocabulary in order to pass this on to other gays. The symbolism of transmitting a language from one generation of gays to the next was a powerful way of showing links and continuities with the past.

Brendan, born in Umlazi, Durban (1957)

To pursue the meaning of history for my informants, the life story of Brendan, whom they closely associated with the emergence of this special language, is illuminating. His experiences and insight provide a measure with which to gauge the impact of more recent social change, particularly over the past twenty years. His life had intersected with major urban centres, such as Durban and Johannesburg, as well as smaller towns in Mpumalanga, including Standerton and eMbalenhle. He began to recognise himself as gay while he was in Durban, with the collective and recent memories of gay life in Mkhumbane as a reference point. In Johannesburg he entered gay social life through gay clubs and then into the nascent black-led gay organisations such as GLOW (the Gay and Lesbian Organisation of the Witwatersrand) that started as social support groups and proceeded to play an important political role. His life story provides a framework for a gay history from the perspective of an ordinary individual who became actively involved in the very early days of formal black gay and lesbian activism in South Africa. In this sense, his experiences provide a history 'from below'. Not only were Brendan's reflections on the changes that had taken place on a local level in Sakhile, Standerton extremely insightful, but he had traversed and engaged with gay life in two important urban centres, which had shaped contemporary gay experience in profound and important ways. I will use his life story as a framework for a broader discussion about some of the salient aspects of gay history that have shaped the contemporary life worlds of gays in towns such as Ermelo.

When I first met Brendan, I was struck by the noticeable lines on his face. He had deep furrows on his brow and his mouth was framed by strong lines, which made him appear older than his 49 years. He had a full head of hair that was greying in a uniform way so that his whole head was tinged with white. He was tall and had a stomach befitting a man of his age and stature. He was dressed in black and white and was wearing loose-fitting trousers, a white T-shirt and a trench coat.

Brendan was born in Umlazi, Durban in 1957 and lived there until 1984, when he moved to Sakhile, Standerton. He lived in Sakhile until 1986 when he moved to eMbalenhle, Secunda. There he worked as a process controller for Sasol, the petro-industrial complex, for over a year. Then, aged 30, he migrated to Johannesburg for a short period in 1987, where he worked as a teacher and administrator and became involved in gay activism, before returning to Durban, where he stayed in KwaMashu. He returned to Sakhile in 2004. Brendan thus spent 43 of his 49 years living in Durban, one year in Secunda, one year in Johannesburg and four years in Standerton.

Durban featured as an important urban locus for gays in Ermelo and nearby towns. Several gays had spent time there, either for brief visits or for longer periods. Thando, for example, from Sakhile, had studied in Durban and while there was visited by other gays from Standerton. It was also a source of boyfriends. When Andrew had his engagement party, Tsepo met his blind date from the Durban taxi at the Ermelo taxi rank. Thando was 'promoted' in Durban. He explained that this involved lengthy discussions as well as sex and this was the time when he decided on his sexual role. His partner had told him that 'he would not pass to be a femme' because he was 'too energetic'. Thando had, in turn, promoted others, including visitors from Standerton, such as Wandile. Thando said that it was important for one of the partners to be experienced, so that he could anticipate and respond appropriately to all possible reactions from the sexual initiate. Sipho, from Driefontein, was also promoted in Durban where he was introduced to gay life by a Durban-based priest, who first accompanied him to Adult World, where they watched a gay pornographic movie together.[9] In 2004 Bhuti travelled to Pietermaritzburg, near Durban, to attend the Miss Gay Pietermaritzburg beauty pageant and there he also met a group of gays from Durban, some of whom subsequently attended Miss Gay Ten Years of Democracy in Ermelo later that same year, an event which saw Miss Pietermaritzburg acting as MC. Durban was thus an important node for the extensive networking of gays living in Mpumalanga.

Brendan spent the first 27 years of his life in Durban. It was here he realised that he was gay. He told me that he 'did not have any feelings for girls. I have never had any'. Then an 'old man' in Umlazi called Mr Mkhize gave him a book entitled *Love Without Fear*, and on reading it, he recognised himself.[10] Shortly thereafter he fell in love with someone from Standerton, the town he subsequently moved to. It was in Durban that he began meeting other gays who were also networked with gays living in Soweto:

While I was still in Durban I started to meet different people like people who were staying in KwaMashu who were more advanced as far as gay life is concerned. To such an extent that while I was there they started introducing me to people in Diepkloof [a suburb of Soweto] who were even more advanced as far as gay life is concerned. Then I started to orientate myself in the life of gays.

It was in Durban that Brendan learned *isingqumo* and heard about the story of Mkhumbane. As mentioned earlier, Mkhumbane played an important role in the development of gay life in the Durban area from at least the mid-1950s. Central to the public face of gay life were regular wedding ceremonies. Brendan said that it was in Mkhumbane 'where gay men were getting married. That is where we could find a man living with another man'. According to the participants at the weddings in Mkhumbane, the marriages would take place between an effeminate *isikhesana* and a masculine *iqenge*. Importantly for Brendan, this represented a nascent gay community. *Isingqumo* was the lingua franca that gays used to conceal their relationships from their partners' wives. This form of marriage between *isikhesana* and *iqenge* has strong echoes of the gendered ordering of relationships between *ladies* and *gents*, in which *gents* were viewed by my informants as essentially heterosexual (see Chapter 2).

Historical antecedent?

In Chapter 1, I presented an overview of some of the historical documentation of male same-sex experience in South Africa, especially as this relates to migrant labourers on the South African gold mines. The questions that concern me in this chapter are to do with antecedent. For example, can one draw direct links with the documented experiences of African labourers contained in the 1907 government commission of inquiry into 'unnatural vice' on the mines, or with the institutionalised sexual practices of prison gangsters first recorded in Nongoloza

Mathebula's personal testimony to the director of prisons in 1912? Do the experiences of Mozambican mineworkers in 1915 have any direct bearing on the lives of gays living in Ermelo or Standerton today? Did the practice of mine marriage in the 1930s, 1940s and 1950s relate to the engagement ceremony that took place in Ermelo in 2003? Or were the marriages that took place in Mkhumbane from the mid-1950s to the early 1960s the antecedent of that ceremony? Epprecht (2004) has grouped diverse historical evidence under the rubric of 'dissident sexuality', a term that suggests both commonality and subversion in same-sex practices in southern Africa. Certainly, as Brendan's recollections reveal, there is a memory (and an emerging mythology) about the same-sex weddings in Mkhumbane, for example. But is there a line of continuity between contemporary expressions of gay identity, as found in my fieldwork, and these older forms of same-sex practice?

Dunbar Moodie (1989) has argued that male same-sex relationships were essentially functional and served to shore up traditional norms. On the mines, same-sex relationships (and more rarely, marriages) would take place between an older, more senior mine worker and a young, junior recruit. In this way, Moodie argues, male same-sex relationships reflected and sustained patriarchal arrangements in rural areas from which the mineworkers came and to which they would return. By being a wife on the mines, young men were able to accumulate sufficient resources to 'achieve masculinity' back home, by taking a wife and establishing an independent homestead. These relationships were predicated on principles of seniority, authority and control. In this context it is understandable that the younger partner would be deferential to the elder and would be expected to perform the domestic duties of a wife and maintain a sexually passive role. As Isak Niehaus (2002) has pointed out, the persistence of male same-sex relationships on the mines (despite the erosion of the migrant labour system and the accessibility of women) can best be understood in terms of the intimacy and domestic comforts that these relationships offer, which make them more appealing to many men than transitory sexual liaisons with women. What is perhaps more surprising in the testimonies on which Moodie bases his observations is the extent to which younger men took on and performed the role of wife: 'Indeed, mine "wives" took on the behaviour of women or servants in their relations with their "spouses"' (1989: 235).

There is a striking continuity in expected gender roles between older men and their mine wives – *tinkonkana* – as described by Moodie (1989) and the norms associated with *ladies* and *gents*; *skesana* and *injonga* (or *iqenge*). What they have in common is a systematic construction of same-sex relationships between opposite genders, between masculine and feminine partners.

Clearly, contemporary gays in Ermelo turn to the past for role models or cultural forms that can be emulated and adapted to current circumstances. The ongoing practice of same-sex marriage is testimony to this, as are forms of feminine self-styling. However, the strongest continuity of experience lies in the tenacity of the gender order, where there is a persistent pattern of male same-sex relationships that is based primarily on gender differentiation and role separation in which one partner is indisputably feminine and the other masculine. This is by no means unique to South Africa. As Moodie remarks in relation to notions of masculinity in societies where 'patriarchal modes predominate', 'the importance of power, of conquest and control, seems a fundamental aspect of male sexuality in the construction of the self' (1989: 247). In fact, cross-cultural and historical studies of homosexuality show that gender-based models are the norm. It is the egalitarian ideal of the West that is the exception.

In this context, opportunities for acceptance, even veneration, within the broader social order are to be found in the successful negotiation of local gender norms. *Gents* can escape social opprobrium, despite ongoing sexual relationships with *ladies*, because in this model the gender order remains intact.

And *gents* usually continue to fulfil their masculine social roles of getting married and, importantly, fathering children. *Ladies*, on the other hand, take on the role of women and are thereby afforded the advantages and the drawbacks of this social position. In the example of same-sex relationships on the mines, this is a temporary and transitory social position of the *tinkonkana*, whereas for the *ladies* it is a more fixed gender role.

This puts a particular slant on the fact that gays are seen to be threatening and undermining to patriarchal arrangements (as evident in the opposition to the legalisation of same-sex marriage, for example) and are condemned as being un-African. While gays in the ambit of my fieldwork went to great lengths to demonstrate that they are authentically African (as the role of a sangoma demonstrates), they are commonly accused of being 'untraditional'. To complicate this further, 'untraditional' can shade also into 'modern' and this can offer certain advantages. It can mean, for instance, that gays, because of their modern identity, are supported by other groups who have benefited from social transformation, especially those women who have experienced vast improvements in their social, legal and economic position. According to Brendan, this produces a natural alliance between women and *ladies*, which he sees as a consequence of social change: 'I can say that the community is willing to accept gays. I have experienced that here in Standerton because I have seen a very big change, especially amongst the ladies [women]. This one [Dan] has many friends amongst the ladies.'

However, as shown in the first four chapters of this book, male same-sex relationships tend to display the same inequalities and even gender-based violence of heterosexual relationships. While a hyper-feminine, modern persona can be used to social and economic advantage, being feminine in a context of male dominance and even violence also renders *ladies* vulnerable. Research shows that violence directed at gays in KwaThema and Soweto is almost invariably directed at effeminate gays and that the nature of the assaults is often sexual, more so than in comparative studies elsewhere in the world (Reid and Dirsuweit

2002). This correlates with the high levels of rape in South African society.

Moodie argues persuasively that amongst many other factors, there is an economic rationale that fundamentally shapes male same-sex relationships on the mines. How then does one explain the persistence of these forms of relationships, characterised by diffidence and authority, power and submission, when the *ladies* are more economically independent than their *gents*? In my fieldwork experience, and in a situation of relative poverty, it is the *ladies* who tend to support the *gents* economically, hence their persistent concern about gold-diggers. Why is it that desire continues to be so strongly predicated on gender difference, requiring an essentially heterosexual dominant male (a *gent*) and a submissive female (a *lady*)? Aside from the fact that the sexual partners are both anatomically male, can these usefully be understood as 'dissident sexualities', as Epprecht suggests, when they so closely mirror patriarchal arrangements of power and control?

Social and economic emancipation for women and gays has produced new forms of discourse and behaviour that encourage a more assertive approach by *ladies* in their dealings with men. This was evident in the series of workshops held in Ermelo. It is understandable that these workshops were attended almost exclusively by *ladies*; it is, after all, the *ladies* that stand to benefit from the constitutional provisions on sexual orientation and gender equality. Heterosexual men and *gents* might bewail the loss of masculine privilege that the political and legal commitment to gender equality suggests.

Brendan goes to Jo'burg

When I moved to Jo'burg, still following those people that they introduced me to, then I started to get involved now trying to be somehow open to myself. Accepting myself first because that is what is the most important thing as far as life is concerned, is to accept yourself . . . So then I oriented the gay life with people who were

very, very much experienced in as far as this life is concerned. Then they introduced me to many kinds of
people that were living in Jo'burg, to such an extent
that I met Simon Nkoli who was the president [of
GLOW] by that time. They also introduced me to Linda,
then to Tsidi, Beverley and many more.

Brendan lived in Sakhile from 1984 to 1986, maintaining links
with his gay friends in Durban. As he recalls, he knew of only
two other gays living in Sakhile at the time and both of them
were very young. When he moved to Johannesburg in 1987,
Brendan used what might be considered a gay 'homeboy
network'. He was introduced to gays living in Soweto through
his friends in KwaMashu and through this network began to
mix with individuals, such as Simon Nkoli, who were at the
forefront of a new type of gay and lesbian organisation to emerge
in South Africa.[11] In 1988, following his acquittal on charges of
treason, Nkoli founded GLOW, which emerged as a robust new
player in the field of sexual identity politics. The predominantly
white and self-consciously apolitical Gay Association of South
Africa was dwindling and teetering towards collapse, out of
tune with contemporary South African political developments
and mired in internal problems. By contrast, GLOW was at
home in the anti-apartheid movement, affiliated to the United
Democratic Front and participating in political protest. GLOW
attracted a new breed of politically savvy activists who combined
a strong anti-apartheid agenda with public assertiveness regarding
lesbian and gay identity (Reid 2005b: 28–32). Brendan participated in the organisation during these formative years, recalling
Lee's Place and the proprietor who, like MaThoko in the East
Rand township of KwaThema, opened her home as a social
meeting place and shebeen frequented by gay men and lesbians.
It was at Lee's Place in Orlando East, Soweto that the early
discussions about the formation of GLOW took place.[12] Brendan
remembers the proprietor fondly: 'It was the only place where

the gays were highly honoured and also highly accepted. She was the only woman who could understand the gays more than anyone else. So that was a wonderful woman, that one, Lee.'

Don Donham (2005) argues that the 1976 youth uprising that began in Soweto was a critical turning point, not only for the country as a whole, but also for the emergence of new forms of gay and lesbian identity. Traditionally deferential treatment of elders was swept away by the defiance of youth who went on to take on unprecedented leadership roles in the anti-apartheid struggle. This would support Achille Mbembe's (2000) suggestion that the reaction against homosexuality in many African countries is a symptom of broader concerns about a decline in gerontocratic social relationships. The Soweto uprising of 1976, aside from being a potent symbol of political resistance and the marker of the beginning of the end for the apartheid state, was an unmistakable sign of the new role that the youth would play in the political arena. It was this that Donham suggests also created a climate in which the emergence of a modern gay identity amongst township youth took place. Political activism did not connote tolerance of sexual diversity, as underground activist Paddy Nhlapo recalled about his own reaction to transgendered youths, before he realised that he himself was gay. In an interview with Zackie Achmat he reflected:

> Well the first time I saw gay people it was in my school. They were – I could call them now because I have an understanding – they were transgendered youths who were at my school, who I hated so much. I hated them, they know me very well, Bennie and Themba, why I hated them. Because I thought they are behaving like girls. They think they are women, they're putting make-up on and the way they behave. They only hang out with girls and all that. So I had that very strong hatred against them (Hoad, Martin and Reid 2005: 68–70).

In the mid-1980s, the African National Congress (ANC) was also divided on the question of sexual diversity, as the controversy surrounding the statements by spokesperson Ruth Mompati indicate (see Chapter 4). The history and background to the ANC's ultimate inclusion in its Bill of Rights of 'sexual orientation' as an express category for protection against discrimination has been well documented (see, for example, Gevisser and Cameron 1995; Hoad, Martin and Reid 2005). Briefly, the arguments include the presence of well-known gay figures within the anti-apartheid struggle, in particular Simon Nkoli; a broad public consensus on inclusivity in the aftermath of apartheid, captured in the idea of the 'rainbow nation'; the absence of strong opposition from the church and indeed, its opposite, the support of key figures such as Archbishop Desmond Tutu; gay and lesbian equality as a litmus test for a modern constitutional democracy – one which South Africa was eager to demonstrate; and the influence of the exile years on the leadership of the liberation movement, especially the influence of feminism and the gay and lesbian movement, and the effectiveness of the lobbying process that took place in drafting the Constitution.

The political transition has been coupled with new consumer trends and a renewed emphasis on fashion and style after the austere struggle years and the consumer boycotts that characterised the last phase of militant struggle against apartheid. Amongst township youth, style has acquired a particular significance, whether in the form of the latest designer labels, cell phones or hairstyles. If political activity was a marker of status for many youth living in black townships during the apartheid era, the material trappings of success became the dominant aspiration in post-apartheid South Africa. The status symbols of the new order are aptly summed up by the 'three Cs' (cash, car, cell phone), a phrase commonly used by young women in evaluating the worth of a potential partner (Hunter 2002).

There has also been a certain blurring of the gender order. Mine 'wives' were expected to make themselves look effeminate by shaving or concealing their beards, through their style of dress and in their personal demeanour. Young men in Standerton from 2004 onwards differed from the preceding generation. In 1984, if a man wore a perm, it would have provoked male hostility. Twenty years later, in a context where the accoutrements of economic success, rather than political credentials, became a defining feature of urban youth culture, fashionable clothes and hairstyles, including the perm, were not only unremarkable but a defining feature of emerging forms of youth masculinity.

When Ruth Mompati remarked in 1987 that being gay 'seems to be fashionable in the West', she was echoing a common refrain that sees homosexuality as a fashion (Reid 2003). One of the ways in which gays in Ermelo and surrounding towns have managed to carve a niche for themselves is in the black hairstyling industry. As shown in Chapter 4, it is through a form of hyper-feminine display that gays have built up a reputation for being especially talented and skilled in a highly competitive informal industry. The close association between gay lifestyles and 'fashion' is thus an ambiguous one. On the one hand, the word is intended to suggest that being gay is a transitory identity of choice, an implicit reinforcement of the idea that gays exist beyond the ambit of tradition and culture. On the other hand, the idea that being gay is 'a fashion' plays into the idea that gays are at the forefront of fashion and style, and this can be advantageous in post-apartheid South Africa. For Brendan, talents (such as hairstyling) were one of the keys to social acceptance and yet in the past these had to be suppressed in the interests of discretion. As far as Brendan could remember, the visible presence of gays in the black hairstyling industry was a recent phenomenon. He attributed this to the need to hide: 'Before, the gays could not expose themselves to the society; they were having an inferiority complex. So I am hiding the

talents that I have got which was going to make me accepted in
the society.'

The nurse at the local government hospital in Ermelo placed
Nathi in the women's ward because she was aware that gay rights
are protected in the Constitution. Nathi's appointment card
was filled in as 'Ms', so as not to offend his sensibilities. During
the chaotic arrangements leading up to Miss Gay Ten Years of
Democracy, local government officials were available on their
cell phones on a weekend, willing to try and sort out the confusion regarding the venue. These are examples of the sometimes
unexpected consequences of a Constitution that guarantees
equality on the basis of sexual orientation, which challenges the
concern that the benefits of the Constitution may only be
accessible to the well-resourced and privileged few (Barsel 2006;
Cock 2005; Jara and Lapinsky 1998). As Brendan comments:

> So I also think for gays to have the marches and all
> of those things it has made a great influence. On the
> government's side, that has made the government, even
> now, introduce this legislation . . . The political point
> of view has played a big role. There has been a change in
> ideology of people towards the gay life.

When the three friends Siyanda, Dumisani and Ayanda arrived
at school wearing make-up and in drag, it was not the dressing
up and adornment that was something new – as Henri Junod's
(1927) alarm at what his colleague witnessed in 1915 testifies –
but the legal, political and social context that created the space
for new forms of public assertiveness. As Brendan reflected, 'Gay
life, these days, it has spread.' The increased visibility and public
assertiveness that he refers to are intricately linked to South
Africa's transition to democracy – as events such as Miss Gay
Ten Years of Democracy beauty pageant demonstrate.

The Miss Gay Ten Years of Democracy beauty pageant
The following description of the beauty pageant, Miss Gay Ten Years of Democracy, is based on my field notes and observations of the event.

When Thulani announced that he was dropping out as an organiser of the pageant, just hours before the doors of the Wesselton Hall were due to open, he left Bhuti to take care of all the arrangements. And most of them still needed taking care of. For one thing, the hall was locked and, we were told, the caretaker who held the keys was at that moment in a shebeen adjacent to the taxi rank in town. Furthermore, the event had been advertised for a different venue. Although the fine print on the receipt read 'Wesselton Hall', Bhuti was under the impression that he had booked the Gert Sibande Hall. 'Gert Sibande' was printed on all the posters and everyone would need to be redirected.

Thulani said that he was too stressed. Boyfriend trouble, he explained. He had tried to be respectful, but things had gone horribly wrong. When his handsome boyfriend, Vusi, told Thulani that he would be travelling from Vosloorus to Ermelo for the weekend, Thulani had carefully removed all evidence of his current Ermelo boyfriend, Phumlani, from his room. By the time Vusi arrived, his framed photograph was back in its place at Thulani's bedside, while all photographs of Phumlani, together with two pairs of his underwear and a couple of other personal effects were in a shoebox, under the driver's seat of Thulani's car. But the previous day, on Friday, shortly after he arrived in Ermelo, Vusi, a passenger in Thulani's car, had found the shoebox and opened it and he was furious. He beat Thulani and Thulani cried out 'Don't do it! No, Phumlani!' calling out the wrong name in his pain, fear and panic, which led to more beating and arguing. He told me that things had calmed down and they had made passionate love that night and the next morning, too. Vusi told Thulani that he would give him something that would stop any other man looking at him for the whole weekend and, indeed, Thulani sported an unmistakable love bite on his neck. But all this had left Thulani drained and exhausted and he was no longer in the mood to help with the pageant.

So Bhuti and I drove around looking for the caretaker, who was not in the shebeen. Meanwhile a small bakkie had arrived with all the scaffolding for the stage. There was shopping to do for the meal at the after-party, which would take place at the Back of the Moon nightclub, owned by lawyer Roy Ledwaba. The nightclub prided itself on its cosmopolitan clientele and it was one of the venues frequented by gays in Wesselton. So Bhuti popped R5 for the man who was cleaning cars outside the hall and asked him to get the keys from the caretaker, if he saw him, while we went shopping. At the vegetable shop, which consisted of a large warehouse of cheap fresh produce, the white woman behind the till asked Bhuti what he needed all the vegetables for. He told her that it was for a gay beauty pageant. She was curious to know where it would be held and if it was for everyone. 'Will white gays also participate?' she asked. 'We don't even know one white gay here in Ermelo,' Bhuti told her. That was a shame, the cashier said.

By the time we had dropped off the groceries with the cooks, who would have to prepare the food using Bhuti's small pots borrowed from his kitchen, the hall was open. But it was a mess, empty bottles everywhere and it was already 5.30 p.m., half an hour after the official opening time. So Sizwe, one of the *gents* who was to act as bouncers and sell tickets at the gate was roped into cleaning the hall. He saw an opportunity in the urgency and negotiated an astronomical fee of R50 to clean the hall. But there was no choice, so Bhuti agreed and Sizwe got cleaning. The *gents*, boyfriends of the gay *ladies*, were the DJs and the bouncers, while the *ladies* were organisers, contestants and cooks.

By 10.30 that evening, five and a half hours after the scheduled start, the event was in full swing. The *ladies* were on stage, parading in casual wear, then traditional wear and finally, formal wear. The judges, from Pietermaritzburg and Johannesburg, were having a hard time because the identifying numbers pinned to the contestants had been written with a borrowed pen on small scraps of paper and were almost illegible. Bhuti, who had not had time to style his hair was wearing a headscarf and doing a lip-sync impersonation of Brenda Fassie, as part of a series of tributes made to 'MaBrrrr', 'Madonna of the townships' and gay icon, who had died three months previously, in May 2004.

The main DJ was a boyfriend of one of the contestants. He was assisted by two other *gents*: Vusi, Thulani's lover from Vosloorus, and Mandla, Bhuti's boyfriend. The beers kept flowing and the sound system kept crackling and then screeching into silence, while the contestants waited patiently for the show to resume. When Tsepo took to the stage for the all-important formal wear, the sound system broke down once again. There he stood, poised in limbo between backstage and the catwalk, too late to retreat and in no position to promenade into a room that was filled with the noisy cheering of the audience, but had no music. He stood there for several minutes, while the *gents* tried to fix the sound system. He smiled at the responsive audience and gave short impatient glances at the *gents*, as if to say, 'What can you expect?' It turned into a mini-pantomime, as Tsepo devised a way of rising above circumstances, retaining his poise and sustaining a moment of glamour amidst the unfolding chaos of the pageant. It seemed to me that it was at that moment that he clinched the title of Miss Gay Ten Years of Democracy.

Before the event Bhuti told me that they were looking for someone to work as an ambassador for gay people in the Mpumalanga province. 'A PRO [public relations officer] for gay people,' he added. In recent years, Tsepo had taken part in another pageant, Miss Ithafa High School, where he competed against the young women in his class, but intense rivalry amongst the contestants' supporters in the audience meant that the pageant was foreshortened and the results were never announced. Hairstylist Nathi had participated in several pageants in the region and was bitterly disappointed not to be chosen in this pageant, even as a princess. After all, he had won Miss Dube by Night in 1998 and had been placed as first princess in the two subsequent pageants at the same nightclub. This pageant, Bhuti told me, was different in that it was organised by gays themselves in a community venue, rather than by the proprietor of a shebeen for commercial purposes. Nathi had also competed alongside women in other pageants in Ermelo and was rumoured to have been prevented from rising above the top five when someone informed the judges that she was in fact he. Nathi told me that, as he had feared all along, the judges at Miss Gay Ten Years of Democracy were obviously not looking for a real lady at all. They admired something else altogether, someone with male features who could impersonate a woman, whereas Nathi saw himself as feminine enough to compete against other women.

When Bhuti collected the cake at the bakery section of the Spar supermarket and paid the R70, he was disappointed. He had discussed the cake with me on the phone. Did I think that it should be in the colours of the South African flag, or the rainbow flag? His vision of the cake was as follows: It would be a rainbow cake, symbolising both the rainbow nation, as well as alluding to the international gay rainbow symbol. On the one side would be an image of banner-waving people, marching and protesting against apartheid. The cake would be divided in the middle by the new South African flag. And on the other side of the flag would be scenes of joyous celebration, images of emancipated individuals. What was produced by the confectioner was much more modest. The icing was multi-coloured and there were generous sprinklings of hundreds and thousands that suggested a rainbow. On the cake itself, emblazoned in icing was the legend 'Happy Ten Years of Gay Democracy'. It was a large cake and it formed the centrepiece of the gathering the following morning that took place in front of Bhuti's rooms, where the more serious business of the weekend took place. There were speeches. Martin, who had been sent as a representative of the Hope and Unity Metropolitan Community Church (HUMCC), led the small group in song. Norman from the Johannesburg-based gay and lesbian information website, 'Behind the Mask', said, 'You are the first township to have celebrated ten years of democracy in style. I know in KwaThema, where I come, it has a gay history, but Ermelo has outdone us . . . We never even thought of that.' Two young men hovered around. One declared his love to one of the judges from Durban and asked to share his plate of food, echoing Martin's caricature of the straight men of Ermelo. He said that based on his experience of the party the previous night, their favourite saying was 'I love you, buy me a beer'.

Bhuti, still wearing his party gear from the night before, concluded his speech by saying:

> Today we are celebrating ten years of democracy, as the rainbow nation and as a diverse culture. Don't ever set limits for yourself because you are gay. No. *uNkulunkulu* [God] created you for a purpose and a nice purpose. You are an apple and don't ever pretend to be a banana, because you will be a second-rate banana.

Thulani could not make it. Vusi had left town and made off with his cell phone and several items from his wardrobe.

Bhuti's concept of the cake captured many of the issues that I have grappled with in this book. Should it represent a rainbow flag or a South African flag, he wondered. Ultimately, it was both – the backdrop was rainbow, the specifics were South African and the divider down the middle was the end of apartheid and the realisation of democracy. Although it failed in the detail, the modest confectionary of the cake and the context in which it was served alluded to the interrelationships between global gay identity politics, the influence of the anti-apartheid struggle (and gay activism within and alongside that broader struggle), the foundational influence of constitutional democracy, and the role of glamour and style – this was, after all, the cake for a gay beauty pageant. And yet, despite all these new elements, the local obsession with gender in same-sex relations remained very present.

In Durban Brendan found a new sense of gay community, but in Johannesburg this sociability took on a political edge when he became involved in GLOW. These are the two legacies of Brendan's life story that can be seen as analogous of the position of gays in towns such as Ermelo and Standerton. The gender-structured relationships evident in the Durban weddings and the activism of organisations such as GLOW have combined to create a unique environment for self-identification. On the one hand, the inclusion of sexual orientation in the Constitution represents a political development in South Africa that could not have taken place without the activism of groups that organised around gay and lesbian identities. On the other hand, there is a strong tradition of same-sex relationships that are structured along gender lines and that are embedded within an essentially heterosexual (and patriarchal) paradigm.

Brendan has pointed out that much has changed to improve the lives of gays in a town such as Standerton. In the twenty years since he last lived there, he noticed that dramatic changes had taken place. There is no doubt that the liberalisation of the political climate and everything that goes with it (including, for example, increased media attention on gay and lesbian issues) has opened up new spaces for gays to function in public spaces. Some of these have been explored in this book. What is interesting about the form of this modern gay identity is that although it is based on a language of identity politics, it remains embedded in a gender order that has strong historical antecedent. A modern gay identity and egalitarian forms of relationships are often cast as synonymous, with the assumption that other forms of relationship patterning (for example, age-structured or gender-structured) are somewhat less modern. Yet it is clear that the gays of Ermelo and surrounding towns regard themselves as modern and are seen by others as modern. In fact, in some respects, they are icons of modernity.

Notes

1. For an autobiographical account of a lesbian sangoma's quest for cultural affirmation through an exploration of same-sex desire in South African history, see Nkabinde (2008).
2. Like Themba, Thulani made a written note of his sexual liaisons, although his list was constructed from memory and covered the period of only one year. In January 2004 while I was driving with Thulani and others between Piet Retief and Ermelo, he showed me a list that he had compiled, indicating 29 sexual partners in

the previous year, 8 of whom were for the December/January period. One name had been cut out of the list following a serious disagreement.

3. According to Bhuti, women or *ladies* would be paid between R20 and R50 for sex, depending on the kind of sexual services provided to the truck drivers.

4. I had come across other references to the language during my fieldwork. For example Thando, from Standerton, had mentioned it and had shared a few terms with me.

5. This was the rationale for the establishment of the Gay and Lesbian Archives of South Africa (GALA) in 1997 and the various projects associated with GALA that were designed to uncover hidden histories.

6. This was evident in Chapter 6 where the idea that homosexuality was alien to African culture was promulgated at the public hearings on same-sex marriage, that were organised by the National House of Traditional Leaders.

7. Different gay dialects that emerged in parallel spoke not only to language differences, but also to racial cleavages in South African society. Different dialects were used, one by blacks, another by whites and Coloureds. One dialect, known as 'Gayle', was used primarily by Afrikaans- and English-speaking whites and Coloureds in urban centres. Gayle was formulated around a basic linguistic strategy of using women's names as verbs and adjectives and was drawn from an American model of gay vernacular and is similar in some respects to Polari in the United Kingdom. But Gayle is also distinctive in that it is peppered with typically South African words and phrases. The dialects also had a number of terms referring to race. *Isingqumo* has terms such as *udayi* (from dye and meaning a white person); *Imbaha* (an Indian person); and *Ikuki* (a Coloured person). In Gayle, racial references include Wendy (a white homosexual); Zelda (a Zulu homosexual); Natalie, originally Natalie Native (a black homosexual); Iris (an Indian homosexual); and Clora (a Coloured homosexual). There were at least two words on Thulani's typed list that were common to both dialects. These were Nora, which no one in Thulani's room that night knew the meaning of but which means 'stupid' or 'a stupid person', and *ebhuyula* (derived from Beulah) which means 'beautiful' or 'a beautiful man' (McLean and Ncgobo 1995; Olivier 1995; Cage 2003).

8. Mkhumbane is also known as Cato Manor.
9. Adult World is one of the many adult chain stores that have opened since the liberalisation of South African censorship laws, coinciding with the transition to democracy.
10. Presumably, *Love Without Fear* by Eustace Chesser, first published in 1940.
11. For a fuller discussion of this important period in gay social history in South Africa, see Gevisser and Cameron (1995); Donham (2005) and Hoad, Martin and Reid (2005).
12. Brendan appears in a photograph taken at Lee's Place that depicts the first executive committee of GLOW (Simon Tseko Nkoli Collection AM 2623, University of the Witwatersrand Libraries).

CONCLUSION

Country and City Styles
Being Traditional and Modern

This book explores gay spaces and identities in rural and small-town South Africa in a time of transition. It is about shifting forms of self-understanding and social organisation amongst gays living in the South African countryside in the light of the Constitution. It is about the raw materials that gays draw on in reimagining themselves and forging their life worlds. These raw materials include traditional and historical ideas about gender and same-sex practices, a Constitution that upholds the principles of gender equality and non-discrimination on the basis of sexual orientation, as well as increased access to the discourses and practices of international gay and lesbian social movements. These intersections on local, national and transnational levels are evident in the everyday practices of gays living in towns such as Ermelo.

The results of my research serve to moderate the global sex hypothesis, which posits that modernity has produced a hegemonic model of gay identity that is rapidly becoming a universal norm, replacing other traditional models of same-sex practice. Dennis Altman argues that, generally speaking, there is a 'rupture between traditional and modern forms of gay identity' (1996: 88–9). A specific aspect of the setting where I did my research might be that, especially after the inauguration of the new Constitution, local models are directly confronted with more modern definitions of what it means to be gay. The result is not seamless replacement of earlier tradition, but rather bricolage and syncretism: a gay identity that in many respects is modern – albeit in different ways – and that is couched, by gays themselves, in terms of tradition. This is particularly evident in relation to gender norms (where traditional roles are venerated) as well as in debates about what it means to be African.

Gender norms and practices

A strong dichotomy between masculine and feminine underlies the organisation of gay social and sexual life in the small towns of my research. Based on her study of the sex lives of young men and women in Nairobi, Rachel Spronk observes: 'If sex is constitutive to people's feelings of being either "woman" or "man", then experiencing being feminine and masculine is partly related to normative expectations based on existing gender roles' (2006: 261). These remarks could equally be applied to the apparent need for *ladies* to experience femininity through appropriate sexual and social practices and, similarly, for *gents* to experience masculinity. These gendered norms are clearly ideals, much like the related dichotomy of town and country, although in practice, the boundaries are not as clear-cut as the hypothetical models suggest. Nevertheless, the dichotomy between masculine and feminine has a profound effect on processes of self-identification. Making a clear distinction between who is a *lady* and who is a *gent* – and the related idea that *ladies* can only be sisters to each other and only fall in love with a *gent* – had an almost obsessive quality for nearly all my local informants. The example of Clive, who was torn between becoming a husband or a wife in a context in which, in his own words, 'a man is a man completely and a wife is a wife completely' illustrates the power of these categories.

Clive's remark also points to another aspect of my fieldwork in relation to gender. He speaks of 'a wife' and 'a man': femininity is described in relation to a social position – 'a wife' – while masculinity – 'a man' – refers to gender. This research confirms what other studies of masculinity have shown, namely that masculinity is a relational concept usually defined as 'not feminine' or 'not female' (Connell 1995; Morrell 2001). In this context, where there is a strict gender division in male same-sex relationships, masculinity is also defined as 'not gay'. In Chapters 3 and 4, I explored the advantages and dis-advantages of feminine self-styling amongst gay hairstylists. Femininity renders gays vulnerable in the same way that women are vulnerable. The experience of gender-based violence, in-cluding sexual assault, is an extreme aspect of this vulnerability. This is what Bhuti alluded to when he made a speech coinciding with Miss Gay Ten Years of Democracy:

> There have been gays who are being attacked. Themba was attacked a few weeks ago by people who are hating gays. Nathi was stabbed and was assaulted and lost his cell phone, just because he is gay. Dumisani was raped and he just arrived at home naked. You can see how difficult it is to pass through these experiences. But through it all we must celebrate our rights. They are rights and I am stressing we must exercise every right that we believe we deserve.

Ladies' vulnerability also makes them susceptible to HIV-infection. Like many women in similar circumstances, *ladies* are not always able to negotiate condom use, since the decision on this is often the prerogative of *gents*.

However, a hyper-feminine performance can also be deployed to social and economic advantage. The celebrity status of some gay hairstylists is indicative of the way in which a hyper-feminine persona can generate popularity and fame – an important ingredient for success in an oversubscribed informal economy, such as hairstyling. Gays are perceived to be particularly adept at producing femininity amongst their female clients, precisely because they are constantly performing femininity themselves. Brendan observed: 'When it comes to hairstyles, they are the experts.' This has also the undeniable consequence that *ladies* are often richer than their friends. In practice, many maintain their boyfriends. The economic position of *ladies* in relation to *gents* is the reverse of that experienced by economically vulnerable mine 'wives' who sought the patronage of older men. Economic vulnerability was an important component of the 'situational homosexuality' argument, which offered a functionalist explanation for the existence of male same-sex relationships in single-sex mine compounds.[1] This argument does not hold in the context of my research.

What is apparant, is that the relative economic advantage of *ladies* in Ermelo can itself lead to gender-based violence. Strict adherence to gender roles can be seen as part of a strategy for managing vulnerability: by performing as *ladies*, gays situate themselves within the existing gender order; they do not threaten hegemonic masculinity or undermine patriarchy. In this scenario, as the human-rights based model of the Constitution gains ground – stressing individual rights and protection on the basis of sexual orientation – one would expect a waning of gender as a defining feature of sexual identity. But this does not appear to be the case; instead gender continues to play a pivotal role in male same-sex relationships. Indeed, my research reveals the difficulties of using constitutional provisions to gain protection. There is also an understanding amongst *ladies* and *gents* that difference and inequality is an essential component of erotic charge and sexual passion. This runs counter to the dominant logic of the Western egalitarian ideal and to the aspirations to gender equity reflected in the Constitution.

Numerous historical and anthropological studies have shown that while a gendered model of homosexuality seems to be quite common worldwide, rather than exceptional, an egalitarian ideal is regularly cited as a defining feature of modern homosexualities that tend to eschew age- or gender-structured models. Yet what my research shows is the overarching importance of gender ideals as the main principle for organising same-sex practices in an indisputably modern context.

Kgomotso, Scalo,
Bafana, Vusi and
Tony, 2009

Couple Bheki and Sipho, 2009

Kgomotso and his three days date, 2008

Madlisa, 2009

Palisa, 2009

Innocentia aka Sakhile, 2009

Lincoln Mkhatshwa, 2009

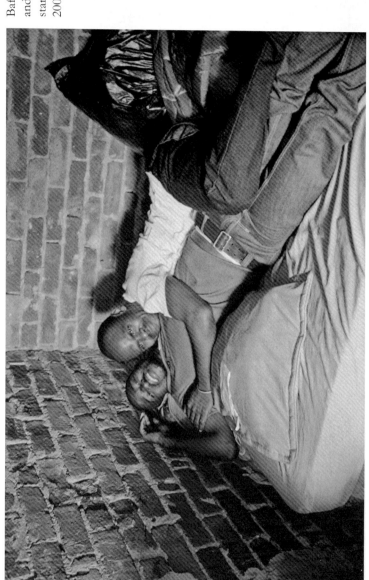

Bafana Mhlanga and his soccer star boyfriend, 2009

Kgomotso, Scalo, Bafana, Vusi and Tony, 2009

Talent and his
girlfriends, 2009

Oupa 'Konke
enginakho
nengiyikho
kuyintando
KaJehova', 2009

Kgomotso, Palm Dove Lodge, Ermelo, 2008

Piet Retief, 2009

Mandla from Piet Retief at Miss Ten Years of Democracy, 2003

Bheki on ramp, 2008

Innocentia
and Bigboy
with friends
from Carolina,
Ermelo, 2009

uMakhosi Gadisa,
2004

Gay spaces

In this book, I explore three gay spaces. Central in my research was the hair salon, as a gay space associated with style and modernity. The gay hair salon functions both as an important site of interaction between highly visible gays and the broader community and as a place where gay identity is reproduced, particularly through informal apprenticeships, into the skills of hairstyling and ways of performing a gay style.

A comparison can be made with a more traditional niche profession, as exemplified by the role of the sangoma, where gender ambivalence is acceptable as part of a liminal position between the world of the living and the world of the ancestors. In fact, gender liminality can be seen as a source of strength and ritual power (Morgan and Reid 2003). The traditional role of the sangoma is emphasised by gays as a way of staking claim to an African gay identity.

There are also the emerging gay spaces produced by gay activism. In the wake of the Constitution, a particular form of gay identity that conforms more to a modern model is strengthened. This is the globally hegemonic model of sexual orientation reproduced through the media and promoted by gay and lesbian organisations. On a local level, it was evident in the workshops on 'how to be a real gay', which represented a self-conscious attempt to promote new forms of self-understanding amongst gays living in the hinterland and to provide an identity-based vocabulary. These new possibilities for self-identification were evident in the reactions of workshop participants who recognised themselves in new and unfamiliar terms, such as 'butch'. Similarly, the debate about whether individuals are gay or transgendered showed how these forms of categorisation are both new and contested. Taking over these ideas has clear advantages. The modern gay is more able to tap into national and international networks. Aside from the social prestige that this can bring to individuals such as Bhuti, there are also increased possibilities of accessing resources allocated to gay and lesbian organisations. For example, donor funding has become a realistic possibility for gays who can show that they are part of an organisation that is promoting gay and lesbian interests in the countryside. Urban-based organisations are paying increased attention to gays living in outlying districts as part of their outreach programmes, encouraged by the donor agencies that support them.[2] Increasingly, there are economic advantages to a particular way of styling the self, a way of being gay that draws on an international register of gay and lesbian social movements. In a similar way that hairstylists are able to perform femininity to economic advantage, so is it increasingly viable to perform as a modern gay and reap social capital and donor funding. It is also significant that several gays work in local government departments. The government policy of non-discrimination on the basis of sexual orientation makes state employment an attractive option for gays living in small towns.

While I have drawn a distinction between local style and global activism and there are palpable tensions between individuals who espouse different approaches, there is also considerable overlap. One of the ways in which the mutual influence of these two approaches was keenly felt was in the workshops, where the rhetoric drawn by a modern gay social movement was adapted to a traditional gender configuration, between *ladies* and *gents*. Such combining has its paradoxical implications. One of the characteristic features of modern homosexualities is 'a differentiation between sexual and gender transgression' (Altman 1996: 83), while in a traditional view, 'the "real" homosexual is the man who behaves like a woman' (82). Yet in Ermelo, gays who see themselves as modern and who are able to use the rights secured in the Constitution to their advantage do so in the context of traditional gender norms and practices, which hold that a 'real' gay is a *lady*. This was evident, for instance, at the local state hospital where Nathi managed to secure a ward in the women's section. The hospital administrators obliged precisely because they were aware that gay rights were protected in the Constitution. Another example of this interplay was the three stylists who came out at school by wearing variations of the girls' uniform and make-up, combining a feminine style with a nascent form of gay activism. Similarly, small-town beauty pageants were couched in a language of activism, as an outlet for expressing a gay identity and as a way of educating the broader public about gays. Certainly the organisers and participants in Miss Gay Ten Years of Democracy saw the event as part of a broader activist programme. Clearly, it would be too simplistic to see such emphasis on a gendered version of being gay as a traditional rudiment that will fade away in the face of more modern views emphasising equality. My informants seemed to be intent on exploring their own forms of a modern gay identity. To them, emphasis on categorical difference, in this case gendered, seemed to remain essential for an eroticisation of same-sex relations, despite the direct impact at the local level of the Constitution and the ideas of the global gay movement.[3]

African versus modern and old versus millennium

In this research, I also explored the figure of the sangoma – particularly in the somewhat paradoxical role this figure plays in debates on the question as to whether homosexuality should be seen as un-African. Of special relevance in this respect is the striking contrast my informants made between 'old' and 'millennium' sangomas. Indeed, the sangoma figure can be used as evidence to show that gays are part of African culture and tradition. Paradoxically, even amongst gays, some sangomas are perceived to be 'too gay' or, as my informants put it, 'millennium' (too modern or even fakes). Such a contrast inadvertently reinforces the popular perception that being African and being gay are incompatible.

There is a similar ambivalence in responses to gays in the light of parallel debates about fashion and modernity. The other side of being seen as un-African is that gays are regarded as modern and fashionable. This is evident in the fact that gay lifestyles are often referred to as a fashion, or part of a modern way. Again, my research suggests as a conclusion that being closely associated with fashion and modernity has positive as well as negative connotations. Spronk (2006) has shown how young professionals in Nairobi negotiate an identity between being African and being modern and attempt to reconcile the two. A similar dilemma exists for gays who are perceived as both modern and un-African.

There is an increased attention to style, even in rural areas, where designer clothing and other accoutrements have an increasingly important role to play as expressions of material success in post-apartheid South Africa. One of the ways in which an increased attention to style is evident is in the proliferation of the range of hairstyles on offer in black hair salons. As a form of fashion, contemporary black hairstyles in South Africa reflect both African and cosmopolitan identities. Gays are able to occupy a special niche as sought-after stylists, precisely because they are widely regarded as icons of modernity. Fashion, when applied to gays, might suggest a transient identity of choice, but it also has a particular appeal in the hairstyling industry, where few people want to be seen as unfashionable. To the extent that gays embody modernity, ambivalent public responses to homosexuality as fashion probably reflect broader ambivalences towards modernity, which is both a source of aspiration as well as a threat to traditional norms and practices. The price such modern gays pay for being so fashionable is clear: it exposes them all the more to accusations of parading un-African values and, therefore, to gendered violence.

How to be a 'real' gay

Debates and discussions about what constitutes a 'real' gay highlight similar ambivalences. The workshops (Chapter 5) offered an example of an explicit and self-conscious intervention, with the aim of creating new possibilities for self-identification and self-styling. The discussions about 'old' and 'millennium' sangomas (Chapter 6) reveal a different, but related, set of concerns: To what extent is a modern gay identity compatible with African culture? These are the broad parameters in which contemporary gay identities are being forged in towns such as Ermelo. On the one hand, gays feel the need to situate themselves within a framework of traditional values and cultural norms – 'country style', in my informants' terms. This is a way of showing that to be gay is compatible with African culture. Gender norms and practices are one of the ways in which traditional values are evoked and performed. In this debate, the figure of the gay sangoma also plays an important role.

On the other hand, 'city style' offers many advantages. Through a close association with fashion and style, gays have managed to carve a special niche within the hairstyling industry and, increasingly, the rights secured in the Constitution are having a tangible impact on the lives of gays in the countryside. In Chapter 2, I described an engagement ceremony that took place at a time when same-sex unions had no legal status. The ceremony had a strong performative aspect and, as one of the speakers put it, 'we must show that we are not faking it'. As of 30 November 2006, the legal situation regarding same-sex marriage changed when the Civil Unions Act was signed into law, so there is no longer any need to show that 'we are not faking it'.

On 2 December 2006, I attended a party held in Ermelo to celebrate the passing of the Civil Unions Act. This party illustrates some of the ways in which increased interaction with other, urban-based gay organisations as well as broader legal changes continue to make an impact. It also shows how change continues to be received by gays (and increasingly lesbians) in Ermelo on their own terms. This particular party was more organised than usual. Guests had to pay to get in and if one did not, or could not, one was turned away, like the two youngsters who were hanging around outside. Local activists were modelling events differently from the haphazard events that I was more familiar with. A young woman was managing the finances and authorising the purchase of additional liquor from a shebeen nearby. The celebration was modelled more closely on the social events that coincided with the highly organised Out in Africa Gay and Lesbian Film Festival that had taken place in Ermelo in 2005 and 2006. Aside from bringing gay films to the country-side, the film festival also served to hone existing organisational skills amongst local gay activists. A sign-language interpreter had been present at one of the events linked to the festival and, while Bhuti made a speech, one of the *ladies* did a mock sign language interpretation, until Bhuti pushed him aside in bemused annoyance. The party was in town, held in a room rented by a *lady* in a converted former convent. Many gays had in a short space of time moved out of the township and into nooks and crannies, such as rented rooms, in the formerly white town. Another striking feature was the presence of more lesbians than was usual at these events in the past. One woman dressed in shirt and trousers similar to that worn by the *gents* helped with the cooking of the meat, while the two other lesbians present were with the *ladies* who were making salad, cooking vegetables and partying in the former convent room. There was much speculation as to who would be the first to get married.

The countryside is an ambivalent environment for gays, as it can be both hostile and accepting. During the course of my fieldwork, I came across a strong rhetoric that declared homo-sexuality to be un-African and, in terms of which, gays occupied a vulnerable social position as *ladies*. Yet, in practice, a wide spectrum of people engaged with gays in everyday and ordinary ways. Gays were accommodated, accepted and even venerated in small-town communities. Even conservative social groups, such as church communities, could be affirming for gays. My informants were active agents in creating gay spaces and making optimum use of the opportunities that presented themselves, notably in the hairstyling industry, in the realm of traditional healing and through new forms of activism and community organisation.

A distillation of the life worlds of gays in Ermelo could be seen in this party held to celebrate the Civil Unions Act. Gays were responding to the possibilities brought about by social change. They exercised a high level of innovation and agency in forging new identities, a process that remained open ended and in flux. The party was held to celebrate a significant development, the legalisation of same-sex marriage. The sexual orientation provision of the Constitution had opened up previously unimaginable possibilities. The influence of ongoing interaction with other city-based gay and lesbian organisations was also evident. Yet *ladies* and *gents* remained at their respective posts. Gender was still central to gays' strategies of integration into conservative worlds and it was also at the heart of emerging activist models of gay identity.

Epilogue
This book presents a slice of life in rural gay communities a decade after political transformation in South Africa, the dawn of democracy and the protection of gay rights. What has happened since then to the people who appear in this book? Some have moved on. Many – far too many – have died. And evangelical Christianity is flourishing.

AIDS has devastated communities, even after anti-retroviral drugs were finally made available through the public healthcare system. But drugs were no immediate panacea. Stigma kept people from testing and many did not learn their HIV status until it was too late and they were too ill and too weak for life-restoring treatment.

Nathi, whose soprano voice made her 'the leading lady' in her church community, died in 2009. Nathi belonged to a healing church, the Ethiopian Holy Baptist Church in Zion, and her beautiful voice created an atmosphere in which healing occurred. She was seen as a pillar of the church and the Archbishop came down from Soweto to bury her – an honour reserved only for the most devout and revered. Siyanda, winner of Miss Gay Ten Years of Democracy died within two weeks of Nathi's passing. Siyanda's First Princess from the same pageant also died. Colin, tormented by the stark choice he needed to make – would he be a *lady* or a *gent*, has also died. Brian and his senior wife Zithembe died too.

AIDS-related deaths have affected everyone in the region and gays have been particularly hard-hit. But attitudes are changing and stigma is diminishing. Nhlanhla combines his work as a sangoma with outreach work, offering counselling and advice on HIV and AIDS prevention and treatment. Nhlanhla has recovered his own health and vitality.

So-called millennium sangoma, Themba, is now a police constable. He has a boyfriend and continues his healing work on the side. Wandile, who placated his demanding boyfriend with domestic chores in order to be allowed to attend the engagement ceremony, is now married with two kids. Gays say that he is a double adaptor, or a micro-wave and convection oven all in one. Ayanda, once inseparable from Siyanda, moved to Johannesburg and is rumoured to be working in an upmarket salon in affluent Sandton. Tsepo also moved to Johannesburg and works for an accounting company. Thulani, who had a penchant for keeping lists (both Zulu gay vocabulary and sexual partners) moved to Kimberley, where he works as a safety officer for a major mining company. Rumour has it that he married under South Africa's same-sex marriage provisions.

Bhuti tells me that few gays have married in this region of the country, but several lesbians have. An exception to this is the charismatic pastor of the evangelical church community based in Nelspruit who married his male partner in a large ceremony attended, he tells me, by gay and straight alike. In August 2012, I attended an Ark of Joy church service in Nelspruit. The church hall was filled with hymns and packed with young men and women, eager to hear Bhuti's preaching that Sunday, to create community and share faith. By day, the founder of this church community is an educator, training people how to use massive earth-moving equipment needed in the mining industry and, in his spare time, he moves mountains of a different sort – preaching to a growing community of gay men and lesbians in Mpumalanga and KwaZulu-Natal, for whom his message of salvation has particular resonance.

Notes

1. See more detailed discussion of this issue elsewhere in this book and, for a qualification of this argument, see Niehaus (2002) who shows that male same-sex relationships remain common on the mines, despite increased access to women.

2. In 2006, the international donor agency that provides the most generous funding to gay and lesbian organisations in South Africa (the Atlantic Philanthropies) together with HIVOS initiated the Multi Agency Grants Initiative, a special fund specifically aimed at grass-roots and community based initiatives. A component of the fund is intended for emerging LGBTI organisations in rural areas and small towns, such as those in Mpumalanga.

3. For more on 'eroticisation of difference', see Chapters 1 and 2; see also Sinfield (2004) and Van der Meer (2006).

Select Bibliography

Achmat, Z. 1993. ' "Apostles of Civilised Vice": "Immoral Practices" and "Unnatural Vice" in South African Prisons and Compounds, 1890–1920'. *Social Dynamics* 19 (2): 92–110.

Alberton, P. and G. Reid, directors. 2000. *Dark and Lovely, Soft and Free*. Produced by Franmi (Brazil) and Gay and Lesbian Archives of South Africa.

Altman, D. 1996. 'Rupture or Continuity? The Internationalization of Gay Identities'. *Social Text* 14 (3): 77–94.

Altman, D. 2001. *Global Sex*. Chicago: University of Chicago Press.

Barsel, S. 2006. 'What Are We Marching For?' In *Pride Protest and Celebration*, eds. S. de Waal and A. Manion: 174–75. Johannesburg: Jacana.

Berger, J. 2004. 'Re-Sexualising the Epidemic: Desire, Risk and HIV Prevention'. *Development Update* 5 (3): 45–67.

Besnier, N. 1997. 'Sluts and Superwomen: The Politics of Gender Liminality in Urban Tonga'. *Ethnos* 62 (1–2): 5–31.

———. 2002. 'Transgenderism, Locality and the Miss Galaxy Beauty Pageant in Tonga'. *American Ethnologist* 29: 534–66.

———. 2003. 'Crossing Genders, Mixing Languages: The Linguistic Construction of Transgenderism in Tonga'. In *Handbook of Language and Gender*, eds. J. Holmes and M. Meyerhoff: 279–301. Oxford: Blackwell.

———. 2004. 'The Social Production of Abjection: Desire and Silencing among Transgender Tongans'. *Social Anthropology* 12 (3): 301–23.

Bhana, D. 2005. 'Violence and the Gendered Negotiation of Masculinity among Young Black School Boys in South Africa'. In *African Masculinities*, eds. L. Ouzgane and R. Morrell: 205–20. Pietermaritzburg: University of KwaZulu-Natal Press and New York: Palgrave Macmillan.

Blackwood, E. 2005 [1998]. 'Tombois in West Sumatra: Constructing Masculinity and Erotic Desire'. In *Same-Sex Cultures and Sexualities: An Anthropological Reader*, ed. J. Robertson: 232–60. Oxford: Blackwell.

Boellstorff, T. 2005. *The Gay Archipelago: Sexuality and Nation in Indonesia.* Princeton: Princeton University Press.

Botha, K. and E. Cameron. 1997. 'South Africa'. In *Socio-Legal Control of Homosexuality: A Multi-National Comparison*, eds. D. West and R. Green: 5–42. New York: Plenum.

Bourdieu, P. 1984. *Distinction: A Social Critique of the Judgement of Taste.* Cambridge, Mass.: Harvard University Press.

————. 2001. *Masculine Domination.* Stanford: Stanford University Press.

Brubaker, R. and F. Cooper. 2000. 'Beyond "Identity"'. *Theory and Society* 29: 1–47.

Burke, T. 1996. *Lifebouy Men, Lux Women: Commodification, Consumption, & Cleanliness in Modern Zimbabwe.* Durham: Duke University Press.

Busby, C. 2000. *The Performance of Gender: An Anthropology of Everyday Life in a South Indian Fishing Village.* London: The Athlone Press.

Butler, J. 1990. *Gender Trouble: Feminism and the Subversion of Identity.* London: Routledge.

————. 1991. 'Imitation and Gender Insubordination'. In *inside/out*, ed. D. Fuss: 13–31. New York: Routledge.

————. 1993. *Bodies That Matter.* New York: Routledge.

Cage, K. 2003. *Gayle: The Language of Kinks & Queens: A History and Dictionary of Gay Language in South Africa.* Johannesburg: Jacana.

Cameron, E. 1994. '"Unapprehended Felons": Gays and Lesbians and the Law in South Africa'. In *Defiant Desire: Gay and Lesbian Lives in South Africa*, eds. M. Gevisser and E. Cameron: 89–98. New York: Routledge.

Carrier, J.M. 1995. *De los otros: Intimacy and Homosexuality among Mexican Men.* New York: Columbia University Press.

Chauncey, G. 1994. *Gay New York.* New York: Basic Books.

Chetty, D. 1995. 'A Drag at Madame Costello's: Cape Moffie Life and the Popular Press in the 1950s and 1960s'. In *Defiant Desire: Gay and Lesbian Lives in South Africa*, eds. M. Gevisser and E. Cameron: 115–27. New York: Routledge.

Cock, J. 2005. 'Engendering Gay and Lesbian Rights: The Equality Clause in the South African Constitution'. In *Sex and Politics in South Africa*, eds. N. Hoad, K. Martin and G. Reid: 188–209. Cape Town: Double Storey.

Comaroff, J. 1985. *Body of Power, Spirit of Resistance.* Chicago: University of Chicago Press.

Connell, R.W. 1995. *Masculinities.* Berkeley: University of California Press.

D'Emilio, J. 1993. 'Capitalism and Gay Identity'. In *The Lesbian and Gay Studies Reader*, eds. H. Abelove, M.A. Barale and D. Halperin: 467–76. New York: Routledge.

Di Leonardo, M. 1991. 'Introduction: Gender, Culture, and Political Economy: Feminist Anthropology in Historical Perspective'. In

Gender at the Crossroads of Knowledge: Feminist Anthropology in the Postmodern Era, ed. M. di Leonardo: 1–48. Berkeley: University of California Press.

Donham, D. 1998. 'Freeing South Africa: The "Modernization" of Male-Male Sexuality in Soweto'. *Cultural Anthropology* 13 (1); 3–21.

———. 2005. 'Freeing South Africa: The "Modernisation" of Male-Male Sexuality in Soweto'. In *Same-Sex Cultures and Sexualities: An Anthropological Reader*, ed. J. Robertson: 261–78. Oxford: Blackwell.

Douglas, M. 1966. *Purity and Danger: An Analysis of Concepts of Pollution and Taboo*. New York: Frederick A. Praeger.

Douglas, M. and B. Isherwood. 1979. *The World of Goods: Towards an Anthropology of Consumption*. New York: Basic Books.

Ellis, H. 1948 [1933]. *Psychology of Sex*. London: Heinemann.

Entwistle, J. 2000. *The Fashioned Body*. Cambridge: Polity Press.

Epprecht, M. 2004. *Hungochani: The History of a Dissident Sexuality in Southern Africa*. Montreal: McGill-Queen's University Press.

Eribon, D. 2004. *Insult and the Making of the Gay Self*. Durham: Duke University Press.

Ferguson, J. 1999. *Expectations of Modernity*. Berkeley: University of California Press.

Fester, G. 2006. 'Some Preliminary Thoughts on Sexuality, Citizenship and Constitutions: Are Rights Enough?' *Agenda* 67: 100–11.

Foucault, M. 1978. *The History of Sexuality: Volume 1: An Introduction*. New York: Vintage.

———. 1992 [1984]. *The History of Sexuality: Volume 2*. Harmondsworth: Penguin.

Fuss, D. 1991a. 'Inside/Out'. In *inside/out*, ed. D. Fuss. New York: Routledge.

Fuss, D., ed. 1991b. *inside/out*. New York: Routledge.

Geschiere, P., B. Meyer and P. Pels. 2008. 'Introduction'. In *Readings in Modernity in Africa*, eds. P. Geschiere, B. Meyer and P. Pels: 1–7. Oxford: James Currey (for International African Institute with Indiana University Press and UNISA Press).

Gevisser, M. 1999. 'Homosexuality in Africa: An Interpretation'. In *Africana: The Encyclopedia of the African and African American Experience*, eds. K.A. Appiah and H.L. Gates: 961–63. New York: Basic Civitas Books.

Gevisser, M. and E. Cameron, eds. 1995. *Defiant Desire: Gay and Lesbian Lives in South Africa*. New York: Routledge.

Giddens, A. 1992. *The Transformation of Intimacy: Sexuality, Love and Eroticism in Modern Societies*. Cambridge: Polity Press.

Gimlin, D. 1996. 'Pamela's Place: Power and Negotiation in the Hair Salon'. *Gender and Society* 10 (5): 505–26.

Goffman, E. 1986. *Stigma: Notes on the Management of Spoiled Identity.* New York: Touchstone.

Gopinath, G. 2005. *Impossible Desires: Queer Diasporas and South Asian Public Cultures.* Durham: Duke University Press.

Gordon, C.D. and A. Clermont. 2006. 'Belles of "Bont"'. *Sunday Times Lifestyle,* 2 April.

Hallam, P. 1993. *The Book of Sodom.* London: Verso.

Halperin, D.M. 1995. *Saint Foucault: Towards a Gay Hagiography.* New York: Oxford University Press.

———. 2002. *How to Do the History of Homosexuality.* Chicago: University of Chicago Press.

Hammond-Tooke, W.D. 1981. *Boundaries and Belief: The Structure of a Sotho Worldview.* Johannesburg: Wits University Press.

Harries, P. 1990. 'Symbols and Sexuality: Culture and Identity in the Early Witwatersrand Mines'. *Gender and History* 11 (3): 318–36.

Hekma, G. 2009. 'Review: Queer Masculinities'. *European History Quarterly* 39 (1): 168–69.

Hoad, N. 2005. 'Introduction'. In *Sex and Politics in South Africa,* eds. N. Hoad, K. Martin and G. Reid: 14–25. Cape Town: Double Storey.

Hoad, N., K. Martin and G. Reid, eds. 2005. *Sex and Politics in South Africa.* Cape Town: Double Storey.

Houlbrook, M. 2005. *Queer London: Perils and Pleasures of the Sexual Metropolis, 1918–1957.* Chicago: University of Chicago Press.

Howard, J. 1999. *Men Like That: A Southern Queer History.* Chicago: University of Chicago Press.

Hunter, M. 2002. 'The Materiality of Everyday Sex: Thinking beyond "Prostitution"'. *African Studies* 61 (2): 99–120.

Ingram, G.B., A. Bouthillette and Y. Retter. 1997. *Queers in Space: Communities/ Public Spaces/ Sites of Resistance.* Washington: Bay Press.

Jara, M. and S. Lapinsky. 1998. 'Forging a Representative Gay Liberation Movement in South Africa'. *Development Update* 2 (2): 44–56.

Johnson, M. 1997. *Beauty and Power: Transgendering and Cultural Transformation in the Southern Philippines.* Oxford: Berg.

Judge, M., A. Manion and S. de Waal. 2008. *To Have and to Hold: The Making of Same-Sex Marriage in South Africa.* Johannesburg. Jacana.

Junod, H. 1927. *The Life of a South African Tribe.* London: MacMillan.

Kuckertz, H. 1990. *Creating Order: The Image of the Homestead in Mpondo Social Life.* Johannesburg: Wits University Press.

Kulick, D. 1998. *Travesti: Sex, Gender and Culture among Brazilian Transgendered Prostitutes.* Chicago: University of Chicago Press.

Lancaster, R.N. 1988. 'Subject Honor and Object Shame: The Construction of Male Homosexuality and Stigma in Nicaragua'. *Ethnology* 27: 111–25.

Laubscher, B.J.F. 1937. *Sex, Custom and Psychopathology: A Study of South African Pagan Natives*. London: Routledge.

Louw, R. 2001. 'Mkhumbane and New Traditions of (Un)African Same-Sex Weddings'. In *Changing Men in Southern Africa*, ed. R. Morrell: 287–96. Pietermaritzburg: University of Natal Press and London: Zed Books.

MacRae, E. 1992. 'Homosexual Identities in Transitional Brazilian Politics'. In *The Making of Social Movements in Latin America*, eds. A. Escobar and S. Alvarez: 185–203. Boulder: Westview Press.

Manalansan, M.F. 2003. *Global Divas: Filipino Gay Men in the Diaspora*. Durham: Duke University Press.

Matebeni, Z. 2011. 'Exploring Black Lesbian Sexualities and Identities in Johannesburg'. Ph.D. diss. Johannesburg: University of the Witwatersrand.

Mbembe, A. 2000. 'An Essay on the Political Imagination in Wartime', trans. S. Rendall. *CODESRIA Bulletin* 2–4: 6–21.

McLean, H. and L. Ncgobo. 1995. '*Abangibhamayo Bathi Ngimnandi* (Those Who Fuck Me Say I'm Tasty): Gay Sexuality in Reef Townships'. In *Defiant Desire: Gay and Lesbian Lives in South Africa*, eds. M. Gevisser and E. Cameron: 158–85. New York: Routledge.

Meyerowitz, J. 2002. *How Sex Changed: A History of Transsexuality in the United States*. Cambridge, Mass.: Harvard University Press.

Moodie, D. 1989. 'Migrancy and Male Sexuality on the South African Gold Mines'. In *Hidden from History: Reclaiming the Gay and Lesbian Past*, eds. M. Duberman, M. Vicinus and G. Chauncey: 411–25. New York: New American Library.

Moodie, D. with V. Ndatshe. 1994. *Going for Gold: Men Mines and Migration*. Johannesburg: Wits University Press.

Moore, H.L. 1994. *A Passion for Difference*. Cambridge: Polity Press.

Morgan, R. and G. Reid. 2003. ' "I've Got Two Men and One Woman": Ancestors, Sexuality and Identity among Same-Sex Identified Women Traditional Healers in South Africa'. *Culture, Health and Sexuality* 5 (5): 375–91.

Morgan, R. and S. Wieringa. 2005. *Tommy Boys, Lesbian Men and Ancestral Wives: Female Same-Sex Practices in Africa*. Johannesburg: Jacana.

Morrell, R. 2001. 'The Times of Change: Men and Masculinity in South Africa'. In *Changing Men in Southern Africa*, ed. R. Morrell: 3–37. Pietermaritzburg: University of Natal Press and London: Zed Books.

Morris, R. 1994. 'Three Sexes and Four Sexualities: Redressing the Discourses on Gender and Sexuality in Contemporary Thailand'. *Positions* 2 (1): 15–43.

Muller, C., director. 2004. *Four Rent Boys and a Sangoma*. Produced by C. Muller.

Murray, S.O. 2000. *Homosexualities*. Chicago: University of Chicago Press.

Niehaus, I. 2002. 'Renegotiating Masculinity in the South African Lowveld: Narratives of Male-Male Sex in Labour Compounds and in Prisons'. *African Studies* 61 (1): 77–97.

———. 2005. 'Masculine Domination in Sexual Violence: Interpreting Accounts of Three Cases of Rape in the South African Lowveld'. In *Men Behaving Differently*, eds. G. Reid and L. Walker: 65–87. Cape Town: Double Storey.

Nkabinde, N.Z. 2008. *Black Bull, Ancestors and Me: My Life as a Lesbian Sangoma*. Johannesburg: Jacana.

Olivier, G. 1995. 'From Ada to Zelda: Notes on Gays and Language in South Africa'. In *Defiant Desire: Gay and Lesbian Lives in South Africa*, eds. M. Gevisser and E. Cameron: 219–24. New York: Routledge.

Posel, D. 2005a. '"Baby Rape": Unmaking Secrets of Sexual Violence in Post-Apartheid South Africa'. In *Men Behaving Differently*, eds. G. Reid and L. Walker: 21–64. Cape Town: Double Storey.

———. 2005b. 'Sex, Death and the Fate of the Nation: Reflections on the Politicization of Sexuality in Post-Apartheid South Africa'. *Africa* 75 (2): 125–53.

Povinelli, E.A. 2006. *The Empire of Love: Toward a Theory of Intimacy, Genealogy, and Carnality*. Durham: Duke University Press.

Prieur, A. 1998. *Mema's House*. Chicago: University of Chicago Press.

Reddy, G. 2005. *With Respect to Sex: Negotiating Hijra Identity in South India*. Chicago: University of Chicago Press.

Reddy, V., T. Sandfort and L. Rispel. 2009. *From Social Silence to Social Science: Same-Sex Sexuality, HIV & AIDS and Gender in South Africa*. Cape Town: HSRC Press.

Reid, G. 2003. '"It is Just a Fashion!" Linking Homosexuality and "Modernity" in South Africa'. *Etnofoor* 16 (2): 7–25.

———. 2005a. '"A Man is a Man Completely and a Wife is a Wife Completely": Gender Classification and Performance amongst "Ladies" and "Gents" in Ermelo, Mpumalanga'. In *Men Behaving Differently*, eds. G. Reid and L. Walker: 205–29. Cape Town: Double Storey.

———. 2005b. 'Fragments from the Archives'. In *Sex and Politics in South Africa*, ed. N. Hoad, K. Martin and G. Reid: 28–32 and 174–77. Cape Town: Double Storey.

———. 2010. *Above the Skyline: Reverend Tsietsi Thandekiso and the Founding of an African Gay Church*. Pretoria: UNISA Press.

Reid, G. and T. Dirsuweit. 2002. 'Understanding Systemic Violence: Homophobic Attacks in Johannesburg and its Surrounds'. *Urban Forum* 13 (3): 99–126.

Retief, G. 1994. 'Keeping Sodom out of the Laager: State Repression of Homosexuality in Apartheid South Africa'. In *Defiant Desire: Gay and Lesbian Lives in South Africa*, eds. M. Gevisser and E. Cameron: 99–111. New York: Routledge.

Rofel, L. 2007. *Desiring China: Experiments in Neoliberalism, Sexuality, and Public Culture*. Durham: Duke University Press.

Rubin, G. 1975. 'The Traffic in Women: Notes on the "Political Economy" of Sex'. In *Toward an Anthropology of Women*, ed. R. Reiter: 157–210. New York: Monthly Review Press.

———. 1993. 'Thinking Sex: Notes for a Radical Theory of the Politics of Sexuality'. In *The Lesbian and Gay Studies Reader*, eds. H. Abelove, M.A. Barale and D. Halperin: 3–44. New York: Routledge.

Rule, S. and B. Mncwango. 2006. 'Rights or Wrongs? An Exploration of Moral Values'. In *South African Social Attitudes: Changing Times, Diverse Voices*, ed. U. Pillay, B. Roberts and S. Rule: 252–78. Cape Town: HSRC Press.

Sang, T.D. 2003. *The Emerging Lesbian: Female Same-Sex Desire in Modern China*. Chicago: University of Chicago Press.

Sedgwick, E.K. 1990. *Epistemology of the Closet*. Berkeley: University of California Press.

———. 1992. *Between Men: English Literature and Male Homosocial Desire*. New York: Columbia University Press.

Sideris, T. 2005. ' "You Have to Change and You Don't Know How!" Contesting What it Means to be a Man in a Rural Area of South Africa'. In *Men Behaving Differently*, eds. G. Reid and L. Walker: 111–37. Cape Town: Double Storey.

Sieber, R. and F. Herreman, eds. 2000. *Hair in African Art and Culture*. Munich: Prestel.

Simpson, G. and G. Kraak. 1998. 'The Illusions of Sanctuary and the Weight of the Past: Notes on Violence and Gender in South Africa'. *Development Update* 2 (2): 1–10.

Sinfield, A. 2004. *On Sexuality and Power*. New York: Columbia University Press.

Sinnott, M.J. 2004. *Toms and Dees: Transgender Identity and Female Same-Sex Relationships in Thailand*. Honolulu: University of Hawaii Press.

Spronk, R. 2006. 'Ambiguous Pleasures'. Ph.D. diss. Amsterdam: University of Amsterdam.

Trumbach, R. 1998. *Sex and the Gender Revolution: Volume 1: Heterosexuality and the Third Gender in Enlightenment London*. Chicago: University of Chicago Press.

Tucker, A. 2009. *Queer Visibilities: Space, Identity and Interaction in Cape Town*. Chichester: Wiley-Blackwell.

Valentine, D. 2002. 'We're "Not about Gender": The Uses of "Transgender" '. In *Out in Theory: The Emergence of Lesbian and Gay*

Anthropology, eds. E. Lewin and W.L. Leap: 222–45. Champaign: University of Illinois Press.

———. 2007. *Imagining Transgender: An Ethnography of a Category*. Durham: Duke University Press.

Van der Meer, T. 2006. '"Are Those People Like Us?" Early Modern Homosexuality in Holland'. In *Queer Masculinities, 1550–1800: Siting Same-Sex Desire in the Early Modern World*, eds. K. O'Donnell and M. O'Rourke: 58–76. Basingstoke: Palgrave MacMillan.

Van Dijk, R. 2003. 'Localisation, Ghanian Pentecostalism and the Stranger's Beauty in Botswana'. *Africa* 73 (4): 560–83.

Van Onselen, C. 1984. *The Small Matter of a Horse: The Life of 'Nongoloza' Mathebula, 1867–1948*. Johannesburg: Ravan Press.

Walker, L. 2005. 'Negotiating the Boundaries of Masculinity in Post-Apartheid South Africa'. In *Men Behaving Differently*, eds. G. Reid and L. Walker: 161–82. Cape Town: Double Storey.

Walker, L., G. Reid and M. Cornell. 2004. *Waiting to Happen: HIV/AIDS in South Africa: The Bigger Picture*. Cape Town: Double Storey.

Warner, M. 2002. *Publics and Counterpublics*. New York: Zone Books.

Watt, J. 1996. 'Year of the Black Hair Revolution'. *Mail & Guardian*, 24 December 1996–9 January 1997: 35.

Weeks, J. 1977. *Coming Out: Homosexual Politics in Britain from the 19th Century to the Present*. London: Quartet Books.

———. 1985. *Sexuality and its Discontents: Meanings, Myths and Modern Sexualities*. London: Routledge.

———. 2003a. 'Necessary Fictions: Sexual Identities and the Politics of Diversity'. In *Sexualities and Society: A Reader*, eds. J. Weeks, J. Holland and M. Waites: 122–31. Cambridge: Polity Press.

———. 2003b. *Sexuality*. London: Routledge.

Wekker, G. 1999. '"What's Identity Got to Do with it?" Rethinking Identity in Light of the *Mati* work in Suriname'. In *Same-Sex Relations and Female Desires: Transgender Practices across Cultures*, eds. E. Blackwood and S.E. Wieringa: 119–38. New York: Columbia University Press.

———. 2006. *The Politics of Passion: Women's Sexual Culture in the Afro-Surinamese Diaspora*. New York: Columbia University Press.

Whitehead, S.M. and F.J. Barrett 2001. 'The Sociology of Masculinity'. In *The Masculinities Reader*, eds. S.M. Whitehead and F.J. Barrett: 1–26. Cambridge: Polity Press.

Wilson, E. 1985. *Adorned in Dreams*. London: Virago.

Wood, K. and R. Jewkes. 2001. '"Dangerous" Love: Reflections on Violence among Xhosa Township Youth'. In *Changing Men in Southern Africa*, ed. R. Morrell: 317–36. Pietermaritzburg: University of Natal Press and London: Zed Books.

Index